THE MIND AND HEART
IN HUMAN SEXUAL BEHAVIOR

THE MIND AND HEART
IN HUMAN SEXUAL BEHAVIOR
Owning and Sharing Our Personal Truths

Alan Bell, Ph.D.

JASON ARONSON INC.
Northvale, New Jersey
London

Director of Editorial Production: Robert D. Hack

This book was set in 11 pt. Galliard by Alabama Book Composition of Deatsville, Alabama and printed and bound by Book-mart Press, Inc. of North Bergen, NJ.

Library of Congress Cataloging-in-Publication Data

Bell, Alan P., 1932–
    The mind and heart in human sexual behavior : owning and
sharing our personal truths / Alan P. Bell.
        p.   cm.
    Includes bibliographical references (p. 371) and index.
    ISBN 0-7657-0135-9 (alk. paper)
    1. Sex (Psychology)   2. Sex (Psychology)—Case studies.
I. Title.
BF692.B385   1997
155.3—DC21   97-33435

Printed in the United States of America on acid-free paper. For information and catalog write to Jason Aronson Inc., 230 Livingston Street, Northvale, New Jersey 07647-1726. Or visit our website: http://www.aronson.com

Contents

Preface

In his recent biography of Alfred C. Kinsey, James H. Jones[1] contends that Kinsey's ideology, fueled by his own sexual proclivities, influenced his sampling and data analysis to such an extent that he found exactly what he wanted to find in the sexual behaviors of American males and females. Much of what has been said about Kinsey's "secret life" is supposition, but there is no question that this pioneering giant in the field of human sexuality, whose contributions were so enormous and whose findings had such a monumental impact on Americans' sexual attitudes, focused primarily on people's sexual *behaviors* and their relationship to demographic variables such as age, religion, marital status, and social class. By collecting and classifying sexual histories just as he had done with gall wasps during his career as a taxonomical entomologist, Kinsey and his distinguished associates established the fact that American men and women were engaging far more frequently in various sexual behaviors than had previously been supposed. Their findings, painstakingly reported in statistical tables and graphs and discussed without moral judgments, shocked the

---

1. Jones, J. (1997). *Alfred Kinsey*. New York: Norton.

nation. The unexpected news of many people's engaging in sexual behaviors, hardly ever discussed in polite company, was given attention everywhere, not only in scientific journals but in the popular press as well. There seemed to be no end to the debates over how many people were "really" engaging in what kinds of sexual behaviors at any given point in time. Sexual conservatives remained convinced that Kinsey and his associates at the Institute for Sex Research had overestimated the number of people in the various categories of behavior. Liberals, on the other hand, took the Kinsey figures as gospel and as justification for their efforts to reduce the effects of what they saw as a crippling erotophobic environment. Private citizens, meanwhile, uncertain if their own sexual practices and patterns were quite typical, were quick to look up Kinsey and colleagues' graphs and tables for an implicit judgment of their "normality." Regardless of how exact the figures were, numerous men and women who had ever masturbated or engaged in premarital or extramarital coitus or in sexual behaviors with a person of the same sex could now at least be sure that they were not alone in what they did.

Long before I became the Senior Research Psychologist at Kinsey's Institute for Sex Research at Indiana University, approximately fourteen years after his death and at the time that the so-called Sexual Revolution had just begun, I had been greatly impressed by what Kinsey and his cohorts had achieved. I had welcomed their reports as a reason to be less harsh in my judgments of those whose sexual patterns were not similar to my own. I had seen too often the ravaging effects of shame and guilt in those whose sexual lives did not conform to what they and others thought was the psychosexual or spiritual ideal. My plea then as now, one perhaps shared with Kinsey and his colleagues, was that we celebrate our sexual diversity instead of wringing our hands over it. Thus, after earning my doctorate in Counseling Psychology, I welcomed the opportunity to join others at the Institute for Sex Research to learn more about the nature of human sexuality. I shall remain forever grateful for being given such an opportunity and can do nothing but applaud the Institute's first efforts in this important field.

I did not come to the Institute, however, without certain misgivings. Like others of my ilk, I had been somewhat critical that the

Institute appeared to focus on sexual behavior exclusively. Counting orgasms or estimating the number of people who could be scored a certain way on the so-called Kinsey Scale was simply not my cup of tea. Sexual practices of various kinds, whether they involved anal intercourse or sadomasochism, were of little import to me. The huge array of pornographic films I found at the Institute were of only passing interest to me. My curiosity lay in a different direction: I was far more interested in the *psychology* of sexual behavior, in the *meaning* of sexual events to those participating in them, in the very complex *covert* responses, involving the mind and heart, to be found in those sexually engaged with each other. What do our sexual behaviors tell us about ourselves, our histories, the nature of our emotional development, the quality of our interpersonal relationships? Where, in those behaviors, do we find the needs and issues and motivations that give rise to them?

Upon my arrival at the Institute in the summer of 1967, I was immediately made field director of a study of gay males that was then being conducted in Chicago. In helping to construct the questionnaire we were to use in one-to-two hour interviews with some 500 individuals it did not take me long to realize that the final version of our research instrument did not even begin to tap the dimensions of sexual experience of most importance to me. These dimensions were not what Kinsey and his associates came to include in their innovative interview procedures, nor were they to be found in what we had concocted ourselves. While our questionnaire, unlike Kinsey's primary focus, did include certain measures of psychological and social adjustment in addition to sex-related behaviors, it sought no information about the deeper aspects of sexual experience. Thus, on more than one occasion, I found myself apologizing to respondents for our failure to inquire about the most crucial elements of their sexual behavior.

My frustration with what happened in Chicago followed me to San Francisco, where we interviewed more gay men and lesbians, black as well as white, than had ever been interviewed before. Regardless of the improvement we made in our interview protocol this time, making it possible to identify five different types of homosexual men and women and to compare them with their heterosexual counterparts, my misgivings about multiple-choice questioning and the lack of any opportunity to get to a level of inquiry where what matters most—thought and feelings—is going on, did not abate. Perhaps Margaret Mead, who accused Kinsey and his associates of reducing sexual behavior to a simply physical event, was asking too much of what amounted to a hugely significant, but only a first, step. In the same vein, perhaps Lionel Trilling, informed by the psychodynamic understanding of human behavior, expected far more than could possibly be delivered in the first Kinsey Reports.

But almost five decades have elapsed since those initial inquiries were made, and the time has come to shift our focus. Looking up tables and graphs to see where we stand as compared with others in our sexual behaviors will no longer suffice. It is not what we *do* sexually that matters most. It is what we are up to, our needs and motivations and our feelings about our sexual deeds, that chiefly distinguishes us from others. I am convinced, for example, that while homosexuals and heterosexuals differ in the nature of their sexual attractions, certain homosexuals are far more like certain heterosexuals than they are like other homosexuals when it comes to the meaning and place of sexuality in their lives. The same, of course, would be true in comparing men with women, large numbers of whom are far more similar to those of the opposite sex than they are to their own.

During the course of my career as a sex researcher, I have become convinced that if we are to gain a better understanding of sexual behavior, we must include both qualitative and quantitative approaches in our methodology. While the deftly crafted questionnaires generally employed in survey research can provide us with information that allows us to see the forest for the trees, qualitative research, involving in-depth, quasi-clinical interviews with a smaller number of respondents, allows the researcher to see not only a certain number of trees but their roots as well. When it comes to sexual behavior, the terrain encompassed by a person's mind and heart may not be easily discernible, but if it is not our primary focus, we shall miss the point entirely and fail to grasp the vast complexity of what it means to be sexual.

Acknowledgments

My gratitude to others who have contributed so much to this book is beyond any bounds. There are so many of them. Most cannot be recalled by name.

This would not be the book it is without those who gave permission to be interviewed by me and my students regarding their sexual whereabouts. Their highly personal accounts illustrate in no uncertain terms the wonderful diversity of sexual experience. They were told that reporting the details of their sexual exchanges and accounting for them would be no easy task. Still, they were willing to risk the inevitable awkwardness of their uncommon transparency, secure only in the knowledge that they would never be publicly identified. Of course I know and remember well the interviews I personally conducted, in homes I would never visit again and in my own office, from which the book's clinical vignettes emerged. I shall always regard the participants as heroes.

The graduate students in psychology or counseling who helped me out on this project could be considered brave as well. To be sure, it might be assumed that would-be clinicians would be forthright and reasonably comfortable with their own and others' sexuality, but such an assumption, I have learned over the years, is not always warranted. Too many professionals are ill-prepared to take on the sexual circumstances of their clients: When it comes to asking others questions about their sexual experiences or telling about their own, they often hesitate, lest their questioning be misinterpreted or their self-revelations offend the listener. Thus, my hat goes off to those graduate students who not only conducted interviews with strangers but also made their way each week to the office I constructed in my barn to address sexual matters with me and their peers (our heated exchanges interrupted only occasionally by the sight of my horses peering through the windows or by the sounds of geese flying by). For several years we met to discuss the many different nuances of our own and others' sexual behaviors; sometimes the students listened as I thought out loud. Without such opportunities, this book would not have been possible. In addition, these graduate students helped develop the exercises that appear at the end of the book, fine-tuning them with their friends and colleagues. They also went out of their way to read and describe popular works dealing with the topic at hand. I hope the entire enterprise proved to be as energizing for them as it was for me, and I only regret that my records do not include the names of every student who contributed, so they could be acknowledged individually as well as collectively.

One person who shall not remain nameless is Patt Stowers, a long-time friend and colleague, who helped me teach my course in human sexuality for many years at Indiana University. Her experience as a sex therapist and her endowments of great humor, forthrightness, and ease in the sexual domain made her presence at our weekly discussions invaluable. Driving to the barn in a Honda bedecked in sexually suggestive slogans and sometimes joining the group with a garland of condoms around her neck, always ready to share her latest personal anecdote, Patt led the way in our considerations of matters sexual. Especially sensitive to the fact that every person's sexual needs, attitudes, and behaviors are unique, she constantly warned us against the tendency to label others' sexual whereabouts as "normal" if they coincided with our own and "abnormal" if they did not.

Another on this list is Patricia Chambers who typed each of the seven revisions of the manuscript without complaint. She prided herself, as indeed she should, on being one of the few persons who could begin to read my handwriting! Her devotion to my work over the years is perhaps best exemplified by her efforts to get the final version of the manuscript in on time after being stricken with a detached retina in one eye while nursing a cataract in the other! Following her surgery, she accompanied me every evening and over a weekend to the office and piloted her hastily recruited substitute through the computer file, remaining close by to help out whenever the computer refused to cooperate.

Linda DuPlantis is another friend and colleague whose expertise I came to rely on throughout this project. I consider her an editor without equal, just the kind of collaborator I need to keep my language more precise. In addition to all her editorial changes, she made extremely useful suggestions (which I almost invariably followed) in regard to the order and structure of the book. I happily deposited various chunks of the manuscript behind her storm door out in the country, knowing that she would do magic and return a draft in much better shape than what it was when I delivered it. I cannot thank her enough for all she did to make this book what it is. Besides, it is nice to know that when it comes to its possible shortcomings, there is someone besides myself to blame!

Finally, there is Shirley, my wife of thirty-three years, who has always felt called upon to keep me grounded in reality. She fancies herself to be my toughest critic, and if I did not know that her heart were really in it, I would have discharged her long ago. It is out of our sexual relationship that many of the questions and issues addressed in this book have arisen. Our own efforts to come to terms with who we are sexually and to make the most of our sexual partnership have made me well acquainted with both the sexual heights and the sexual doldrums. Shirley's honesty and good will throughout our marriage have contributed more to who I am and think and feel than she could possibly know.

By way of a final note, I have been especially pleased and grateful to my publisher and to his associates for their generous reactions to what has been written here. It took more than marketing prospects for a publisher to enthusiastically embrace the manuscript I sent to him. He never blanched at the language of the book. He never retreated from the substance. He was struck most by what he termed "clinical gems," which he thought would be useful, if not inspiring, to professional and non-professional readers alike. His enthusiastic engagement with what is offered here restored my confidence in what I had undertaken when there was no guarantee that it would ever see the light of day. I shall remain forever grateful to him for that.

Introduction

We do a callous injustice to the sexual moments of our lives whenever we take what we or our partners do at face value, whenever we leave unexplained what is really going on in our minds and hearts and what we think is really going on in theirs. If we are ignorant of ourselves, we cannot share much-needed information with our partner, and our sexual exchange will inevitably remain uncertain and unclear. If we do not identify what elements in our sexual experiences make up the poignant and exhilarating drama of sexual need and contact, we shall remain strangers to our sexual circumstances.

This book invites you to broaden your view of sexual experience, to look far beyond your loins in considering your sexual circumstances, and to deepen your understanding of what occurs sexually to a point where you find yourself confronting core convictions about yourself and the company of others. Our sexual fortunes or misfortunes are chiefly determined by how we construe our sexual circumstances, not by what "actually" transpires. If we ignore what is going on between our ears—our deeply held convictions about what the stakes amount to in the sexual domain—our sexual lives cannot be completely fulfilling.

There are vital questions we all must answer.

- Why is sex so important or unimportant to us?
- What things are we really after in a sexual exchange?
- What do we expect of ourselves and our partner?
- What makes us pleased or displeased?
- What needs can we easily declare and why? What needs do we scuttle?
- Which of our sexual proclivities can we talk about?
- What is our bottom line in a sexual partnership?

These are all a part of the woof and warp of sexual experience, and we need to broaden and deepen our consideration of them. Truncated versions will never do.

There are always reasons for sexual troubles. They usually consist of deep personal truths we would rather not acknowledge to ourselves, much less share. In fact, it can sometimes feel dangerous to examine how we perceive our partner or how we experience our partnership, so that often enough we disregard our mind and heart and seek cheap solutions—new moves—avoiding deeper truths. There are plenty of self-help books happily ready to cooperate with us in this self-deception. Their suggestions are glib: take the phone off the hook or put a lock on the door; go off on a cruise; try pornography; plug in colored lights; do it in different ways, places, clothing. Even well-meaning sex therapists may define their patients' problems chiefly in *sexual* terms and propose primarily *sexual* remedies, but this only helps the patient ignore the roots of their problems. Sexual difficulties arise in the secret recesses in our hearts and minds, and that is where most damage to sexuality is done. This book is a call to put first things first.

During my fifteen years as Senior Research Psychologist at the Kinsey Institute for Sex Research at Indiana University, I conducted surveys of people's sexual behaviors and attitudes and concocted countless statistical tables. I eventually became convinced that such methodology barely scratched the surface of respondents' sexual lives. What does it matter what percentage of men and women engage in non-marital sex or masturbate with a given frequency or are sexually dysfunctional in one way or another? What people *do* sexually does not begin to tell the story! It is how they *construe* what they are doing, how they explain their behavior to themselves and perhaps to others, that portrays them.

Why is it, for example, that sex outside of marriage is shrugged off by some people and bitterly resented or repented by others? How is it that frequent sex is satisfying for some couples and not others? What causes some individuals with a major sexual dysfunction to be relatively pleased with their sex lives while others, technically proficient in every way, are profoundly disappointed? Clearly, sexual behaviors do not in themselves tell us anything about emotional effects on a person or on a relationship. The sexual domain is not defined by what happens between two bodies, by the dimensions of the bed, or by the texture of the bedsheets. Rather, it is marked by hidden assumptions as to what *should* be taking place during a sexual act, by hidden evaluations of ourselves and our partner, by hidden determinations, by echoes from the past, by wishes barely formed in our minds, by conclusions drawn with or without evidence, by needs that may or may not be entirely compatible.

Anyone who reads these pages will be struck by how differently people view, experience, think about, and evaluate the sexual moments they share with others. There are hugely various descriptions of why sex took place when it did, what truly matters about ourselves or our partner, what we think drives our sexual impulses and needs, what fears or confidence we have in communicating with our partner, how much or how little focus there is on reaching orgasm and why, how we enact ourselves before and during and after a sexual exchange, how we defend ourselves against total self-abandon, how far we feel emotionally connected to our partner. We are widely different in how we want to appear to ourselves and to our partner, how we understand our sexual fantasies or lack of them, what it feels like being stuck in the sexual doldrums or exalted to sexual heights, the quality and meaning of our sexual partnerships, and the remedies we envision for improving our sexual circumstances. Each of these differences, combined in countless different ways, makes up the unique tapestry of our sexual past, present, and future.

I did not set out to illustrate the diversity of human sexual behavior. It just emerged during open-ended interviews, originally conducted in order to identify the principal parameters of sexual experience, with approximately one hundred men and women. With no particular interest in correlating responses with age, socioeconomic status, religious affiliation, or anything else, we cast as wide a net as possible. Some participants were friends and acquaintances, some were students, others were colleagues; a goodly number were clients or ex-clients whom I had seen as a psychotherapist, sex therapist, or marriage counselor. Most were heterosexual, some were gay; most but not all were married or involved in a serious relationship. Most were not sexually dysfunctional and, in fact, were reasonably happy with their sexual lives; only a few found their sexual circumstances unbearable. I personally collected only some of these extensive interviews; my students recorded the rest. Individual responses were selected for inclusion here on the basis of how well they illustrated the issues addressed. Exactly who said what was of no importance. What mattered was the depth and the eloquence of the descriptions of sexual joys and pain. Those descriptions reminded me again of how much is missing from statistical reports, and of what an affront it is for survey researchers (such as I once was) to claim that they have defined the American Sexual Scene, indeed that their "how many times" counts for very much at all!

When I initiated the interviews, I did not plan to cover any particular themes. It was only after sifting, again and again, through the transcribed tapes, that I began to see what forest these trees made up. The chapters of this book summarize what was found, comment on how, and possibly why, sexual experience is so diverse, and illustrate these points with word-for-word excerpts from our respondents' stories. Each of us has our own unique sexual reality; our sexual history, our gender, our age, our temperament, our hormones, our ways of behaving so as to feel safe in our contacts with others, what we think we have a right to, how we go about making life meaningful to us, what we value most. All these combine to make an individual sexual being.

For readers who want to try a voyage through their own sexual whereabouts, some words of advice and warning. Try not to be quick in your reading of what follows. Feel free to lay the book aside;

indeed, by all means do so whenever you think you may have run across yourself or certain parts of yourself in what is said in what others report about themselves. Perhaps a notebook and pen within easy reach would prove useful to you as you jot down whatever strong reactions you have and want to think further about.

In my own clinical practice, clients are invariably assigned tasks to be performed between sessions. I have found the contents of this book to be extraordinarily helpful in the effort to facilitate self-awareness and deeper communication. Because the topics addressed are so deeply personal and the material so challenging, I ask couples to proceed slowly and cautiously into territories seldom explored in even the best adjusted partnerships. I ask them to read a chapter or two at a time and always at the same pace; I ask them to write down their reactions and, at first, to save discussions for the clinical hour with me.

The emphasis is on owning their individual personal truths, first and foremost, and then on becoming increasingly transparent with each other. These efforts become the major focus of our sessions together, with no attempt on my part to get the couple to change any of their ways. I sometimes encourage the couple to make use of the various exercises that can be found at the conclusion of the book and to examine their resistances to them—as much can be learned from a couple's trepidations as from their ease in coming to terms with their sexual whereabouts.

Try your best to be brutally honest with yourself. If certain themes repeatedly emerge as you move from one chapter to the next, so much the better. This will mean that you are in the process of identifying what truly matters or concerns or gratifies you in the sexual domain. And by the end you will find yourself among the fortunate few who have more than a vague idea of where they are coming from, sexually, and of what they need in a sexual partnership. Consider, also, at the end of each chapter what thoughts you are ready to share with your partner and how that might be done and, of course, how your admissions will be received by a partner willing to listen to them. Perhaps, and this would be ideal, you and your partner will decide to work your way through the book together, sharing your notes as you move along, perhaps even reading to each other out loud the entire text.

As you find yourselves joined in a common enterprise, the two of you may decide to make use of the exercises in the final chapter. These activities have been tried, tested, modified, and retested, and have been found useful in promoting sexual self-awareness. Some of the people who have benefited from them have supplied comments that suggest ways to go beyond the text. Of one thing I can be sure: Any couple who takes these tasks seriously and has the courage to own and declare where they are coming from will never be the same again in the sexual domain. Out of fears or painful revelations can emerge a radically different experience of sexual partnership and a resolution of issues rarely addressed by couples anywhere. There is no satisfaction quite like the relief of owning who we are and what we mean by our sexual conduct. Nor can there be any substitute for self-awareness when it comes to speaking from the mind and heart to a partner who truly matters to us. If we are not in touch with our true selves, how can we speak in utter honesty? And if we cannot communicate what is authentic, how can we ever feel comfortable and confident with our partner?

The Sexual Journey:
Getting There From Here

When was the last time you wished that things could be different in your sex life? There are, of course, people who are content with their sexual circumstances, who find little or nothing wrong with them, but they are probably a minority. Most of us wonder, from time to time, if there might be something missing. Sex has become too routine. Something is not quite right. The erections may be there. Orgasms are taken for granted. There may even be a kiss goodnight when the sexual exchange is over. But still there is a feeling of "Is that all there is?" Resignation to the status quo, no hope at all that things will ever be much different, has come to characterize many sexual partnerships across our land. This "disorder of sexual desire," as sex therapists term it, appears far more intransigent than the so-called sexual dysfunctions that occupied center stage at sex clinics in past decades.

Not all couples are passive in the face of sexual ennui. Some are keenly aware of feeling sexually spent, and their pain leads them to sex therapists who are impressed by their candor and eagerness to improve.

In conventional sex therapy the first step is to look at the client's history for various clues; the therapist will often recommend a medical exam to rule out physical causes. Efforts will be made to help the client become more sex-affirming. Clients are taught "desensitization" exercises, in which they undertake various kinds of physical contact without sexual relations; it is hoped that in this way they will become more comfortable with each other in intimate contexts. Sometimes clients will be given videos to watch at home, from which they can learn both sexual and non-genital contact techniques; it is hoped that exposure to such materials will relax the couple's inhibitions and expand their sexual imaginations. In addition, attention is often given to couples' communication skills and self-assertiveness, so that each of them can ask for what they want and refuse unwelcome suggestions from the partner. So far, so good. But is it good enough?

To be sure, there are some individuals, or so I have been told, whose sexual difficulties are swiftly cleared up by the therapist who, as Father or Mother Surrogate, gives them permission or even encouragement to be sexual. The magic words may go something like, "No matter what you have been previously told, you have a right to your sexual needs and interests." With a look of relief, no longer shrouded in doubt by "shoulds" from the past, such clients leave the therapist's office transformed. Similarly, others are said to need little more than basic information about their sexuality. This might be given directly by the authoritatively informed therapist, or it might come from a wise and kindly book that the couple is told to read. Usually, sex therapy encompasses both of these features and adds a third: instructions or suggestions designed to make the individual or couple less afraid, less critical, less antagonistic and more transparent to each other. Homework assignments, usually behavioral, incorporate the risks that new learning requires. And finally, if all these interventions are not enough, more extensive psychotherapy is used to bring about further changes that may be crucial to a successful outcome.

The shortcomings of this sequence of interventions are only too obvious to battle-weary clients and the experienced clinician. It is not enough to simply give an adult "permission" to be sexual. The logical question is, why does this grown-up person need that permission in the first place? What does this need tell us about the client's failure to forge a viable moral value system of his or her own? As for imparting the fundamentals, what kind of life has this person been living that up till now he or she has not sought sexual information? Can this be associated with much deeper sexual disinclinations? If so, should they not be examined?

It is at the level where clients experiment with new ways of relating to each other that avenues of deeper inquiry emerge—and where, despite the couple's best efforts and the therapists' boldest interventions, things often run aground. Every stop may be pulled out on the cognitive-behavioral pipe organ, but to no avail. The program of sharing thoughts and feelings in "real" talk, conducted in a particular place at particular times, is too soon forgotten in the wake of other distractions and priorities. They have been told exactly what they must do if their sexual circumstances are ever to improve. They may have even signed an agreement to carry out exercises that would promise change and relief. But they cannot keep up with their schedule of sensate focus exercises, accompanied by candle flames and wine, perhaps conducted in a sexual sanctuary, away from the kids; their everyday schedule intrudes. Special risks and new sexual experiences, such as seducing or being seduced, making love with one's eyes open, or going to bed in the nude, initially welcomed, fall into disuse and now are hardly considered at all. Over time, one by one, the old habits with their painful circumstances finally reappear, like weeds that finally take over a neglected garden.

It would appear that all too often behavioral prescriptions are simply not enough to get couples off dead center. Far more important—and the point of this book—are efforts that must be made to uncover each individual partner's *personal truths*. These form the bedrock of all that occurs in the sexual domain. It is here, in the mind and heart, that sexual needs and interests and torments can be more clearly understood, and only then, sometimes, changed.

- What does your sexuality mean to you, what is its purpose, how does it fit into your life, what part would you have it play in your partnership?
- How do you understand the importance or lack of importance you assign to sexual intimacy?

- What goes on in you at various junctures of your sexual exchanges: What are you feeling, what are you thinking, what do you wish?

Questions such as these are raised on just about every page that follows. You will be invited again and again to address them, to burrow more and more deeply into the *core* of your sexual experience, and to own, without apology, the personal truths you discover there.

If you go far enough, chances are you will come face to face with an enormous ambivalence, and it is your ambivalence that makes the changes you seek so difficult. You must come to see how you embody competing versions of the truth—about yourself, about your partner, about what might happen if things were different—in order to get off dead center. It is simply not enough to focus on the pain your "symptoms" cause. All your efforts to rid yourself of them will come to naught until you become acutely aware that you also greatly fear what might happen should your circumstances change to any significant degree.

For example, a large part of you (especially if you are female) may wish that you were far more interested in sex than you are. You may think that your partnership would blossom if only you felt more like making love or if only you had it in you to initiate sexual contact or if only you were more easily aroused and could communicate your sexual excitement to your partner. If this—your lack of interest in sex—is your chief complaint or "symptom," you probably are only too aware of its cost to you and your partnership. You wish you could be enthusiastic in bed: "Why can't I change? If I could, it would make all the difference in the world. What's the matter with me, anyhow?"

Or take another example: "I know that badgering my wife about sex does no good at all," you may tell yourself. "I feel like a predator. She knows I know she doesn't want it, and she resents my approaches. She ends up feeling used. I end up either feeling deprived when she 'wins,' or else ashamed of myself if I 'win.' But I can't help it! I have the needs that I do, and it's not unnatural, and I won't just sit and masturbate." If this man is you, you may blame your partner for your sexual misfortune; however be aware that you contribute to your sexual impasse by being so insistent. You can't help but demand sex, despite worrying that if you do, your relationship may fast go down the drain. What can you do?

What are *both* people in these examples to do? The chances are that neither of them has gone far enough in their burrowing for their deepest personal truths of all. They have yet to discover more central versions of reality that make their current "symptoms" not only difficult to dislodge but absolutely necessary to retain. They are not yet aware of how much they fear the consequences of change. They have not yet discovered that they hold an array of convictions about themselves and the world, about what would happen should their circumstances change. They do not realize yet that their "symptoms" have been designed to protect them from what their deeper truths warn them of: consequences far more fearful and involving far more suffering than they presently endure.

These deeper truths, described throughout the book, usually stem from whatever we needed to do and believe and wish for in order to feel safe, in childhood and, later on, among our peers, when we form convictions about who we are and who we must be and how we must act and what we are not free to acknowledge about ourselves and others. These convictions are not all verbal by any means, since the deepest ones were engraved in us before we could even use words: by a mother's touch, by sounds, by all manner of sensory input.

Our earliest experiences, together with the nature of our later exchanges with those who mattered most to us, are part and parcel of our *organismic* experiences and response to whatever occurs in our lives. The phrase "mind and heart," which you will see used over and over in this book, affirms that thoughts and feelings inevitably inform each other in constituting organismic experience. It is out of that experience that each of us constructs our personal realities.

This book is an invitation to probe the innermost recesses of heart and mind deeply enough to determine those emotional truths that govern our sexual life. The exercises at the end of the book help the explorer tease out interconnected avenues of thoughts and feelings, motivations that drive one's sexual activity, wishes that need to be acknowledged and voiced, behaviors that get chief attention, sensations that please or displease, desired changes in the sexual routine, what various features of one's sexual life are attributed to, what sexual difficulties are the greatest hindrance to the sexual partnership, the nature of one's sexual peaks, hidden assumptions that may be making sexual difficulties even more upsetting than they might otherwise be, and, finally, the most-loved features of one's sexual partnership. Anyone who takes the time to carry out these exercises will find that the benefits far outweigh any aversion there may be at first. They go straight to the core, touching on those aspects of sexual experience that really matter. But the journey is not for the faint-hearted.

There does remain the possibility that even those readers who are intent upon making radical changes in their sexual lives will end up unrewarded, even if they have tried out every behavioral measure in the therapist's repertoire and examined attitudes of which they were previously unaware. Going back to our examples, the woman who wishes she were more interested in sex and the man who can't help but badger his partner for more than she can possibly give might still be stuck where they are.

It is at this point, if not long before, that a shift in focus would be very much in order. Instead of making all kinds of efforts to change the troublesome symptom—whether it be a lack of sexual interest or compulsive behaviors in the bedroom or just a generally unhappy and dissatisfying sexual partnership—the individual or couple would do better to examine what convictions they hold that make the symptom more important to have than *not* to have. The new focus, still on matters of the mind and heart, would lead to the following questions:

- What does the sexual discontent *do* for me in my world?
- To what problem or concern is the *lack* of sexual fulfillment a solution?
- What unwelcome consequences might occur if I lived *without* my sexual dissatisfaction?
- What would I have to change, in behavior or attitude, for sexual dissatisfaction to cease?
- How important is it to me to make such a change?

According to Bruce Ecker and Laurel Hulley, the authors of *Depth-Oriented Brief Therapy*,[1] whose views I enthusiastically espouse, the chief reason clients do not relinquish their grip on clearly painful circumstances is that to do so would involve the prospect of consequences even *more* fearful than the ones they are living with. Until clients come to own and accept whatever version of reality makes their present "symptom" necessary, important, and meaningful, the changes they seek so desperately will elude them.

Ecker and Hulley suggest that the client describe in detail the worst features of his or her present predicament. The client's wish to change is taken seriously and sympathetically. But then the client is asked to imagine what it would be like if, by some miracle, the symptom or complaint disappeared—if the woman in our example now suddenly became interested in sex, if the man were now able to take his partner's sexual needs into account and not insist on his own. ("Try to imagine what it would be like if your sexual situation were remarkably improved," the therapist might say to the client. "What does that feel like? Note the changes in your experience of yourself and your partner. What can you detect that is different about your sexual exchanges?") At first the client may be full of hosannahs, supremely grateful for the change. But the therapist knows differently and waits patiently for some unwelcome aspect of the change to appear in the client's report. Sooner or later, the therapist is convinced, the greater evil that makes the client's present pain and predicament more tolerable than the change he or she consciously seeks will emerge. The client's hitherto unrecognized emotional reality will make the symptom readily understandable and provide themes to help the therapist account for the client's resistance to change.

How does the symptom outweigh its costs? How does it keep the client from having to face more fearful truths? In what ways and to what extent would change of any kind come to challenge the client's long-held views of reality, of who he or she is and amounts to, of how much power or control is required for safety, of all the "shoulds" and "musts" and "ought tos" in the client's life? In the case of the woman

---

1. Ecker, B. and Hulley, L. (1996). New York: Jossey-Bass.

with a lack of interest in sex, it may turn out that as long as she maintains her lack of interest, she will *never* have to experience herself as defying parental prohibitions and thus can always remain the good girl of her childhood; she will *never* have to experience rage over her parents' control and punishments when she was growing up, *never* run the danger of being a sexual predator instead of a victim, *never* have to contend with making sexual choices, *never* find herself vulnerable to a partner's rejection, *never* run the risk of being sexually out of control, *never* engage in sexual fantasies which she might find deeply troubling, *never* have to confront her anger over all that is missing in her sexual partnership or her sadness over all that she has forfeited throughout her life by unnecessary self-control. Sooner or later must come the discovery that for this woman there are things far worse than her lack of sexual interest.

According to psychodynamic formulations, oftentimes our chief complaint masks our deepest wish, and it is the latter that must be owned and understood before any progress can be made. This is exactly what I hope will happen for the reader who pursues what I refer to as his or her "ideational trails" and "hidden assumptions." Sometimes, with or without the help of a therapist, such radical inquiry into the heart and mind can be conducted by completing a sentence such as, "If, all of a sudden, I found myself full of sexual interest and eager for my mate, it is possible that. . . ."

I hope this book will help you become less afraid to take at least a peek into what may be hidden beneath your sexual complaints and problems. Your goal, beyond self-discovery, must eventually include profound respect for what you find out about yourself. Therein lies the change that can be extraordinarily worthwhile. It is only when we honor the selves that we are that we can understand and celebrate the Zen master's saving wisdom: "Complete acceptance and profound change are one and the same." The woman with a lack of sexual interest must do far more than wring her hands; she must pursue her various ideational trails to uncover the array of consequences more dreadful than those she now struggles with. Suppose one is the fear that if she were to awaken her sexual interest she might become sexually promiscuous: One strategy would be for her to write down on a 3 x 5 card, "As much as I suffer from my lack of sexual interest, I'd rather live with it than run the risk of becoming a whore, and I shall make sure to avoid this risk by doing all I can to control myself sexually." This woman has followed her ideational trail to identify a "focal construct"—an important concept that is part of her emotional reality. By writing it on a card, along with other constructs on other cards, she acknowledges that it exists for her: "This is me. This is part of who I am."

If and when we can daily face and own the deepest versions of our reality, we can now make a conscious choice to change or to stay the same. It is up to us, we are ready, and at least we know where we are. We are no longer trying to get someplace with no good idea of where on the map we are starting from. We confront our profound ambivalence and recognize parts of ourselves at odds with each other, each fostering its own version of reality. ("I know this in my head but not in my gut.") Intellectual truths and emotional truths are often not the same, but until the differences become clearer to us, until both are embraced equally, we "can't get there from here." This may be especially so in the sexual domain, where the stakes feel so high, where there are major consequences for how we conduct ourselves, and where we keep our deepest convictions about what is possible or necessary.

Interlude:
Eva and Charles

Charles and Eva are a perfect example of a couple stuck in the sexual doldrums. Married eight years and with two young children, Eva finds herself increasingly hamstrung by rage over not having her sexual-emotional needs met, while Charles has grown bone-weary by the energy he expends in avoiding issues. Their sex life is badly derailed, as we see from how they describe their latest exchange. Eva relates it this way:

> That afternoon he came home from work, gave me a big hug and a squeeze, and said, "Let's see what we can do about tonight." That made me a little nervous, but I thought it was great. To make a long story short, in the evening he came home with an X-rated porno film which I found very distasteful. It was awful! But as long as we were there, I thought I'd go along, and I guess I got excited enough to reach orgasm. After I was done, I was done, but I wasn't done because he wasn't done. I was wishing he would come. I remember thinking, "I wish this was over," so I said, "OK, honey, you can go ahead." But he said, "No, I want to wait." He was obviously enjoying himself, waiting to the end of the video. He wasn't looking at me. There was hardly any kissing or fondling. He grabbed my bottom and stuff every once

in a while, but that's not what I wanted. It's the upper part of my body that is sensitive, my breasts, my neck, my ears. I'm just a very sensuous person, and it's killing me to be shut out like this.

Charles saw the experience quite differently:

That particular night I brought home a pornographic movie. We both enjoy movies like this. It can be a turn-on. So I put in the tape, got into bed, and we started touching. It was a real treat and by the way she was reacting, I could feel she enjoyed it as much as I did. We didn't talk about specifics afterwards. I hate going into details. I guess I enjoy things that are more unspoken.

It is not just this one episode that reflects Charles and Eva's widely disparate views. Eva is plainly dissatisfied with their sexual circumstances:

I'm really down in the dumps about not being a sexual being. I guess you could say I have a passion for passion, and I have absolutely none in my life right now. When I tell him this, he just says, "OK. You've said this to me before." I've just kind of given up. I try not to think about it, because it's not part of my life. But every now and then I'll say to myself, "Is this what it's going to be like for the rest of my life?" I can't believe it will ever change.

But Charles sounds quite contented:

We touch as much as we can, and I really like that. When you touch a person, you always feel like something came out of you that is directed at that person, a kind of energy that comes out of your body and into theirs. The other day I gave her a big hug, and it felt good. It was just a fleeting moment, but we connected. Our hug said a lot. Her mind may have been a million miles away, or she could have connected exactly the way I did. I didn't ask. It wasn't necessary. When I hugged her, what I was saying is that I was glad we were together, glad that we have two such wonderful boys, that I was there for her. On our wedding anniversary I got us a park bench so that I can sit with her and put my arm around her, so that we can be together and forget the worries of the outside world.

How does Eva account for the void she feels and deeply resents in her marriage?

He's so wound up in his work! Work and food are his passions. He's rather eat than make love.

And, according to Eva, Charles' passion for food has had other consequences.

He's up to 290! When I look at pictures of him in the past, it becomes obvious that he keeps going up, up, and up. You can tell by the notches on his belt. He's got big folds in his back. Any time I put my arm around his waist, I can hardly get it around. If we're walking I can't even hold on. I can tell in my bones that he's not going to live a long, happy, healthy life, and I worry about that. I wish he were as concerned about his weight as he is about the way his glasses look or about his clothes. But when I bring it up, he shuts me out.

Although Charles does not mention it, Eva supposes that he is as turned off by her body as she is by his. He seems to rely on porno tapes and magazines to get him going, so she is convinced that he does not find her sexy enough:

I don't have big, firm breasts. My body is not real firm and young. My legs, my arms, my stomach. I've had two kids!

She blames herself, as well as him, for her failure to be alluring:

He might say, "She never does anything to turn me on!" And that's true. I don't come out of the bathroom all gussied up and coming on to him. The last time I tried that it was a disaster. My friends had given me a really skimpy outfit for my birthday. So I showered, put on some makeup and perfume and got dressed in the outfit. By the time I got to bed, he was snoring away!

What is the remedy for Eva and Charles? How will they ever find their way out of the sexual doldrums? Eva thinks that if her husband did a better job of grooming himself, it would make a big difference or, as we have seen, that it would help if her body were more appealing to him. Both agree that the pressures of work and of raising children are hugely distracting from a fulfilling sexual relationship. As Charles puts it:

> When we're at home, the phone rings or the laundry has to be done or the grass has to be cut. The kids are a handful. We need to get away from the house so we don't have to look over at the table where the diapers got changed or look at the toys on the floor. We've been to Mexico a few times. What a difference! We were both relaxed. Let it rain. Let the sun come out. It didn't matter. The smells, the tastes, the warmth, the beauty of the place were a real turn-on.

Unquestionably, exotic settings in faraway places can sometimes stimulate more sexual and emotional intimacy between two people than they find at home. But such retreats provide no lasting solutions unless the couple finds opportunities to make themselves known to each other in accustomed quarters. Any proposed remedy that does not include the effort to genuinely communicate their fears, their worries, their expectations, their perceptions of each other, the impact of their engagements with one another, will come to naught. Besides being unsure whether she has the right to more than she now is getting, Eva hesitates to assert herself sexually for fear of how Charles might react if she laid her cards on the table:

> If I said anything at all, it would totally crush him. He gets hurt and indignant so easily. Whenever I bring anything up, he immediately puts up a wall. He doesn't want to hear it. He wants to gloss over all the things that matter. It's hard for him to deal with feelings. If I really let it out, he probably would never approach me again, and then where would I be? It's just easier to go to bed and forget it. I'm exhausted as it is. I need to deal with that, too? It's easier to pretend that everything is O.K.

Charles' report confirms Eva's impressions of him:

> I hate the idea of having to talk about the details of my sexual life, even with her. I guess we talk about it, but it's not a really exhaustive discussion. We don't get into what turns us on, like

bikini briefs or garter belts. She'll ask me, "What would make you happy?" and I usually respond, "The things that you do make me happy." I sometimes get the feeling that she thinks I'm not telling her everything. But it's hard for me to respond. She satisfies me sexually just fine. Why do we have to get into the specifics of exactly what I'd like her to do? That's a line of questioning that I don't feel comfortable talking about. I used to play tennis a lot when I was in high school. When I started thinking about the way I served, all of a sudden I couldn't serve the ball worth shit! When it comes to sex, I just want to be with her, touch her, feel her, connect with her, make love to her. That's good enough for me.

But not for her! And can we believe what he says when, in fact, he continues to masturbate three to four times a week and manages sexual intercourse with his wife but several times a year? Meanwhile, he continues to work himself into exhaustion, while Eva fantasizes lovers she has had in the past and seriously contemplates divorce.

I

SEXUAL
TRANSPARENCY

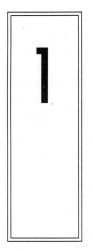

1

Making Sense of Things: CONSTRUALS

From the moment that a sexual exchange is about to begin, to not begin—indeed just to be thought of—the partners' hearts and minds are already busy shaping the moment. What we think and feel before, during, and after the exchange make up the essential core of our sexual experience.

IDEATIONAL TRAILS

Suppose that one night a man feels sexual desire for his partner who lies just inches away from him. What he makes of this wish, the thoughts he has about it, the explanations he gives for it, will reflect his entire history as a man and as a sexual being and will determine what happens next. It is not sexual desire in itself that is particularly noteworthy; rather, it is how a person construes sexual desire at the moment that directs what will take place.

- This hypothetical man may think, "It's been three days since we've had sex. It's about time we had it again. Couples like us are supposed to average two or three times a week." Concerns about whether or not he is sexually "normal" may actually affect him more than his desire does.

- Perhaps, though, a closer look would show that expressed concerns about "normality" serve only to justify his approaches to his partner. Underlying them may be even deeper fears— that the sexual relationship is losing its zest and may peter out entirely if they are not careful, or that his partner has lost desire for him, or that he must "use it or lose it."
- Or these fears may be overshadowed by still graver ones—that the relationship, overall, is no longer what it was and may soon end if every effort, sexual and otherwise, is not made to remedy it; or that his partner may be looking for another man; or that his aging or his medications are taking away his sexual prowess.

At the end of this particular "ideational" trail is the grievous fear that time is passing all too quickly, that he must face the prospect of death, wondering whether he has ever fully lived.

On the other hand, this man's interest in sex on this particular occasion may not be laced with any of these concerns at all.

- Perhaps he feels gratitude for special kindnesses his partner showed that day, or an enduring delight that things are going so well between them, or deep contentment in being reunited with his partner after an absence.
- He may consider that tonight she is looking or acting especially sexy.
- Or, he may simply believe his desire arises naturally from generous amounts of androgen; he might explain that his parents were sexually affirming or that he inherited his father's great sexual capacity.
- He might go on to assert that an interest in sex is a male trait and therefore is never remarkable; it merely should be taken as proof-positive evidence of his masculinity.

All these explanatory efforts take him no longer than an instant, based as they are upon long-held assumptions and beliefs about his sexuality which are carried over from one moment to the next.

Let us now suppose that this man's partner does not want sexual contact. She, too, is inevitably producing explanations. If her disinterest is momentary, she may think that they should wait until bedtime or that her menstruating would make sex messy or that she is tired and needs to get up early. But if she has never felt much sexual interest, generally, or in this particular partner, she might consider low interest as normal for women. She may ascribe it, as well, to repressive parents who inhibited her or to feeling unattractive or to sexual trauma in the past. More deeply buried than these explanations may be disgust or fear at submitting to a larger, stronger person, arising from a shaky sense of autonomy. Each explanation, sufficiently explored, usually uncovers a further one.

REASONS, REASONS EVERYWHERE

When we first met, there were no holds barred, but that's changed quite a bit. Now she doesn't like to perform oral sex the way she used to. She says she feels like she's choking or being smothered. . . . Maybe something happened in the past that really fucked her up. In the beginning of our relationship, we had sex every day, sometimes twice a day. Maybe she just got to the point where she thought it was just for the sake of having sex, that there wasn't any love in it.

*

My father would try to touch the side of my leg with his penis. Sometimes he'd try to put it in my underpants, and I'd back away or crawl under the bed or go to my mom. I think that really has affected my sexual relationships with men. I don't trust them even though some of them could probably have been trusted, but I wouldn't, I couldn't. I was too afraid.

*

He won't hold my hand. He has a hard time being affectionate. But I don't take it personally. I could be wrong, but I think it's *his* hangup.

In the mind of each of us can be found an entire array of convictions that determine our sexual behaviors and attitudes, beliefs about ourselves that are drawn from every one of our life experiences. They start with our earliest experiences of our parents, our childhood associations with male and female peers, memories of our first sexual arousal or interest, all that we have ever learned about ourselves and the world that beckons us. They may or may not be conscious or easily identified, but we can be sure that with sufficient introspection we can unearth almost all of our interpretations of what is happening in our sexual lives. Here is where we enact all that we think we know. What we expect to happen, how we explain what does happen, and how it all makes us feel, together lend to the sexual enterprise a kind of majesty that is missed by those who regard sex merely as what body parts do together.

> "Our emotional response follows from our interpretation, rather than from the act per se." (Beck 1988, p. 140).

Of course, sexual interpretations and explanations account for far more than whether we feel sexual desire. At every juncture in a sexual exchange we challenge ourselves with numerous questions:

"Why am I always the one to initiate things?"
"Why is it so hard for me to make the first move?"
"Why can't I just let *go*?"
"Am I doing this right?"
"How come it's all fellatio for him and no cunnilingus for me?"
"Do people actually *enjoy* this?"
"Why can't she just tell me what she likes?"
"Who is he thinking about right now?"
"Doesn't he even notice I'm not turned on?"
"Why can't I hold off ejaculating?"
"Why can't I get as hard as I used to?"
"What does it say about me as a woman, that I don't have an orgasm?"
"Why isn't this the fun it used to be?"
"What's he doing, jumping off me and grabbing a cigarette?"
"Why does it make me want to cry at the end?"

The answers we find may be slow in coming. They may be tentative; they may be irrational. But to ask questions, and to search for explanations, is to affirm our humanity: Human beings seek meaning in all the events of their lives. Our suppositions represent our attempts to bring order and predictability to our lives. They constitute the warp and woof of what we see as reality—the basis of our decisions, judgments, and emotional responses. Not understanding what is going on can deeply frighten us, so we are quick to reduce ambiguity by applying beliefs and convictions to make sense of things.

Nowhere is a human being's need for making sense of what is going on more evident than in sexual matters. In this domain, no gesture goes unnoticed. We fashion from what transpires a reality that reflects and fosters extremely important conclusions about ourselves and our partner and about the nature and quality of the relationship. The judgments we make touch the very core of who we think we are and have the power to affect our deepest sense of what it means to be truly alive. In a sphere where clear communication between partners is notably absent and much is unclear to ourselves, we fill in the gaps with a mortar of highly subjective and inaccurate notions of what is going on, assigning meanings of great consequence to every nuance of the sexual exchange.

Since the same sexual event can be interpreted so differently by either partner, it follows that what literally occurs may say very little about the quality of the sexual relationship or about its impact upon the persons involved. In other words, it is not *what* happens that is of sublime importance to the actors but rather their *explanations* for its happening. For example, a woman may attribute multiple orgasms to plenty of estrogen or to feeling free to fantasize or to a recent business success or to the absence of interruptions from children or to her efforts in overcoming sexual inhibitions, and not necessarily to the love she feels for her partner or to his physical attractiveness or sexual skills. Likewise, sexual difficulties may or may not be understood as a function of our partner's ineptitude or as a sign of a deteriorating relationship. They may be viewed by both partners as the result of aging or of medications that dampen libido or of stress or of a history of terrifying abuse. Our partner's sexual dysfunction may make his or her willingness to engage in sex at all a mark of heroism or a sign of uncommon love and caring, while the triumphs of the sexual athlete may be viewed as merely the sign of narcissistic needs, having little to do with love or caring or intimacy.

No wonder so little is known about exactly how sexual experience relates to the quality of the partnership. Up until now, sexuality has been defined far too narrowly. It has less to do with what people *do* than with what people *think* is being done and why. To complicate matters even further, two given partners frequently have quite different explanations of their sexual contacts—their own idiosyncratic views rooted in their own quite separate realities. When I interview two partners separately I sometimes find myself amazed by the differences in their accounts. Neither is necessarily misrepresenting anything, but they are individually committed to the reality they have fashioned and highly resistant to any attempts to change it. Nothing seems to matter more to us than the conviction that we know what is really going on, that our interpretations are correct and unassailable. There can be no safety, no sense of empowerment, no confidence in ourselves if our perceptions are found wanting. Thus, between sexual partners, as with other types of partnerships, there is often an ongoing struggle as to who gets to define what is happening, whose interpretation will gain sway.

All that can be said with certainty about people's sexual circumstances is that they differ from moment to moment and to such an extent that new names must be invented to describe what is truly happening. What is "figure" for one partner may well be "ground" for the other. That is, a prominent element in one partner's sexual event may not even be present in the other's, and vice versa. Individual differences in the sexual domain may be so pronounced that sexual partners actually remain strangers to each other at the very moment in which a mystical union appears to occur. More often than they would like to believe, they assume that they understand what a sexual transaction means to each of them, but miss the mark.

IT MUST BE ME

Some of us tend to emphasize our personal responsibility for whatever occurs in the sexual domain. We may see our personal traits or characteristics as prescribing the behaviors we engage in; our thoughts and feelings can influence the process and the outcome. Our reflexive reaction to *any* event may be, "It's because of me." This attitude takes a malignant form in manic-depressive episodes or psychotic breakdowns, but in its more frequent and benign form, it can denote what is termed an "internal locus of control," in which people view themselves as agents in lives of their own making and not as inordinately affected by forces beyond their control. They may congratulate themselves for what others might view as simply good luck and, as well, seek reasons in themselves for misfortunes. Thus, a favorite question of mine is to ask people what they think is responsible for their sexual peaks and valleys. Answers to such questions tell us a great deal about the individuals involved and about the nature of their partnerships.

Sexual peaks—those times when sex is especially gratifying—we can attribute to ourselves in countless ways. It could be that we felt unusually eager for sex that day. Or perhaps we were at a high point emotionally, at the top of our form and ready to celebrate:

> It all had to do with my good mood. It had been a long time since I wasn't feeling like I was sitting and watching or I wasn't thinking about work the whole time or "God, I hope this gets over with because someone's coming over," or "We really need to be doing something else." All I wanted to be doing was having sex with him.

*

> I always like it if I'm feeling particularly good or relaxed.

*

> I feel different when I stop taking the Pill. I start thinking, "God, I'd like to have a penis inside."

Other ways in which people might ascribe sexual peaks to themselves have to do with efforts they have made to overcome their inhibitions:

> Last night it felt real good because my wishes were being gratified. It was like icing on the cake. I'd felt real dissatisfied

because we just weren't having sex, so I spoke up, and now we're having sex a lot more.

*

The quality is a lot better than it was at the beginning. I've learned that I'm not a bad person if I enjoy having oral sex with him. I used to have a lot more guilt about being sexual.

We might explain successful sex in terms of what stimulates us best, irrespective of our partner:

It's the rape fantasies I have. I don't imagine violence or getting hurt. Just the whole idea of the woman not wanting to do it but the man making her do it and her ending up liking it.

*

When I can think that sex is forbidden, it becomes more exciting.

*

When sex is forbidden then there is no obligation to go through with it, and without a sense of obligation things go easier for me. There's no pressure to become sexually aroused.

On the other hand, we may attribute sexual peaks to ourselves when our partner provides what we require:

I enjoy it most when it's with someone I'm not trying to put the make on, when it just kind of happens. I like that. When I don't have to force it to happen, when I don't have to bullshit my way into it.

*

When I feel loved and adored, it builds up the lovemaking.

*

It's so much easier for me to let go and be myself with someone I know and love.

*

My experiences lately have been so good because I think I finally know what it means to be in love. I can't believe how much love changes sex!

Finally, we might explain our sexual fortunes as resulting from the technical ability we have developed:

> I think the fact that I've had many different lovers has helped me be uninhibited in my sexual expressions. You learn from other people you're with. You come to create your own style of how to be with someone.

IT'S ALL MY FAULT

The comments above, illustrating how men and women might account for their sexual fortunes and the part each plays in them, hint at opposite reasons why the sexual moments in their lives have not been rewarding or are downright negative: the *absence* of love, the *presence* of tension, guilt, inhibitions, detachment; feeling or invoking an obligation to submit; a lack of sexual experience or of permission to fantasize. We are more likely to think about the reasons for our sexual difficulties than for our sexual pleasure, unless, of course, the latter represents a long desired change. Sexual difficulties, especially when they are viewed as unique or atypical, require explanations of one sort or another, all of which clearly depict the images we have of ourselves as sexual partners:

> Our sex life started declining after the first three years. It was never bad until the kids came along, and I never got out of the house. I was boring even to myself, so my self-esteem was piss poor.

*

> I was very anxious about my performance. She had a lot more sexual experience than I did, so I wondered, "How will I stack up to her former partners?"

*

> By the end of the day, I don't feel clean, and I don't want him poking around down there.

There are other explanations for sexual woes that are more global and more permanent features of one's sexual functioning, none of which enhance the partnership and most of which do it harm. Some people describe what amounts to a fear of intimacy:

> For me to enjoy sex, I have to be with a partner I trust; otherwise I don't enjoy it very much. But it's hard for me to trust anyone. In fact, I think there's only one man in my life — my ex-husband — whom I really enjoyed sex with. Even when I hated him, I still trusted him, and the sex was good. I knew he wasn't going to reject me or say that I was strange.

*

> Even though I'm attracted to her and think about sex, it's like it's almost forbidden because we're friends. I wonder if getting more and more intimate sexually will mess up the friendship. For me the sex gets scarier as the intimacy grows, and it gets worse. I admit it. I have a fear of intimacy.

*

> I don't feel as turned on to him as I once was. I sort of pull back to protect myself and use a lot of fantasy to turn myself on.

*

> I don't like people to touch me unless I want them to. I'm not a real touchy person except with kids. I prefer my distance. I can't relax completely if I feel like I need to respond to somebody else.

How can we ever feel safe and comfortable in closeness if we cannot declare ourselves? For some people, sexual disenchantment comes out of their inability to be assertive:

> When it comes to sex, I often feel like it's expected of me. I never feel that there is any other answer but Yes, something I have to do!

An overall lack of self-assertiveness often goes hand in hand with difficulty in telling our partner of our sexual needs. This communication problem is another reason we might give for lackluster sex:

> I'm not very expressive. It's hard to tell her what would feel good to me.

*

I can't communicate what I want as much as I'd like. One reason is that I feel I'm not confident. It's easier to say "This hurts" than to say what I want more of.

Or we may find in our sexual past the basis for a mind-set that prevents us from living up to our sexual promise:

My sexual addiction has led to a lot of fucking, and women get irritated with that. To me it's seventy percent fucking and only thirty percent lovemaking, and women dislike my pressure on them to fuck all the time. I guess I need to continue my recovery.

*

I'd rate myself as not too bad a lover, but certainly not extremely good. I was a good Catholic girl with very little sexual experience. It was all new for me. He's had to teach me a lot. I didn't have much self-confidence, especially now that I've gained weight.

*

I have screwed a lot of women. I mean, just hundreds, and I think that's been detrimental. It's kept me from having a more mature sense of sexuality.

*

Even though he reassures me that he's not going to die from deadly sperm buildup, I can't say No. I'm wimpy that way.

Some people are less self-critical, and attribute sexual difficulties not to a characterological aberration of one kind or another but to factors that can be easily remedied or expected to disappear eventually. Chief among these is mental or physical exhaustion:

I think our sex drives are equal, but sometimes I'm tired. If I'd feel more energetic, we'd probably make love better.

*

Our frequency went down to, like, nothing. I was just exhausted. Those kids were all *over* me. I just needed some space.

*

I've been impotent from time to time, probably because I'm fatigued. I've been working my butt off here lately to make ends meet.

*

I'm physically tired from school. I'm just channeling my energies into other things. Being real tired or preoccupied can make it hard.

While weariness may indeed account for sexual difficulties of one kind or another, people frequently prefer to disregard any other possible factors and leave it at that. Especially among those who suffer sexual fatigue fairly often, it may mask a variety of less obvious but more important issues. It may bespeak a more generalized depressive state. It may denote feeling a duty to our partner, no matter our mood. It may speak volumes about a disenchantment with our partner that is easier to handle if we do not admit it. Regardless, a continual tendency to go "dead in bed" calls for further explanations, some of which involve crippling self-images:

I've got a lot of shit carried around from when I was little and fat and ugly and never thought I'd have a boyfriend, let alone a husband. It doesn't go away.

*

Maybe I'm just too demanding a partner.

*

Sometimes I'm just not interested because I don't feel good about my body. I got to thinking, "Oh, my stomach is sticking out so far, and it's gross." When I'm heavy, I'm sure he feels he can hardly breathe.

*

I have this problem of not being able to let go and relax.

THINKING TOO HARD

William Masters, of the famed Masters and Johnson team, contended that a person's physical equipment is typically in good working order but is vulnerable to one's *mental* equipment. That equipment includes the negative messages we have received from our parents about sexuality in a culture that sets strict limits on sexual expression and renders many of our sexual capacities, interests, and impulses highly questionable. Helen Kaplan, likewise, stresses the fact that mental events can make it all but impossible for an individual to yield to a sexual opportunity. Cognitions, be they preoccupied with other areas in our lives, performance anxieties, or other fears, can rob a moment of its erotic potential and sabotage a sexual exchange.

Even without any overriding worry or preoccupation, we can still be aware at some level of time passing, of minor distractions during the sexual exchange, and if we are not fully immersed in what is happening sexually, we are surely inviting some disappointment and perhaps also setting up a dysfunction for which there will be no easy remedy. Indeed there may be no greater sexual mistake than half-hearted participation:

> During sex I keep wondering if I'm having a hard time enjoying it. I start worrying and that delays my orgasm even more, which makes him frustrated. I guess it says something about how insecure I feel in the relationship.

> *

> Sometimes I'm not really in it. I have school pressures. I'll start thinking about my paper, or I'll start getting worried about homework right in the middle of sex. That's a turn-off, a real distraction.

> *

> Sometimes I'm not as involved as I should be. I have so much else going on in my life, and other responsibilities are on my mind.

> *

> Sex is not as good when I have an agenda, when I approach it with the thought, "What would she be excited by? What could I do to make her want me?" It's not as intimate, somehow. I'm thinking of her more as an object.

Some aspects of a negative self-image may be of long standing. These are convictions difficult to shake, a panoply of thoughts and feelings that may emerge at any time, inevitably darkening our sexual moments. They can be particularly difficult for us to acknowledge, much less share with our partner:

> If anything reminds me of being in a family with my sexual partner, then I'm not turned on by sex. I guess it reminds me of my incest.

*

> It takes a pretty long time for me to come. I start thinking, "Fuck, oh my God, I'm not working hard enough. I'm impotent. Something's wrong with me. Why can't I think sexual thoughts? I'm thinking about the laundry. Oh, my God!" I really torture myself.

*

> In the past few months, I haven't felt comfortable making love: I had a relationship with someone else last year, and I've never gotten over it. I think I harbor a lot of guilt over that.

*

> If I want him to touch me in a certain way, I think, "He's going to think I'm dirty or a naughty girl for wanting him to do that." It goes back to my childhood, this sense of sex as taboo.

*

> I struggle with sado-masochistic thoughts and fantasies. I'm so busy having this political soliloquy going through my head that I can't have good sex.

Clearly, what we think our sexual experiences have to say about us is as important as any other question concerning our sexual circumstances. Somewhere down the attributional trail we are bound to find the conclusions we have drawn about ourselves from what has occurred. They can often be traced to parental appraisals and prophecies made long before we could possibly question them; sometimes they echo childhood peers's treatment of us. Over the years, these inputs lay the basis for beliefs about ourselves that we use to enact and explain our behaviors in every corner of our life. The sexual domain is no exception. Whatever occurs there is colored with personal meanings, chief among which involve telling reflections of who we think we are and why: sexually free or inhibited, sensual or numb, involved or detached, fragile or secure, confident or timid. Taken together, these sexual self-images determine the meaning and quality of any particular embrace or sexual outcome.

In the sexual realm, there is nothing quite so important as your ability and willingness to take stock of yourself as a sexual partner.

- How do I stack up?
- How do I compare myself to others?
- What about my behaviors and attitudes could be changed pretty easily? What with great difficulty? What not at all?
- Is there any area of my life where I feel completely okay with myself?

The further we burrow, the closer we may come to the realization that any disquietude we have about ourselves in the sexual domain stems from earlier years when we were nagged or teased about our faults until, over time, we came to embrace our oppressors' opinions of us. Perhaps we adopted this self-abasement in order to get along with parents and caretakers; even now our "inner child of the past" may still insist that they were right all along. There can be great comfort in what is most familiar about ourselves and others' opinions of us, even when negative, and those convictions are not easily dislodged. As long as I continue to endorse others' appraisals of me, I can remain in a shared reality with those upon whom I depend for an emotional connection. As long as I can continue to view myself as inept or unlikable or troublesome, I don't have to dare blame others for the parts they have played in my pain and dissatisfaction.

Just as a young child will often excuse an inadequate or abusive parent by naming him or herself as the culprit, it may be the case that an adult sexual partner is too quick to seize responsibility for an unfulfilling sexual partnership: "Don't worry. We'll concentrate on *my* shortcomings and not yours. I'll never even begin to suggest that you in any way go along with my hangups." The reason for this resolve would be to maintain a relationship that we think would not easily survive more honest appraisals, as was certainly the case for one of my clients, who preferred focusing on his fears of sexual intimacy to telling his wife that he often saw her as hostile and controlling and sexually unavailable.

Owning our personal truths certainly involves a willingness to assess our own contributions as to what ails our sexual partnership, but it must also include an honest appraisal of how we view the contributions we believe our partner is making to the mix. How about *him*? How about *her*? Is your sexual life only a matter of you and no one else?

2 It Takes Two: ATTRIBUTIONS

The same things that some folks find in themselves to explain their sexual peaks and valleys, others ascribe to their partners. These are people who may be averse to taking responsibility when things go poorly. At the same time, if the circumstances are positive, it is sometimes convenient to view sexual pleasures as the result of the *partner's* special attributes or prowess, especially when we hold the deliberate quest for sensual ecstasy to be taboo.

Sexual behaviors carry with them powerful messages which, when interpreted as positive, can have a tremendous impact on the receiver. They may be viewed as indications of the partner's interest in pleasing, as signs of special caring, as tokens of respect and sensitivity. Behaviors alone, whether or not they are technically superior, do not predict any particular emotional impact.

> I like it when I just lay there, and he spends twenty to thirty minutes pleasuring me. It makes me feel desirable or attractive, that he thinks I'm sexy and wants to have sex with me.
>
> *
>
> I like it when he is really slow and takes a really long time. It's like he's paying attention to my needs and not just getting something for himself.

*

When she initiates or agrees to have sex, it makes me feel wanted, not just as a roommate or a friend or a provider but as a lover and a husband and a potential father.

*

Whenever he's forthcoming and demonstrative, it makes me feel uninhibited and spontaneous. I respond much better when he's feeling confident. I like to be taken. That would free me up to be more sexual with him.

*

A major part of my sexual satisfaction—which may be selfish in one sense—is seeing her response to me.

In addition to what our partners *do*, we might explain our sexual satisfactions in terms of who our partners *are*—their general mood, personality, or capacity for love and caring:

Her personality is very easygoing, and she exhibits that in our sexual relationship. She's also a very loving person, and she wants me to feel that love.

*

His drive excites me, and then, in spite of myself, I have a good time.

*

Our sexual relationship is working real well. Probably because he wants to please me.

*

I'm taken with the fact that I have such a loving partner.

Just as attributing one's sexual gratifications or interests or behaviors to positive actions or attitudes on the part of one's partner can go far in enhancing the sexual partnership, so interpreting one's partner's sexual expressions in a negative light can have highly deleterious effects. And if we go far enough down the attributional trail, we shall inevitably come to bedrock conclusions about what we think we mean to our partner and to our general sense of self-worth.

It is not enough, for example, to state, as one of our respondents did, "*I get a little angry when all of a sudden her attention is gone and she's watching TV!*" This is only the start of the trail. The respondent's rage is determined not by the fact that his partner is watching television but by his *interpretation*—that perhaps his wife is not interested in him and/or that this means that he is a failure as a sexual partner and/or that their marriage is weak. And even these interpretations are not necessarily the end of the trail: He may go on to conclude that the marriage is a mistake, that his wife is basically an unloving human being, that he himself is of little value to anyone. It is these sorts of bedrock conclusions that create such painful sexual circumstances for many of us—conclusions that place our sexual lives in great jeopardy if they are not dredged up, acknowledged, and shared.

It may be equally likely that we ascribe sexual difficulties to our partner, especially among those of us who feel unable to meet what sex demands of us, and cannot see how we might change our own behaviors and outlook. Such people come to believe that if change is called for in order for their sexual partnership to prosper, it must be the partner who does the changing. Criticizing our partner, focusing on the partner's need to change, can represent our only hope of improvement. The indictment of our partner can include "evidence" of either an insatiable sexual appetite (usually if male) or, to the contrary, no such appetite at all (usually if female):

> Often I just want to be close like friends, but I can feel him pushing for more. That's when I shut down and feel like I'm just watching what's going on, as though I'm not really there. I guess it has to do with him initiating it. It makes me feel like an object and not a person.

*

> I really felt like making love, so I said, "Couldn't you turn around?" And she said, "I don't want to . . . Oh, all right!" I thought to myself, "Well, you think you're being so self-sacrificing and so nice to me, but what I want you're not giving me." That's why I get a little grumpy.

*

If my partner is blatant about sex, I can't get aroused at all. Some of my friends will say to each other, "Let's have sex," and then they go ahead with it. For me that's inconceivable. For me it has to be nonverbal. I never talk about it ahead of time.

*

When you keep getting turned down and turned down, you just kind of go, "Fuck! Why should I do it?!" That's why men cheat on their wives.

*

Sex hasn't always been easy. It sure doesn't help that my husband has always been ready to go, like a racehorse!

Sometimes it can be the way our partner behaves in bed that we cite as a turn-off:

Nothing has killed our sexual experiences more than her saying, "Not so hard . . . Not so fast." Whether caressing her or licking her or whatever, she goes, "Not so hard . . . Not so fast." I feel insulted or anxious that I'm not doing this right, as though I'm letting her down.

*

If she's real wild, I'll wonder, "Is she doing this to try to make me feel I'm getting her more excited than she really is?" I'll think, "This ain't right. She can't be that excited," and I'll really get turned off.

*

I went ahead and helped him with his release. Then I rolled over and felt dead. It didn't do anything for me. The word "rape" went through my mind: "Well, you just raped him, and he's happy, but not you." It was all a one-way street!

THE US WE HAVE BECOME

Some sexual partners rightly sense that what happens in their sexual exchanges is not attributable to one or the other of them alone but to the partnership itself, to their *mutual* influence, to what they have fashioned between themselves, which can take on a life of its own. "We" is never simply the sum of two "I"s but rather a creation greater than the sum of its parts. The sexual partnership, like the relationship itself, constitutes a system that represents a host of needs and compromises and accommodations on the part of the two people who make it up, both of whom are responsible for what occurs.

In this view, sexual dysfunction in one partner may be unwittingly encouraged by the other and represent an unacknowledged bargain between them. Initiation patterns, sexual disinclinations, the frequency of sexual contact, the amount of intimacy that occurs, and even the level of sexual drive or urgency can be viewed as an exquisite collusion between two people, a dance of their own choice and making, on which the partnership depends.

Fortunate are those who, in celebrating pleasurable circumstances, can attribute them to the quality of their sexual partnership:

> Sometimes we have what I'd call an ultimate experience. Maybe we've taken a shower before going to bed and our skin feels different. Maybe it's the intensity between us that makes the difference.

*

> The reason sex is so good with us is because I want it, and she wants it, and we love each other.

*

> I've been super horny. It's a real turn-on to touch him. Much more than before. Somehow, since we've had a child, it all feels much more legitimate. The bond between us makes me feel more sexually connected.

*

> It's that sense of belonging, of having someone that's yours. I really feel connected to him. I'm going to be with him forever. I get a sense of forever when he's holding me.

Explanations may be found in behaviors attributable to the sexual partnership:

> Being together at home all day has really helped our sex life. It can feel very cozy and comfortable.

*

> There's a lot of verbal communication, including talking dirty to each other. That's a big turn-on. We're very open with each other. We communicate. That's a very, very big part.

Positive attributions to the relationship may have more to do with thoughts and feelings that get stirred up between partners:

> If we're feeling particularly close, then I'll feel like it.

*

> Having sex is a signal that we're together again and that we're going to stick together. Even if it's routine, it's an affirmation of our relationship.

*

> We're much more responsive when we are rested, relaxed, and away from the world.

Negative qualities in the relationship itself, not the partners, can be used to explain a variety of sexual difficulties. Frequent examples are a lack of bonding outside the bedroom, too little time available for each other, passions directed elsewhere, or an absence of playfulness:

> If it's been a little while since we've had sex or if there's been any dissension, or if too much is going on and we haven't hardly seen each other, then I can't get interested. I need a sense of closeness.

*

> Sex has been more in the once a month range, because we're working quite a bit and seem to be very tired. That can really dampen your sexual interest.

*

> We never seemed to find the time for sex after the kids came along. Even when they were asleep, there was like no motivation. We probably lost a little something between us for a while.

*

> We just don't seem to have much fun together. And when there's no attempt to make sex fun, it can be a real turn-off.

Completely external factors, which partners cannot control or forestall, may also be blamed:

> A lot of the reason we don't have sex more frequently is the weird hours we keep. It's not because one of us is holding out on the other.

If we view sexual difficulties in terms broader than our partner's degree of competence, it may look as if how we are getting along outside the bedroom both affects and is affected by what happens in bed:

> I think any sexual problems we have have more to do with emotional distresses—anger, hurt, disagreements—than with what you'd call a sexual dysfunction.

HOW I WONDER WHO AND WHERE YOU ARE!

The ideational labyrinth that characterizes every sexual exchange between two people is not complete without a consideration of how each partner understands the *other*, where the other is coming from, what accounts for the partner's sexual experience, conduct, and attitude. How we read our partner can, of course, have a tremendous impact on our reactions to our partner's behavior and on the quality of the sexual partnership, but conclusions may be reached on the basis of very little evidence. Where communication is lacking, as it frequently is in the sexual domain, conclusions may be based on nothing more than identification—assuming that our partner is feeling and reacting just like ourselves—or on projection, attributing to our partner feelings and motivations that we deny in ourselves:

> I can't help but believe that sex is not as good as it could be because he's making love to this corpse!

*

> If he ever has a sex problem, I'll think to myself, "He just can't get it up because I'm fat and ugly."

*

With my husband I keep thinking, "I must smell" or "Oh God, I'm fat."

*

I also think that if I were more attractive to him, I could make him forget his work for a time and really get into sex.

*

When he goes off to the couch and masturbates, I feel he's saying, in a snide way, "Well, I sure don't need you any more."

Statements such as these, often made almost unnoticeably, can reflect and maintain the low self-esteem that some sexual partners bring to bed with them. Others reflect the opposite:

He likes having sex with me. He wants to feel closer to me.

*

She likes it best when I'm on top. She experiences me as providing and caring for her that way.

*

From other things he's said, I think his strong turn-ons have more to do with *me* than the fact that I happen to have the body of a female. He's showing his appreciation for me, his interest in me. *I'm* turning him on.

*

He enjoys making love not just as a sexual release but because he enjoys being with me on that level. He likes our intimacy. It's his way of showing how much he cares for me.

*

He likes making me feel good.

When we attribute our partner's negative sexual circumstances primarily to idiosyncracies that have little to do with us or to the partnership, the result is less apt to be destructive. Often the partner's sexual patterns predate our partnership, and we may have known about them even before our sexual relationship was begun. One may feel that the partner has little or no control over certain reactions. They may be characterological or else the result of sexual trauma for which he or she was not responsible. Such involuntary responses are seen to cast hardly any shadow, either upon our self-worth as sexual partners or on the relationship itself. In fact, even when they do not promote sexuality, these responses may evoke sympathy or tenderness:

> She likes to have the lights out when we have intercourse. Having the lights on is a turn-off. She also likes to be covered up. She's just not that comfortable with her sexuality.

*

> Now that he's starting to get older, his body doesn't respond as quickly as it used to. At first I took it personally—"Oh, gosh, he's losing interest in me!"—but now I realize that the aging male can't respond quite as quickly as he used to.

*

> I think our level of interest is equal, but it's hard for her to express her needs and interests. She hasn't learned to trust those kinds of intimate things to other people.

*

> He feels like he'll start something he can't finish, so why start it? His ejaculatory problems make sex a very frustrating experience for him.

*

> When she's not excited, I usually think there are other things in her head that are interfering. She may be worried about something. That's why she's not having a lot of pleasure. It doesn't have to do with me.

*

> Having a lot of sex just isn't *her*!

It helps when we can identify with our partner's responses:

> She might say, "No, I've got to go do something." That's fine with me. I'm like that a lot too. Sometimes I've got this or that to do.

Sorting out our views of what or who is chiefly responsible for our sexual moments is never an easy task. There are no back-of-the-book answers to which you can turn for authority. The deepest personal truths about your sexual life are yours alone and never anyone else's. They are formed by whispers from the past that you would do well to remember more clearly than you may like to do. As we peer more deeply into every aspect of our sexual experience, we shall discover that from the crib to the altar, and beyond, is not much distance emotionally. Inside is still the child we once were, who forged survival strategies to feel safer in a fearful world where parents were never equipped to recognize, let alone meet, all of our needs. Our bedrock notions of what partnership involves, what others' behaviors mean and how they might affect us, are entirely idiosyncratic.

This is why none of our reactions to anything, either in or outside of bed, should be taken for granted and unexamined if we are to learn more and move on. Take the case of the husband who reports that his wife's sexual disinterest is a turn-off for him. While he may view his reaction as unremarkably natural (and so may a sex therapist), it is only by learning much more about this man that his therapist can hope to find remedies that truly hit their mark. The fact is, not all men react this way. Some men suppose it is normal to be more interested in sex than their wives are and they welcome the opportunity to try out their skills at seduction. Others expect to be challenged by an initial rebuff and would find it baffling to meet no resistance. Some men find affirmation of their masculinity in overcoming a feminine reluctance and might even be repelled by an enthusiastic partner. And there are those who welcome their partner's lack of interest as a reassuring sign that she is "getting enough" and will not be seeking fulfillment with someone else.

Just as men are not universally discouraged by their partners' indifference, so, too, do they differ in how much it bothers them and for what reasons. Some may wish with a shrug that things could be different. Others, however, may be distressed if it awakens old fears of being punished or abandoned. Some may be angry that their "rights" are denied, others worried over whether they should persist or not. If a man views his partner's refusal as bespeaking a broader rejection of him, it may become uncomfortably clear to him how much he has come to rely on her validation. Her refusal to cooperate with his neurotic needs and defenses can easily turn her into "The Enemy." Along with any of these reactions, a man who is too easily discouraged in most respects may give up his pursuit before it is ever fully launched and spend his night needlessly alone.

One question I always ask of those who would rather focus on their partner's speck in the eye and not the plank in their own is whether they think their sexual circumstances would be very different if they were with a different partner, if their own behaviors would change and their pain be transformed into sexual joy and ecstasy. Who would that partner be? What would make him or her so much more ideal? In asking such questions, of course, we would both learn much more about the client. After such digging, one of my female clients exclaimed: "I now realize that I married him *because* he was asexual. I felt safe in knowing that our sexual relationship would never get off the ground. If it had, I would have been too fearful of my father's rage toward my being sexual in defiance of his mandate." When it comes to our choice of a sexual partner, there is always far more than meets the eye and usually far more than we would like to admit either to ourselves or to our partner.

IT'S ALL IN OUR MIND

An obvious conclusion from all that has been considered here is that sexual exchanges involve far more than what people do with their body parts. Embedded in every sexual act is an entire history of how we account for our own and others' behaviors, an ideational trail that would make sense of every moment we live. We often reach ungrounded conclusions that are detrimental to our well-being in any domain, or erect defenses against our truest thoughts and feelings, or keep our views vague to avoid the pain of completely honest assessments. Self-evasion in sexual matters is especially perilous. The uncertainty it brings renders our every gesture less authentic and robs our sex life of the spontaneity on which it depends. We cannot advance until we acknowledge where we are.

3

The Point of It All:
MOTIVATIONS

I don't believe the only purpose for having sex is procreation. That's bullshit! It's first and foremost for pleasure.

*

Sex is having fun with someone.

*

It's a way to express the closeness I feel that words can't express.

Few people are at a loss for words to describe obvious aspects of their sexual lives—the activities they employ, their turn-ons and turn-offs, even their sexual difficulties. But should we ever be asked *why* we engaged in sex on any particular occasion, most of us become strangely mute. It seems to be one question we hardly ever ask ourselves, yet probably no definition of reality is more telling than the reasons we give for having a sexual exchange. Why we think we engage in sex and why we think our partner does may, in fact, be the chief determinant of our emotional responses during a sexual engagement and of its final outcome.

This is why I always begin consideration of a couple's sexual circumstances by asking them, in individual sessions, to recall their last sexual encounter. "Why do you suppose you became sexually involved at that time?" I ask. And next, "Why do you suppose your partner had sex with you?" Their first answers are usually unrevealing ("It was the weekend," or "I just happened to be horny"), but as we proceed down the client's ideational trail we eventually uncover a host of reasons and feelings. Some of these hearten the client; others are embarrassing, disquieting, even repugnant, and hard to admit. It becomes eloquently clear, however, that no matter what it evokes, any aspect of a sexual exchange amounts to a great deal more than is easily apparent to the partners.

Especially in sex, we can be sure that our behaviors are prompted by far more than a single or simple motivation. Reasons for engaging in sex can depend so much on the particular moment—the setting, the partner, the mood each happens to be in—that what was true on Saturday might be quite untrue Sunday afternoon. Each of us embodies an astoundingly complex array of needs, goals, and strivings, some of them contradicting others. When we realize that opposing truths about ourselves co-exist, we can be uncomfortably confused. What is worse, we may reject the notion of embracing the ambiguity in our makeup and, instead, conduct ourselves as if we were complete saints or reckless devils, not somewhere in between. Then our pretense leaves us at odds with our core selves, and we feel fake. It may be that those who are most "together" sexually are able to accept in themselves a variety of sexual motivations on which they can act without guilt or shame.

Any single sexual aim can reflect the details of our sexual histories, our personal and interpersonal needs and priorities, and the nature of our sexual partnership. Similarly, the full range of our sexual aims can reflect how well we accept the diverse elements in our natures. This is what determines how we go about a sexual exchange. Our aims determine how we evaluate and respond to what occurs: with joy and gratification or with frustration, disappointment, and despair. Whether we share them with our partner or leave them unshared, perhaps not even acknowledged, they form the basis for a sexual covenant from which the sexual partnership evolves.

Sexual motivations that we find easier to acknowledge and share tend to be those endorsed by the culture in which we are raised. (Both men and women in certain religious subcultures may more comfortably treat sex as procreative than as recreational). In our own, it is thus predictable for partners to declare that our sexual strivings are prompted by love and amount to a celebration of our relationship. What might be much more difficult to acknowledge is that among our sexual motivations may be the need to bolster our self-esteem or to manipulate our partner or to do a tedious duty. Even less acceptable, and therefore not even acknowledged to ourselves, could be such masochistic or sadistic aims as the need to be emotionally trampled or to express unreserved aggression.

Who shares what with whom can also depend upon the partner's gender. It is easier, for example, for a man than a woman to talk in terms of relieving a sexual itch and easier for a woman than a man to speak of deep emotional bonding. In talking with friends, a woman is more likely than a man to construe sexual participation as an obligation to the partner, while a man is more likely to boast of it as a physical accomplishment.

BECAUSE I LOVE IT!

It may be that our changing times have made it easier for many of us to associate sex with personal pleasure, be it emotional or sensual:

Sex makes me feel good, physically and emotionally.

*

It's for enjoyment.

*

I enjoy the body-to-body contact, the wrapping up together like two spoons in a drawer. We usually sleep with some sort of wrapping of the feet or legs, tummy to tummy or back to tummy. I just enjoy the sensuality of it.

*

I get to feel every inch of my being from the crown of my head to my toes.

Fortunate is the man or woman who, from birth till death, feels permitted to delight in sight and sound and smell and taste and touch. We can erect barricades of many kinds. A hectic pace often precludes our even noticing the proverbial flowers, or the dawn's chorus of awakening birds, or the panorama of the heavens. A preoccupation with our problems and chores and ambitions can make it impossible to immerse ourselves in a painting, a concerto, or a poem. The lives of many people comprise masterful attempts to keep feelings of any kind at bay. Spontaneity of any kind is wrung dry. Hearts and heads are divided. Delight defers to caution, sorrow to a callous cynicism. All too many of us learned as children that it was risky to express our feelings or enact our sensual needs and that activities we found intrinsically pleasurable might be dangerous to our reputations, if not our lives. Somewhere along the line, the child whose very life originally depended upon sensual pleasure in the nourishment that nursing afforded, is supplanted by the caricature of an adult who views pleasure-seeking as self-indulgence, who will not own that need or, of course, the anger and resentment that come when it is not fulfilled.

In the sexual domain there is nothing quite so important as the ability to take pleasure in our own or another's body, to savor the comfort of touch and the excitement of passion, to relish the sight and taste and feel and smell of our partner's response, to welcome the delicious relief of impulses discharged. This ability to own and enact and be rewarded by our personal and "selfish" quest for pleasure is the sine qua non of a healthy sexual exchange. Before sex can ever be more than that, at the deepest level it must be "for me," beginning with the craving for physical exaltation.

BRING DOWN THE RAFTERS!

What is being alluded to here is the human quest for passionate experience, the press to move beyond our mundane settings and usual constraints. For all its benefits the civilized world exacts a monumental price from us—the daily denial of what we really are and want and feel, only mildly apparent in our fleeting fantasies, sometimes terrifyingly real in our nightmares. As we grow up our impulses get relegated for propriety's sake, and our freedom to think or to feel becomes seriously curtailed. Most of us become only too adept at drawing on a ready sense of shame to shore up those constraints once applied to us from without.

Given such circumstances, it should come as no surprise that the prospect of a sexual exchange can be at once compelling and fearful. It invites us to submerge ourselves in the sway of our feelings, both physical and emotional. It challenges us to give up control, to set our self-constraints aside, to be caught up in a passion that overwhelms our usual self-consciousness, to stop thinking, to go a little crazy, to be who we are and what we are doing at that particular moment pure and plain, without pretense or wariness. Sexual passion violates everything we have ever been told about what we must do and be in order to survive. It also creates perhaps our best opportunity to affirm ourselves:

> Sex is a big thing. It really is. A lot of people get in trouble over it because they have no control over it. You can get addicted to it and find it's hard to do without.
>
> *
>
> Having his penis inside me is a real primal act. It feels real animalistic. There's an urgency to it.
>
> *
>
> It's a rush of energy and powerful feelings.
>
> *
>
> Sex involves an aspect of yourself you can't express while you're walking down the hall or relating to other people in a conventional way. It's the carnal part of yourself, and I feel very comfortable with it.
>
> *
>
> Sex is an exchange of energy.
>
> *
>
> Sex can be almost equated with life and the passion for living. That's what we really transmit when we make love.

Perhaps, above all, when our hearts and minds are in tune with the moment, sex offers us literal rapture—an utterly absorbing, trancelike state that shuts out rival distractions. Here we are entirely focused on our immediate experience, as musicians or athletes are focused. It could be argued that the truly important, worthwhile moments in life are those when time stands still. Sex at its best has a way of encompassing such moments:

It's when nothing else matters. Everything else is outside.

*

It's something I truly experience rather than just observe or think about. I become aware of who I am and where I am and what everything's about. It's like being able to really feel your soul, your true identity. You're right in the now.

RECREATION

Not unrelated to our need to reach down into ourselves for the reassurance that we are more than a good role-filler and to let our entire selves ring out, is the need to experience life as more than obligation, to shelve the unwelcome gravity of adulthood. As much as anything else, sex can provide us with an opportunity for play not quite like any other.

> "Bed is the place to play all the games you have ever wanted to play." (Comfort 1972, p. 13).

If sex is not fun for us, sometimes at least, then we have missed its essence. The most troubled adults are those who have lost the fascination of making a splendid sand castle, of running down a hill for the glory of it, splashing in puddles, chasing fireflies. The freedom and spontaneity they once knew has become barely an echo, replaced by feelings of resignation which cast a pall on their half-lived lives. "Just for the hell of it" is no longer an acceptable reason for doing something. What does not feel like work or challenge or the discharge of responsibility, what cannot be analyzed, is viewed as dangerously frivolous. For such people, sex is serious business and must be studied carefully. And, of course, as in other areas of their lives, their sexual performance is technically impeccable. They have learned all about their partners' erogenous zones and could diagram them on a blackboard. They have finicky control over their orgasms. They can predict "success" by the length of foreplay, and take every precaution against distractions. They know exactly what to do.

> "Couples seeking to improve sexual functioning should be taught and encouraged to play, playing together in and out of lovemaking activities to learn how much fun sex can really be." (Hartman and Fithian 1972, p. 189).

I KNOW MY JOB

Many people who have not felt the joys that self-discovery sex can bring, who are not drawn to it as liberating, may find it hard to acknowledge, much less honor, so powerful a need. The best account they can give of their sexual interest is to talk of pleasing their partner, to relish vicariously what they do not permit themselves, to watch and try to take in—as if by osmosis—another's passions and gratifications. The sad fact is that for some, this is as close as they will ever come to tasting what is their own right and probably their deepest need:

> It's important to make your partner happy, to please her. I like to see her excited, enjoying herself. It's fun to listen to her moan and groan, losing control of herself.

> *

> "Did you enjoy yourself?" or "Could I have done more for you?" That's always one of his questions.

> *

> I guess a lot of my moves are, "This will please him" or "Will that please him?"

The motive to please one's partner may be viewed as commendable, but sex as *primarily* an act of generosity, or a preoccupation with how the partner experienced it, can often reflect our disinclination to own and enact our own sexual needs and impulses. It may be the result of our inability to ask for much of anything from another, or it may represent an attempt to avoid responsibility for what occurs. Nowhere is this more evident than in those of us who engage in sex mainly because our partner initiated it or out of a sense of duty or in the effort to meet our partner's expectations:

> He had certain ideas of what sex was like, and if I wasn't living up to them, I had to change my ways. I guess I didn't know enough about myself to really know what to say no to or to ask for. So, I thought I should at least try different things. Once he had me dress up in high heels and little skimpy outfits and prance in front of him. I felt more like a whore than his wife. I felt very removed from him.

*

> I think to myself, "I'll have to do it if I want to preserve the peace. It'll just be 45 minutes or an hour, and then it will be over with."

*

> When I first got married, I felt that my role in bed with my husband was just like a duty, something I just had to do to satisfy him, and that there should not be any pleasure there for me. It got to the place where I didn't even want him touching me. I was like a cold fish to him, because I wasn't getting anything out of it. I guess I felt jealous that he was getting all the enjoyment out of it. I just felt empty.

*

> I remember being so tired, feeling dragged down by the kids and all, and after putting them to bed, I knew I still had one more thing to do, and I'd want to get it over and done with so I could be by myself.

The fact that all of the above comments were made by women should come as no surprise. Women have generally been taught by their parents and by every institution in our culture to be reactive rather than proactive in the sexual domain, to wait for male initiatives, and to repulse them from all men but the one whose "right" it is, all the while denigrating their own sexual impulses as wanton. The result is a large number of women who feel they *must* view sexual occurrences as a burden to be borne with clenched teeth, even with a male partner who may actually not be as demanding as he seems to her to be.

NOW I KNOW I MATTER!

In the absence of sexual motivations that stem from the deepest and most human elements in ourselves, which are enlivened and maintained by their authenticity, sex can come to serve other ends that sometimes foster alienation from our own selves and our partner. For example, sex can be chiefly a narcissistic enterprise:

> **It makes you feel as though you're the only person in the world to someone.**

> *

> **I enjoy feeling that I'm turning him on, that he finds me attractive, that he wants me and no one else.**

> *

> **His feeling desire for me, excitement with me, is very important. That I'm the best! Otherwise, I can't make sex.**

> *

> **I want her to be able to say that it was one of the best times she's ever had sexually. That's a real turn on for me, something I really thrive on.**

Narcissistic needs can be reflected in the wish to feel much more powerful than we do in other corners of our lives:

> **It's definitely a little bit of a power trip on my part, because I definitely know that I'm in control.**

> *

Since I've always felt powerless, I've made sex one big power scene, where I get to control and manipulate and dominate a person who is not my equal. I've always insisted that my partner be submissive to me.

*

My ideal sexual experience would be to feel masculine, in control. I want to call the shots, to be in control of what happens, to be the Bull of the Pampas.

*

I feel like the King of Id when she does what I want her to do. When she responds to my desire, I feel dominant.

*

I've made him into this eager little puppy, which is great. I'm in control. That's the way he wants it, and that's the way I want it.

We may engage in sex for such instrumental reasons as manipulating or modifying our partner's behaviors in other spheres: *"After sex, he eases off a little bit. He becomes less picky about the housework or other things."* The aim may be to serve needs that are otherwise unsatisfied: *"It's a way I can have him totally to myself. I really get his attention, at least for a while."* Or it may be to ensure that the present sexual connection will not be the last: *"I want her to like it because I want her to do it again,"* and *"It's one way I can keep him at home."*

All too many couples use sex primarily as what they hope will be a remedy for difficulties in their relationship and as a way of avoiding the real issues between them:

It's the one thing that seems to go smoothly. If we're not getting along in other ways, we can always have good sex.

*

It's the one thing we do well together. So when I'm real angry I'll say, "Oh, I've had enough of all this screaming. Let's just go fool around."

Finally there are those who have no emotional stake *at all* in what occurs. The best they can do is go through the motions: *"Sex has become for me like, 'Here, let me beat you off and get you off my back.' That's about as far as it goes."*

HURRAY . . . IT'S US!

Only those who are relatively free to experience their entire selves in a sexual exchange can forgo sexual motivations that dishonor both themselves and their partner. Such folk bring to a sexual moment a kind of celebration that envelops both of them. Their own pleasure inevitably evokes lavish generosity in pleasing their partner as well. Empowered by the experience itself, they need no reassurance that they amount to something and have no reason to manipulate others in their sexual dealings. Fears have no place in those for whom the promise of sexual experience has been truly fulfilled. As they overcome their self-constraints by daring and doing, so, too, do they overcome whatever sets the two of them apart:

> Sexuality means gratification, sharing love. Our physical and psychological intimacy are tightly intertwined.

> *

> It's a symbol of our relationship, a confirmation of our commitment to each other. It's an integral part of our communication with each other. I really can't imagine not having this part of our relationship active, alive, and good.

> *

> It's how you love your partner and how your partner loves you. There is no faking.

> *

> It seems like the highest form of bonding. When you bond with a lover it's a physical, mental, and spiritual high.

> *

> It's the highest level of being with another human being.

> *

> Sex is a God-given gift and should be used to express love, to express His love, His closeness and commitment to us. When I look at it in this light it becomes even more beautiful than what I ever could have imagined.

> *

I like emotional involvement and commitment. I like security. I like friendship. I like to know somebody. I like to love somebody, not just because they are a good lay, but because of all we have in common, a lot of shared thoughts and feelings, most of all a mutual need based not on sex but on familiarity and love.

*

There is a sense of belonging, a sense of being whole. I need this for my life to function.

*

It's like going to a higher place, like meditating, except you're with another person. It's just very special.

A friend of mine once said, with a wisdom and insight perhaps unknown to him, "Sometimes I fuck to the glory of God, sometimes out of deep affection for my partner, but sometimes just for the sake of fucking!" No two sexual acts are completely alike, and no one sexual act is consistent in itself. The same sexual moment may express various proportions of profoundly diverse motivations, from the noblest to the basest, from the most banal to the most sublime, from an uncommon altruism to an unusual self-absorption. It is important that we ask ourselves if we have ever experienced a sexual exchange as a symphony in which the cosmetic self was shed, in which we knew ourselves and another so surely that our true existence was no longer in doubt and death itself became less threatening. If our sexual histories do not include at least one such moment, then we shall remain more impoverished than we can ever know.

4 Boy/Girl Stuff: CONDITIONING

Perhaps the most pronounced differences in sexual motives are those that purportedly distinguish males and females generally. It should come as no surprise, since it is a familiar stereotype, that males really do tend to explain their sexual desires in terms of physical urgency, and that females most often talk of sex in the context of a particular relationship since they desire sex more and enjoy it more when they feel that their partner is loving and devoted, and they are more likely to attribute bone-shaking orgasms to the love both partners are expressing.

However biologically rooted, these differences certainly also result from differences in preparation for sexual partnering and, especially among males, are reinforced by the encouragement of peers during the dating years. The saying goes, "Men give love in order to get sex; women give sex in order to get love," as if men's interest in relationships and women's interest in sex were all pretense. And it may be this difference that lies at the center of troublesome sexual connections. Like the two blind men each convinced that he alone had the true idea of what an elephant was like—one feeling its trunk and the other its tail—a man and a woman can seem to be on different wave lengths, their entire sexual enterprise shrouded in antagonism over which sexual viewpoint is "right."

THE GUY THING

Men are, of course, correct that sexual exchanges are physical occurrences. After all, human bodies are involved, with their engorgements of blood during sexual arousal, erections and vaginal lubrication, skin blushes, pungent odors, heightened breathing, and inarticulate sounds. For many men the physical components of sexual activity are so paramount that they would be hard pressed to explain or describe their experience in anything but physical terms:

> I love the physical touching, rubbing my cock into her ass or over her teats, putting my finger inside her and rotating it.

> *

> Sex has always been separate with me. It's a physical thing that feels good, but in itself has no meaning whatsoever. Heck you can do it with anybody. As long as they are physically adept at sex, you can enjoy it with them.

> *

> I'd come over and fuck her whenever I wanted. It was like, "Give me a glass of water, and I'll see you next week."

A Fuck is a Fuck

Unlike his female counterpart, a male's history usually includes countless occasions from puberty onward when masturbation, conducted almost anywhere, often daily, and apart from any relational context, led to the alleviation of sexual tension.

> Five times a day was nothing when I was a teenager. I often regarded it jokingly as "Billy Goatitis." Like a billy goat, you just want to come and come and come all the time.

Over the years men learn to view sex as an independent physical impulse, as erections that come and go on the unlikeliest occasions in answer to painful urges that can be set off by the notion of an appealing car or by tight-fitting trousers or by the sight of an attractive female. Many learn that an ejaculation can be a perfect way to end the day, can promise the comfort of exquisite pleasure albeit self-induced, that is nobody's business but one's own.

Solitary masturbation is thus the male's first experience of what it means to be sexual. It is chiefly a matter of an urge that calls for prompt relief whenever, however, and wherever it can be carried out. It requires no particular interpersonal skills; if it is accompanied by looking at erotica such as *Playboy* centerfolds it is focused on bodies, not personalities. And, echoing our prehistorical forebears whose coital activity had to be quick and efficient in order to avoid the possible ravages of predators, masturbation provides a swift discharge of sexual impulses in hardly any time at all.

These sexual habits, amply evident for example in the strutting of a rooster who deposits his semen quickly into any and all hens who happen by, apparently run deep in males of all kinds, even those for whom sex has come to mean far more than the propagation of the species. Rooted in their genetic histories and propelled by their particular hormonal circumstances, males' sexual aims and determinations are supported further by social learning in their youth. Sex is equated with performance, with "getting off" with as many agreeable females as possible and proving one's prowess among male competitors. In this context, quantity is paramount; any aims beyond "getting off" are either denigrated or left unvoiced.

The need for peer approval precludes recalling feelings of vulnerability in closeness, though later on the male may be more open to personal elements in a sexual exchange (*"I'm not sure if it's mostly my sex drive or if she really attracts the hell out of me. Perhaps it's both"*). Clearly it becomes comfortable for him to assert, *"It's just a matter of mutual gratification, just plain old desire on our parts, a matter of appetite, of physical release, and not a matter of, 'I love you so much.'"*

We must remember that sexuality in males approaches its peak at a time when they are most apt to deny any needs or feelings "unbecoming" to their gender. Compelled to establish a sure and certain distance from their mothers to become real men and to renounce any attributes in themselves that could possibly be feminine, young men are apt to define sex for themselves and others as acts of aggression, domination, and conquest, certainly not as the desire for comfort, closeness, and love.

Men who go on to establish sexual partnerships generally learn, with more or less difficulty, that they are expected to attend as well to the emotional contexts of their sexual transactions. But seldom does a man ever really discard the sexual attitudes he developed in adolescence. Thus it happens that in sex, as in other domains, such a man comes to forfeit important truths about himself in order to reassure himself of what turns out to be a costly masculinity. In his workplace he may have to forfeit personal power in order to earn his bread. In the face of world events that he cannot control, he may be all too forcibly reminded of his helplessness. As his formerly unquestioned prerogatives are overtaken by egalitarianism in the family—sometimes, indeed, he sits in the passenger seat!—he may come to rely on sex as the one field that reassures him of his invulnerability, his competence, his strength in conquest, his authority and autonomy. Sexual exchanges may be one of the few remaining venues of "authentic" masculinity.

As long as the male experiences his sexuality chiefly in terms of a physical urgency and of physical relief, he can avoid contact with his basic fears of loneliness and isolation, of insignificance, indeed, of death, though he may not realize that they can sometimes be overcome by a moment of true intimacy. He need never become too aware of the vulnerability his masculine charade has been designed to disguise. But so long as he keeps his sexuality separate from the rest of himself, it is impossible for him to truly engage his sexual partner as well.

I AM WOMAN

Consider the differences between the young male's outlook on sex and that of the typical young female, whose sexual needs and impulses are less obsessive than her male counterpart's. Her separation from her mother does not involve sociosexual identity. Incompletely familiar with her sexual capacities and instructed to associate sexual expression with a committed relationship, the female, unlike the male, is typically introduced to sexual expression by a partner; she most often begins to masturbate only after this. Years of sexual activity may pass before she fully explores her capacities for sexual pleasure. Depending on the intensity of her arousal, she may or may not insist on reaching orgasm;

depending on her mood, she may or may not choose to become highly aroused. Depending on her menstrual cycle, she may or may not be particularly interested in sex. Depending on her partner and the quality of the partnership, she may or may not consider her sexual responses to him as important. And should that partnership come to an end, no matter her age, she may or may not seek a new sexual outlet. Above all else, if she feels no particular urgency about sex it does not make her feel less female. It does not frighten her as it does a male who feels a decline in his sexual drive.

It would appear that females are far more able than males to be sexually selective. This is not a matter of indifference—women are as capable as men of relishing sex and wanting to repeat it—but of opportunity, so that a woman may defer sexual contact until she feels she is in a loving relationship. Her evaluation may balance how strongly she desires the promised physical delights against complex emotional needs: How attractive to her is her partner at this moment? Is his desire selfish? Has he been kind and attentive? Can he be trusted? Is he interested in her or just her body parts? If she refuses, will he make trouble? If she assents, will he love her or disappoint her? Overcoming their socialization to the notion that males are insatiable and that females either bestow or withhold requires women to desire sensual as well as emotional gratification and to feel free to seek it out. Men, for their part, have to learn to develop intimacy, which can be a far more demanding task, especially since there is little in their masculine vocabulary that their partner can use to explain what she needs. It is a little like asking a trumpeter to play the violin.

WE NEED CONSENSUS!

Given these competing perspectives, it is not hard to imagine the kinds of complaints females make about sexually immature male partners. Having failed in romancing a stone, as it were, women are often left with scornful images of the men who share with them a bed and little else:

> **All that blood rushes to the men's penises, and they have nothing upstairs.**

*

For him it's like eating a big bowl of ice cream. Just drop it all in there and go to it.

*

I'll just lay back and let the animal take over. I know that when that is happening he's got no control.

*

Foreplay, in general, is just to get him hard.

*

I could suppose he wanted human contact or closeness or something, but that would be a supposition on my part. I look at it mostly as his sex drive.

Males who emphasize the physical aspects of sex, so far as to construe it in terms of what they get or need or do, are apt to reckon that sex is a right they deserve because of their physical hunger. Sooner or later, such men's partners come to feel more like a handy orifice than a valued person:

I was just there for him to get relief. I began to feel more and more like an object. I needed more love and not just someone going at me.

*

It didn't make any difference who it was, just as long as he got a climax. I felt used, abused, like a gadget. For him it was like taking a drink of water.

*

It's like, "Take off your dress and bend over; I'm going to fuck you."

*

I get into this place where I don't really care what she wants. I get very horny.

If one partner yearns for more than the physical aspects of sex and goes away unfulfilled, she (or sometimes he) is likely to erect her own defenses against the pain of never really meeting, of remaining essentially unknown despite the promise, expectation, and opportunity. She will often adopt his attitude, go through the motions, pretend that sex means no more to her than it does to him. Perhaps not yet enemies, at the end of a sexual exchange they are likely to remain strangers, waiting to be introduced.

To help couples begin to overcome this gender-induced impasse, I assign them to go home and write up their individual versions of an *ideal* sexual scenario involving the two of them.

> "The male's external social conditioning has been so powerful that it has all but destroyed his ability to be self-aware. Yet each denial of his feelings, each faked response, each feigned involvement, and each act motivated by guilt or bravado pushes his destruction further along. . . . The free male will reclaim his total self [and come to] celebrate all the many dimensions of himself." (Goldbert 1976, pp. 190–191).

- What goes on from start to finish? What am I wishing for, what is my mood, how about my partner?
- What gestures are used, and what are the thoughts and feelings accompanying them?
- What is he doing, what is she doing, why?
- What does each want to convey to the other?
- How are decisions being made from one transition to the next?
- Where is each going with all this? Where does each end up?
- How does the scenario finally close?

When the couple returns for the next session prepared to share these scenarios for the first time, the inevitable differences between them begin to be addressed and faced down. There will be no change for the better until those differences are discussed in detail, their manifestations traced to their origins in needs well established before they ever met.

Each of them is asked to assume the attitude and demeanor of a jeweler appraising a fine gem. After the Initiator is finished with his or her account, the Inquirer is invited to ask all the questions he or she can think of about the Initiator's scenario. Questions only, no comments or refutations, only insatiable curiosity about all the elements of the Initiator's ideal. Then they reverse their roles and repeat the task. There is no effort to resolve the impasse; the goal is clarity alone and an honest exchange of much needed information. It is hoped that in the course of this and subsequent exchanges the couple will become increasingly confident that the relationship can tolerate their differences, and that confidence—the sine qua non of any truly successful male–female partnership—will be far more important than the information transmitted in the process.

The panoply of attributions that occupy such a prominent place in our sexual exchanges is well illustrated in the following Interlude.

Interlude:
Kathy and Gilbert

It's been two years since Kathy and I have had sexual intercourse. Before then there was no passion, no joy. Our sexual exchanges were, for the most part, perfunctory. Whenever we got started, it was more like "Time to do the dishes." We may look pretty normal to our neighbors, but the truth is, we've become like brother and sister.

This is how Gilbert describes his sexual circumstances in a marriage of twenty years. As the personnel director of a large manufacturing company, he enjoys occupational success. He is devoted to his three children who flourish at school and among their friends. Quite long ago he had an affair (seldom consummated) with a woman who divorced her husband in order to be free for Gilbert, but he decided not to leave his family and since then has been determined to make his marriage work. Painful memories of that affair ceased years ago to bother him; his involvements are his children's soccer matches, Sundays with his family at a nearby suburban church, and the pleasures of building furniture in his garage-retreat. Kathy, meanwhile, gloomily acknowledges their sexual doldrums. An attractive, energetic graduate student, she has always considered her sexual needs to be exorbitant, her sexual interests excessive, her sexual impulses barely controllable, unseemly in a lady. It has been a long time since she has asked Gilbert for sex:

> Now I have a very hard time even imagining a sexual encounter with him. The idea is actually distasteful for me, almost intolerable. He may find me attractive as a person, but this doesn't translate into an erection.

She has muted her sexual needs and interests, instead busying herself with volunteer work, at which she has won community acclaim. Her sex life is now confined to fantasies that she finds embarrassing to share:

> The most erotic one is where I'm in a room with half a dozen men. They all have erections and are trying to get at me. I'm being fucked orally and vaginally and anally, all at the same time.

Kathy and Gilbert are not at a loss to explain their unfortunate circumstances. They are both bright and perceptive, and they certainly have had enough time to consider what has been going on in their sexual partnership. Kathy traces the time of their sexual decline to her second pregnancy when she was feeling particularly *"unhappy, stupid, and unattractive."* Feeling trapped and powerless, she became more and more angry and critical of Gilbert. She can understand how his experience of her as a *"nagging bitch"* did not help matters. She believes that she does not initiate sexual contact or even try to talk about her sexual needs with him because she has feared that her sexual needs were extravagantly improper, and that if he learned of them he would feel threatened and reject her. So she restrained herself, unwilling and eventually unable to speak up. However, she does not take full blame for their sexual inactivity. She considers Gilbert's sex drive to be strikingly low, and to have been that way since even before the start of their relationship. She notes that it makes him uneasy to talk about sex in any way. She describes herself and her husband as basically different in their needs and outlooks, she being generally more liberal than he, more self-expressive, more inclined toward frank sexuality. In such a partnership, she thinks, there are bound to be sexual struggles not easily remedied.

Gilbert's explanations, as might be expected, have different twists and emphases. He says that in his first marriage as well as this one, sexual activity declined out of his need to control and contain his sexual impulses. This need, he speculates, may have arisen from possible abuse in his childhood. He explains his lack of initiation as a striving to become more autonomous, to be deliberate in his choice whether to accommodate her, like an adolescent rebellion in which he declares his independence from Mommy. He readily admits being angry and disappointed that he does not get all of Kathy's attention and that they do not have any "*true togetherness.*" In part, he says, this is because she is still feeling angry and betrayed over his affair. He thinks he finds it difficult to discuss sexual matters because frank discussions of this kind have always been taboo for him and because he would rather think and talk about his need for intimacy than for sex which is much lower in priority.

Kathy and Gilbert do not clearly understand either their own or each other's sexual activities. Both in his prior marriage and in his present marriage to Kathy, Gilbert has thought that when he consents to sex with his wife, it is primarily from a monumental effort to accommodate her, rather than from actual sexual desire. Then, as he became more confident, less afraid of being abandoned, his need to please his partner abated. He has always been more interested in drawing close to his partner through physical but non-genital contact. When Kathy insisted that this was not enough for her, he came to resent her approaches; he saw her as craving sex for its own sake, without much connection to him or their partnership.

Kathy has shared at least part of her husband's view of her. She acknowledges her physical need for sex, her view of sex as "*an urge to be satisfied,*" and continues to wonder about what other needs her sexual desire may embody—closeness to a man who is otherwise aloof? an affirmation from him that she is attractive, that she is womanly? a need to feel the essential vitality that is missing in her marriage? She perceives Gilbert's sexual motivations far more clearly than her own, and feels they spoil her sexual exchanges with him:

Sex has no emotional significance to him whatsoever! For him, it's like stuffing a sandwich in your mouth, like, "Now I've had lunch today, and I don't need to think about it until I need to do it again." It's to get his rocks off!

There are always exceptions to "facts" about female (or male) sexuality, and Kathy would appear to be one of them. It is indeed her feeling that she is not like ordinary women sexually that has caused her so much trouble. She concludes:

I think I'm weird. According to what I've read or heard on talk shows, it's the man who's supposed to have the much greater sex drive. But in my own experience I've always been the one with the stronger libido. I've always felt I was the more interested, the more passionate partner. In our society, this is unacceptable. It's considered unladylike. I'm not in the role I'm supposed to be in. I keep feeling that I'm not behaving in an appropriate female way.

As to her marriage with Gilbert, "*I often wonder if I want sex too much, if I'm being too demanding.*" Her uncertainty and her shame over feelings and wishes that she views as incompatible with what it means to be female have profound consequences for the quality of her sexual communication, for her ability to initiate a sexual exchange, and for the sense of alienation she experiences in her sexual partnership.

Not many couples suffer worse sexual communication than Kathy and Gilbert do. Kathy recounts:

Early on in our relationship, I'd want to relive what we'd just done, like you do any pleasurable experience. But I could see he didn't want to talk about sex at all, either in bed or out of bed. I'd either get one-word answers or else he'd fall asleep in the middle of our conversation. So I'd think to myself, "He's uncomfortable talking about sex but so are a lot of people. So what if he doesn't want to talk about it?" I just sort of accepted it. Now, 20 years later, I see that that was a biggie!

Like many partners, Kathy has become mute, feeling utterly incapable of declaring her wants, of speaking her mind about any aspect of their sexual relationship:

> When I try to start a conversation with him about our sex life, the words just won't come. I lie there, trying to get myself to say the first few words, but it's too scary. I have to screw up my courage to talk about our lack of sex.
>
> *
>
> I perform fellatio on him, but he's never performed cunnilingus on me. We've never discussed this. I just clam up. I couldn't possibly ask him to perform oral sex on me. I can't even imagine the words coming out of my mouth!

These are things she wants to know but does not ask about:

> I think he probably sees me as a drudge and a bitch, but I don't know for sure because we don't talk. We don't have a clue as to what are turn-offs or turn-ons for each of us. I'd be interested in knowing if he feels any sexual desire at all. Does he find me attractive? He often says he wants to improve our relationship, but I'd like to know what that means exactly and what he'd be willing to do about it.

She sees that their sexual impasse has affected their marriage across the board:

> We've not been able to look into each other's eyes and say what we felt or needed or wanted. I'd keep my anger to myself, and this spread over into other areas of our life together. We've become stuck big-time! I'm certainly not blameless, but his refusal to have any sort of dialogue with me has cut both our throats.

For his part, Gilbert readily acknowledges that he has trouble talking about sex:

Talking about our sexual needs somehow seems wrong or improper. We're not supposed to do that. Telling her which side of my penis I like to have stroked feels taboo to me, almost like we were bridge partners discussing our bidding contract!

Despite their history, it would appear that Kathy and Gilbert have begun to take steps in the right direction. Putting their terror to one side, they have actually begun to talk. Gilbert describes their first attempt:

Recently we went for a walk and had a good talk. We asked each other what we wanted, what our priorities were. Sex was a top priority for her but not for me. It was scary. I brought up how angry she seemed to be all the time, that over the last two years I couldn't think of a single day that she wasn't mad at me over something. The more we talked, the more compassion we began to feel for each other. There's really been a change. We've taken an important step. We'll have to do a lot more talking!

His determination, poetically phrased, bodes well for the future of their sexual partnership:

We may come from very different places and have a long way to go, but this shouldn't keep us from holding hands while we embark on our parallel journey.

————————

Several years ago, Kathy resolved to quit approaching Gilbert for sex. Her earlier attempts had brought her only pain:

It was obvious that he wasn't interested. Sometimes he'd say, "No." Other times he'd just roll over. Most of the time he'd just lie there like a lump.

Unaware that Gilbert's refusal arose from his own inner problems, Kathy concluded that something was wrong with her:

All I knew was that I was unwanted. I came to feel unattractive. My sexual interest felt unfeminine, not proper for a mother. I thought he saw me as carnal, as raw, as raucous. I felt ashamed of myself.

Her unhappiness came to paralyze her:

It got to the point where it became physically impossible for me
to initiate sexual activity with him. I remember lying in bed,
trying to make myself do it, but I couldn't. I physically couldn't
reach out with my hand to touch him. I wanted to, but I wasn't
able to. It was just awful, scary, painful for me to be rejected in
that way.

So, as many another person would do, Kathy determined to risk
no more rejection:

I was turned down so often that I just quit asking. From here on
out it has to be him who makes the first move, not me.

Since they had never really talked about what was happening
between them, Gilbert had left Kathy in the dark. He had not told her
how hurt and angry he felt over having to compete with their children
and friends for her attention. He never described how he felt that she
was simply using him for her pleasure, that he himself hardly mattered
to her. He hid his fear that if he gave in to her sexual requests he would
lose control of himself. He failed to mention that her rancor turned
him off or that her approaches invaded his personal boundaries.
Although Kathy was convinced that he considered her desires unseemly, not once does he report that he rejected her out of disgust at
seeing her behavior as whorish.

More recently, the shoe has been on the other foot. Gilbert
complains:

In the last year, whenever I've made a few tentative advances,
they have been rebuffed. I'll go down and sit beside her, put my
arm around her, and kind of read the paper. But she stiffarms
me. She'll get up and move away for any excuse at all. The phone
will ring or the kids will come in or it's time to get supper.

It is when the lights go out, and she and Gilbert are bedded down
for the night at a familiar distance from each other, that Kathy is

visited by her fantasied lover, the answer to her dreams, the antidote for her unhealthy sexual partnership. The lover she concocts is the antithesis of her husband, and their contact brims over with all that she has not experienced in her marital relationship:

> He gives me permission to be as demanding, powerful, and sexual as I want to be. He affirms me, makes me feel that my appetites are to be celebrated. He takes great pleasure in pleasuring me. In fact, watching me be pleasured is more exciting to him than my coming. In our sexual exchanges I don't have to be quiet. I can be as loud as I want to be. No need to put the brakes on.

Kathy's fantasied lover, at her beck and call whenever she chooses to have him visit her, is the perfect counterpart to a husband who has never tasted her genitals:

> He performs cunnilingus on me for hours, and I come over and over and over again. He asks me if I want him to eat me out, and before I can even answer, he pushes me down on the bed and just does it.

Her invited guest is marvelously experimental, and his daring summons up an ecstasy unknown in her twenty years of marriage:

> Sometimes he'll tie my hands to the kitchen cabinet and play with me, with his hands and tongue and legs. So much so that I can hardly stand it. When my legs give out, he talks me into a kind of sanctuary where I come again, maybe four or five or six times. And after we're through, we're eager to share all of our fantasies.

Unbeknownst to Kathy, Gilbert sometimes can enjoy, up to a point, a sexual fantasy as well. In keeping with his needs for a partner whose sexual energy does not threaten to sweep him out of the confinement to which he clings, Gilbert's fantasies would startle hardly anyone, including himself:

> My fantasies involve having sex with an adult female, occasionally more than one, but that's pretty rare. She's a willing participant but kind of plays hard to get. There's no sex on

demand from her. It's still sex in the box, but I do push the edge a little bit.

Kathy and Gilbert have become acutely aware that they are heavily mired in their unfavorable sexual circumstances. Kathy asks:

Are we just basically unsuited as partners? Would somebody else be a better partner for him? Wouldn't our failure to relate sexually poison any relationship? Am I oversexed and asking for more than any partner could provide?

She remembers:

Over the years he's told me how unhappy he's been about our sexual relationship and that we need to do something to change it. But that's where it ends. Nothing ever happens beyond that. Maybe it's just too scary. Perhaps it's easier to just hang on to how it's always been.

Gilbert not only agrees with what Kathy has to say about being stuck with the status quo, he goes on to explain it in terms of their conflicting needs:

I want to control sex, to keep it in a nice tidy box where it won't get out of control and harm me or someone else. Kathy is asking for almost the opposite: she has no interest in sex that is too well controlled. Thus, so long as our sex life amounts to zero, I don't have to risk moving outside the box, and she doesn't have to engage in the kind of sex which is repugnant to her. As long as we don't have sex both of us feel relatively safe. It may not be the most pleasant situation to be in, but it's also not too painful either. It makes it possible to avoid battles and confrontations that would be far more painful.

II

THE
SEXUAL
EXCHANGE

5 Talk to Me, Baby: COMMUNICATION

We've been married now almost ten years, and it's still real hard for me to talk to my husband about sex. He's always quizzing me: "Are you sure that I made you feel good?" or "Is there anything you want me to do for you?" And me, I'm still tongue-tied after all these years.

*

I've learned that often when I think we're on the same wavelength we may not be on the same wavelength at all. In fact, I've said to him, "You know there are times when I feel like I'd just like to split your head open so I can see what's inside it!"

*

We can talk about sex in a general sense really well, but when it gets down to the specifics, I tend to be hesitant. I feel embarrassed telling him where I want to be touched.

*

These other people I was going with were really sweet and tender and caring, but who do I stick with? The guy who wants to fuck and not talk!

How can it be that between partners who teem with sexual questions, concerns, wishes, or ideas, there is so seldom any discussion of sex? Is one or the other of us too meek to speak up? Does this arise from a general shyness or from modesty reserved just for sex? Perhaps, we think, it is because we are unable to declare ourselves fully sexual people and to charge boldly into unexplored territory. It may be, we suppose, that we are concerned about not upsetting our partner. With a little more candor, however, we may realize that we want to avoid risking rejection or rancor when we try to make ourselves clear to each other. We or our partner may be silent due to hopelessness over sexual circumstances that we think are beyond remedy. On the other hand, to say nothing may be understood as a sign of accommodation to what we see as our partner's needs, regardless of whatever sexual visions we had in the early days of the partnership.

As with any other aspect of sex, communication (or its lack) can be viewed in as many ways as there are viewers. It is probably safe to say that most couples are relatively mute in the sexual domain, unfree to express their deepest needs and feelings, unwilling to reveal a wish or a regret or even a special satisfaction with respect to their sexual exchanges. All they can do is make up stories to themselves that would explain their reticence. Each partner's reasons for their joint failure to make themselves plain will affect the quality of the partnership. When the lights go out, most couples are left in the dark, both literally and figuratively.

DON'T ASK, DON'T TELL

That most of us talk very little about sex with our partners is not surprising. When it comes to sexual matters, even though ours is a sexually preoccupied culture, we find a conspiracy of silence. How many children are permitted to share their sexual interests and feelings with their parents? How many have been taught that even sexual fantasies are shameful, if not sinful? In such a world, young people are not given an opportunity to reflect upon their sexuality in any meaningful way. Frequently unwilling even to acknowledge any particular sexual plans, they find themselves utterly unprepared for what occurs and are simply carried away by heightening sexual arousal.

They seldom discuss any misgivings about what might take place. They cannot articulate their basic viewpoints, let alone undertake negotiation and compromise. They do not explore their sexual motives or share their specific reactions, often out of concern about how they will be viewed and valued as a result of their disclosures.

If they marry, with the accumulation of new stressors and a growing history of unshared hurts and resentments, young people may share even less with each other. Time, instead of healing, usually brings *new* wounds which, when covered over, introduce new perils to the relationship. This is especially true in the sexual domain where couples in longstanding relationships too often end up barely tolerant of each other's advances, engage in sex when their heart is not in it, and use their bed as a battleground.

MAKING THINGS CLEAR

"Real talk" about sexual matters may be both the most vital and the most difficult kind of partner communication. But, especially if you have been reticent before, embarking on real talk may feel like stepping into an emotional minefield. As detailed in the "Communications" section of Chapter 15, ideally one partner would begin with statements about herself or himself using "I" ("I wish . . ." or "Sometimes I feel . . .") to avoid outright criticism ("You always . . ." or "You never . . ."). The other partner, thus tactfully addressed and perhaps praised in part of the statement, may, even so, feel sorry or resentful. It is therefore important to focus on what *behavior* we want changed, and it may assuage our partner's feelings if we stand ready to take our share of responsibility ("This probably says more about me than about you, but I . . ." or "I could

> "Trying to be an effective lover for oneself and one's partner without communicating is like trying to learn target shooting blindfolded. One needs reciprocal feedback to develop a good sexual interaction and to secure and give effective erotic stimulation."
> (Kaplan 1974, pp. 133–134).

> "Many women have unsatisfactory sex lives because they cannot bring themselves to discuss with their partners the subject of what they need in bed."
> (Hooper 1992, p. 58).

be making mountains out of molehills but . . ."). The principles of real talk also require that the one who is listening should pay careful and polite attention, without interrupting, and at the end provide feedback ("What I hear you saying is . . ."). If this feedback is off target, the first speaker restates and then waits for more feedback. This is repeated until both people are sure of what the topic is; then they can discuss it. For people who are awkward at talking about their feelings, or those who find release in letting go their tempers and shouting, or those who escape into banalities to dodge conflict, such dialogue does not come easily:

> "Sweeping feelings under the carpet is the shoddiest kind of emotional housekeeping. The debris is bound to collect, bulge, and spill over in often disastrous ways. Although there's always a risk of seeming too blunt or assertive when communicating, storing up resentments is far more dangerous."
> (Etkes 1995, p. 32).

I'm real open about sexual ideas and opinions, but it's harder for me to talk about my feelings.

*

I really don't blurt out how I feel. I wish I did more often. It's something I'm working on. She does that a lot more.

*

He's not really perceptive about some things. Sometimes he thinks things are just hunky-dory, and they're not. I'm really not a very open person. It's like pulling teeth when it comes to talking about sex and things like that.

*

I found it real hard to open up to him at first in the ways he wanted me to. Whenever he'd ask me what I wanted, it would be like, "Oh, I can't. I never ask for what I want. I'm not supposed to do that." I was always the good little girl who sat back and said, "Thank you very much. Are you done now?"

Sometimes we avoid real talk to protect our partner (or ourselves) from feeling embarrassed, incompetent, or threatened:

> "Communication is often the first and worst inhibition, especially for men." (Chichester and Robinson 1996, p. 62).

I'm always asking her to talk about how she feels, what she likes and what she doesn't like, but she'll say, "I don't like talking about it, I don't want to talk about it."

*

I want him to express how he feels more. Maybe I read too much into how he feels.

*

Sometimes I'll ask her what she wants, and sometimes she'll tell me. She's usually not that open, but occasionally she'll surprise me. She tends to be reserved about sex.

*

I would hope that as the relationship grows and develops she'd be able to talk more and more openly and express more and more of her needs and interests. She's probably held a lot of those back because she hasn't learned to trust those kinds of intimate things to other people.

Some see a lack of sexual communication as a challenge that the partners must work together to meet:

Maybe we should talk more, but it's painful.

*

I think we could work on being a little more clear.

*

I guess it would be nice if we could communicate more. I'm not sure she knows what she'd like me to do.

> "The better the communication, especially the ability to make clear and direct sexual requests, the more satisfying your sexual relationship."
> (McCarthy and McCarthy 1990, p. 82).

ME AND MY BAGGAGE

A major culprit in our failure to communicate with a sexual partner is our failure to make clear even to *ourselves* what we mean by what we do. Particularly in the sexual domain, we find a host of half-thoughts. Just as we are about to make a clear pronouncement about ourselves to ourselves, we cut it off in mid-sentence and stuff it away in the pile of all the unfinished statements of our lives. Notions may suddenly appear and then evaporate, like dream images when the alarm goes off. Thus we end up never quite knowing what we are up to, never quite sure what we feel or what we want.

It could be that for fear of offending or hurting our partner, or out of uncertainty whether our impulses are acceptable, we deliberately keep ourselves uninformed. One result of the secrets we keep from ourselves can be incompletely honest reactions to what occurs. For example, a woman who does not want sex but accommodates her partner out of duty may end up expressing straightforward anger at her partner, all the while sidestepping the greater truth of how fearful it is for her to turn down her partner's requests or how confused she feels about what she is entitled to. Clearly, ignorance and self-delusion preclude the kind of communication required of a truly viable sexual partnership:

> I'm a wimpy, unassertive person. I expect him to read my mind, know what I want in bed even though I don't know.
>
> *
>
> I can't even figure out what I'm thinking about, much less figure out what's on her mind.

*

I can ask her what she wants, and she'll say, "I don't know; just do something!"

ONLY NAME, RANK, AND SERIAL NUMBER

This is not to say that being honest with ourselves is a guarantee of the kind of communication I have in mind. There is the additional matter of sharing our thoughts with a loved one. It is at that moment that many of us draw a blank or bite our tongues. We may become experts at taciturnity. Our minds could be seething with ideas and opinions, wishes extravagant enough to baffle a genie, impulses energetic enough to light a city block. Yet all the while our partners meet inexpressive silence and remain oblivious to the secret drama taking place across the bed. In a couple like this, conversation is merely a tedious travelogue of the day, after which they settle for the boredom which comes to characterize many a relationship. When it comes to sexual matters, their usual silence is occasionally broken by a complaint, an accusation, or an oblique innuendo. What may be on the tips of their tongues never gets shared. For some of us, sharing is painfully hard:

> Sometimes I don't ask for what I need. I have to learn to do that, to express a need when it occurs. I wish I was more comfortable saying, "I haven't had enough caressing or touching. I need a little bit more."

*

> It's real hard for me to talk to my husband, to tell him things I want and need to fulfill myself. He asks me what I want him to do to please me, but I can't even open my mouth. It's hard for me to talk. He has to kind of pry it out of me, bit by bit. It's no wonder we'd been married probably five years before I experienced an orgasm!

*

> I don't make it very easy for her. I'm not open about what I like or about what's happening to me. She has to guess.

One reason we are so cautious in our shaky attempts to tell about our sexual thoughts and feelings may be that we are afraid how our partner will react:

> I can't share much with her because she may end up feeling inadequate even though she's not. I would just screw things up totally, to be blunt. I have to tiptoe a little and structure my sentences very carefully and evaluate her response or read all the verbal and nonverbal signs. I can't just say, "I like having sex with you but we have problem areas we need to look at."

*

> Her thrashing around like that is a big turn-off for me, but I don't tell her because I just don't want to hurt her feelings, especially when I know deep down inside that she's doing it for me.

*

> If I tell him that he's not doing it right, he may leave home.

*

> I tend to be timid. For me, it's inconceivable to say, "Let's have sex." I never talk about it. For me, all the cues have to be nonverbal, fuzzy. That way if the person rejects the cues, you can always retreat without hurting each other.

Some of us tend, in all circumstances, to keep our feelings to ourselves, especially when it seems that to disclose them would be counterproductive, if not downright dangerous, to the harmony we strive for:

> She's able to tell something's bothering me, but I usually hide what it is. It's hard for me to confide what's bothering me. I just hold it in. When we make love it can be very frustrating.

*

> He doesn't give me any indication of how he feels at all. He doesn't communicate. Not only doesn't he talk, there are no sounds for the most part. Sometimes I don't even know that he's ejaculated except for the fact that he slows down.

Almost always, poor sexual communication results when partners cannot assert themselves as they would like:

I used to frequently get angry because I didn't think I could just say "No" outright. So I'd just get pissed off, and he could definitely tell that I wasn't interested.

*

Sometimes I get to the point where I feel like, "Gee, I was ready for intercourse five minutes ago," but I don't always say it. Sometimes I do, sometimes I don't. Sometimes I don't want to say it. I want him to want it. Maybe I feel I'm being selfish.

*

Asking for what you want while you're making love is such a hard thing to do.

*

I'm not a prude, but I am reserved. I'm not very vocal. I don't demand anything, and I don't usually say anything.

*

I want him to do something different, but I don't know how to communicate that to him.

THE CHIPS NEVER FALL WHERE THEY SHOULD

We may, in addition, doubt that our partner will want to know what we have to say about our sexual needs and feelings and reactions. We may fear that our partner will be shattered by the news and/or reject us for the pain that has been inflicted. It may be that honest declarations we have made in the past led to hurts and feelings of estrangement. Partners, in and outside the sexual domain, do have a way of making what they are prepared to hear very well known. With the same respect that kept courtiers from telling the emperor that his "new clothes" did not exist, sexual partners become acutely sensitive to each other's vulnerability, and can end up choking on all that remains unsaid between them.

I see this almost on a daily basis among the couples who come to me for counseling. Before they dare say anything, they often glance furtively at each other, test the waters, try to determine the other's reactions. In fact, the tendency to be controlled by fear of upsetting the partner can be so marked that I sometimes have the partners cover their faces with paper bags, with openings only at the nose and mouth. Such couples are at first made anxious when they cannot "read" the partner's reaction to what they have to say, but eventually they throw caution to the winds and begin to talk in unaccustomed candor. Underneath remains the unanswered question; how much of who we really are—our thoughts, our feelings, our wishes, our needs—can our partner take?

> After we'd been married some time and I finally said, "Look, I'm not having orgasms," it was a real blow to him. I think that happens in a lot of marriages. People are afraid to rock the boat because it may hurt their partner's pride.

> *

> I was never satisfied sexually by my husband. We never did discuss it. I ended up just wanting him to come. I wasn't interested. I didn't want him to think that was my attitude so I tried not to be too transparent. I just wanted him to come, and I didn't get any pleasure out of making him come.

> *

> She's told me that for her the sexual experience is 98% satisfactory. I've never told her this, but I've never felt more than 10% or 15% satisfied. When I was a boy, sex wasn't discussed. Consequently, there wasn't much talk about sex in our marriage. We've grown apart over the years until now it's like we live in two different galaxies.

> *

> I tend to be hesitant about telling him where I want to be touched. I get embarrassed. I'm afraid he'll think, "Well, shoot. I've been doing this wrong all these years!"

For some couples, direct verbal communication between them seems like an insult to the sexual enterprise, as if a true lover should know what we want: Two people should be so highly attuned to each other that to ask for something sexual is not only unnecessary but would even demean their partnership. Thus, their communication is left to nonverbal cues, to hints proffered by bodily responses, awkward or subtle:

We don't always communicate verbally. It's more like he'll grab my hand and put it somewhere he likes it, and I'll do the same with him.

*

I can tell she likes something I'm doing by the way she moves: if she moves toward me or moves against my hand if I'm stroking her or if she sighs or if she breathes a certain way.

*

The other day I tried to seduce her but she gave me a negative cue. She rubbed her eyes with her hands. Whenever she does that I know she's not sexually aroused.

*

If his lips are relaxed, that's an indication that he's receptive, so I'll kiss him more and we'll go on. I'm the same way. If I really relax my lips or stroke his back or something then that indicates to him that I'm receptive.

*

I kind of make a token move of just turning her towards me. It's like saying, "I want you, but I really don't want to have to say that." Sometimes I'll start pressing against her. I'll sometimes just take her hand and motion her down toward me. It sounds horrible, doesn't it?

There are exceptional couples, of course, who feel relatively free to verbalize their sexual thoughts and feelings, for whom such communication presents an opportunity to make what goes on between them crystal clear. Instead of pleading ignorance of what they want, instead of never being quite sure what they are up to and why, they declare themselves in no uncertain terms:

We always tell each other what feels good and what doesn't. Always.

*

He asks for what he needs, and I ask for what I need. In the sexual relationship it works real well.

*

I feel like I'm able to talk to her about anything. Our sex is really, really good, and I think that's why.

*

If I don't feel satisfied or if I want something more, I can always ask. If there's something not working, I can always express myself, and we can move or change. We're both open enough that we're able to make a change if we need to.

*

When you let down those defenses, it's surprising the things that come out of your mouth.

LET THE SUNSHINE IN!

Enough cannot be said about the importance of clear, open, honest, truthful communication between sexual partners.

- How can there ever be a genuine wholeheartedness in our sexual exchanges if we are uncertain about our partner's interests?
- How can our sexual exchanges reach their full potential if we do not know what kinds of stimulation our partner finds especially arousing or repellent?
- How can there be ease and comfort in a sexual exchange if we do not share our fears or difficulties?
- How can partners' deepest sexual motives and interests be ascertained unless we share our dreams and fantasies?
- How can any couple move on from a sexual routine that has outlived its usefulness unless they are able to take stock of what is happening and plan new possibilities?
- How can we enlarge our sexual repertoire without discussion?

In every nook and cranny of the sexual domain there are appreciations, regrets, and resentments that couples need to share to set the record straight, to correct false assumptions, to fill in for our partner what we want or need. Couples run aground on unspoken compromises; giving and receiving accurate feedback is the essence of a good sexual relationship, the lifeblood of a flourishing partnership.

There is obvious merit in no longer being left in the dark about the meanings and effects of our sexual transactions. But more than that, true sexual communication between couples testifies vividly to their trust, in themselves and in each other. When we dare to be honest with each other and risk exposing the deepest aspects of ourselves, we strengthen the very fabric of our life as a couple. This in turn empowers each of us beyond the confines of the bedroom. It necessarily entails an escape from the tyranny of the fears that too often run our lives. It necessarily requires the kind of courage that will stand us in good stead for any enterprise. It is exactly because the stakes seem so high, and because what is shared is so very personal, that we can gain more from the attempt to shed light in this area of our lives than in any other. In fact, the rewards may not even be chiefly sexual.

6

Getting It On:
INITIATION

In longstanding sexual relationships, partners usually establish a pattern for sexual exchange—how it is begun, by which one of them, and under what conditions. This pattern can become quite as familiar as how tasks are shared or vacations planned. Each partner needs deep understanding of what the other's accustomed role feels like, be it that of the one who makes or the one who awaits sexual approaches. Searching for this understanding can expose what they need to know about themselves if they are ever to experience the sexual joy they deserve: the meaning sex has for them, their self-appraisals as sexual partners, what they believe sex amounts to for the partner, and their understanding of appropriate sexual conduct.

We can all produce explanations of one sort or another not only for our current pattern but also for why it may differ from those we've established in past relationships. How we explain both our general rules for decisions to be sexual with each other and our responses in any particular exchange may reveal fears of exploiting another sexually or fears of being exploited. Our explanations may lead to questions and answers about what we feel we deserve, in this and other contexts. They may bare whatever difficulties we have being our true selves, or whether we are comfortable with feelings of power in dealing with

93

others. No matter the sexual initiation pattern we find ourselves in, we can be sure that understanding it will have profound implications for our emotional responses to sex and our assessments of ourselves.

When married couples across America bed down for the night, to the casual observer it may appear that not much of consequence is going on. Whether it be the shower that is taken or the teeth that get brushed or the light that gets turned on or the book that is reached for (perhaps more frequently, the remote control), these nightly rituals are all that can be directly observed. And yet, as with everything else that occurs in the sexual domain, it would be a mistake to conclude that going to bed amounts to no more than the obvious:

> **He'll test me. He'll get into bed and he won't touch me. I'll think he's angry, but I won't make a move toward him. Then, he'll turn over and go to sleep, and I'll be a wreck! The next day, he'll be nasty to me. He'll say, "Well, I really would have liked it if you would have!" I'll answer, "Well, then, why didn't you come out and say it?!"**

This exasperated woman illustrates that what too often occurs among sexual partners is not a simple matter at all. Here we find a wife who thinks her husband is playing games with her and who will not reach out to him, even if not to do so makes him angry at her. She is too daunted by his behavior to confront the situation head-on. Apparently he would like a sexual exchange but needs convincing that she is interested, while she, meanwhile, waits for him to make the first move.

For many people, going to bed with a potential sexual partner involves an assortment of issues, whether or not they are aware of them:

- Do I really want a sexual exchange? If I don't, should I?
- How long has it been since we've had sex? Is it about time we did?
- What does my partner want?
- Dare I approach? What if I get turned down?
- How should I respond if my partner approaches me?

- How can I even be sure that I'm being approached? What if I'm wrong?

Most couples can recall the time when questions like these did not crowd their minds, when "getting it on" was as easy as everything else in their relationship, but that was long ago, that unmarred state when they could have danced or made love or talked all night regardless of the price they might have paid the next day, when sexual passion did not involve a decision at all, was just a given and never a duty, an exclamation point and never a question mark. But all that was before their jobs took their toll on both of them, before the children took attention away from father and sleep away from mother, before power struggles engulfed them both, before resentments and the distances they breed led to ambivalence about just about anything that occurred between them, including sex:

> **In the beginning of our relationship, it was pretty much mutual. Neither of us had to initiate anything because we always both wanted it, so it didn't really matter.**

IT'S WHAT I'M USED TO

If the relationship lasts long enough, the enthusiastic passion that marks its beginning usually diminishes, and couples tend to settle into initiation patterns often prompted by what they view as appropriate masculine and feminine behaviors:

> **He sometimes tells me he has to be the aggressor all the time, and that's probably true. I like to be pursued, probably part of the socialization process. If I'm the aggressor, it feels like a violation of the tapes in my head. I start feeling uncomfortable.**

*

> **I've always felt he's supposed to be the aggressor. That's how we were raised to think. Sometimes I'm the aggressor, but that's not how it's supposed to be.**

*

> Most of the time, I'm the aggressor. I don't know whether I prefer that or not. I think it would be nice if she were assertive, but most women haven't been brought up that way. It's considered unfeminine. So, they wait for the man. If a woman is assertive, then the guy will think, "Oh, hell, here's an easy lay."

Sometimes the role of the male as the sexual pursuer is so deeply embedded that it seems to have a life of its own. Sex then becomes not so much a matter of the male's genuine interest in it as it is the mindless enactment of a mandate that he pursues regardless:

> Once in a while I initiate when I don't really mean to. I'm just not into it. It's more like a habit. Then I'll realize fifteen minutes into lovemaking that Pittsburgh is gonna play the Mets!

A most unfortunate result of clear-cut gender-related roles and responsibilities is the perpetuation of sexist attitudes that harm relationships between males and females, sexual or otherwise. It does not take much to imagine the consequences of such attitudes as eloquently expressed by one of the males in our sample:

> In our relationship, I have the authority to touch her body without looking for clues as to whether it's okay. For me, it's important that I don't have to wait to know.

There is no question but that for most people, sexual desire and interest and advances are the province of the male, and that if a female shows too great an interest it violates her role and repels her partner. An extreme version of this is to be found among the Gensii, a tribe residing in Kenya, where courtship consists of battles between the pursuing male and obstinate female, where the wedding night is marked by a gang rape of the bride by the husband's male friends, and where sexual intercourse between married partners takes on all the qualities of a sadomasochistic enterprise, as the female's determined resistance provokes violent persistence by the male.

In our own culture, where male and female roles are not so exaggerated, spouses enact their sexual rituals with far less certainty. Liberated men do not want to appear coy, nor liberated women demanding. In either case, it becomes difficult for us to declare our sexual needs forthrightly or to act in accordance with them. Sometimes, a person who does not feel fully permitted to own his or her sexuality may not admit a wish or an impulse to conscious thought, much less to the sexual partner. We may find our partner's casual caresses distastefully inappropriate when we are busy feeding the hungry or nursing the sick. We may view sexual hopes as self-indulgent or as unfortunate compromises we are forced to make with the animal side of our nature. It is little wonder, then, that our attempts to connect sexually with another human being are marked by such ambivalence, are so tentative and indirect:

> I told her that when she got done with what she was doing to just wake me up and do whatever. She said, "What do you want?" I said, "Why don't you just surprise me?" She knew what I wanted, but she doesn't like to be told what to do.

*

> I kind of make a token move. I have her turn toward me. The whole thing is embarrassing. It's like saying, "I want you," without having to say it.

*

> I sort of get my message across.

*

> I try to be subtle. I'll start kissing her, start undressing her. It's not a matter of, "Hey, Babe, let's have sex!"

*

> If the cue is too explicit, it doesn't work very well.

THE GHOST THAT WALKS

Note the "kind of" and the "sort of" that mark the attempt to initiate sex. There could be a myriad of reasons for this. Sometimes it expresses a more general unassertiveness. For example, we all know people who cannot seem to make decisions about anything, who leave their lives up to others. In a night on the town, they leave the choice of where to go and what to do up to their partners. Asked to choose a restaurant or a movie, such people are prone to reply, "It doesn't matter to me, wherever *you* want to go." A major component of themselves—what they want, what they would like—is muted, unacknowledged and, therefore, unshared. They tiptoe through their interactions with others, preferring deference to the risk of choosing wrongly. If they know what they want surely enough to overcome their trepidation and let their wishes be known, they may not get what they ask for. Even worse, they might experience a rejection that would hurt too much to be worth the try. Making a request of any kind may feel too imposing, too controlling, too aggressive, even hostile. Feeling unequal to any power struggle, they shelter in habitual evasions. One never knows where such people stand. Their indecision and uncertainty leave them undefined in every way and everywhere, including the bedroom:

> I think she'd prefer my being more aggressive. She's very strong, very forward, direct. I'm attracted to that but also scared. I'm much more of the passive type. I'm less prone to say, "Hey, let's do it tonight," with a force of conviction, like imposing a will. I think I'm afraid of being rejected. It runs through my whole life, as far back as I can remember, this fear of rejection.

This man is not alone. Many people's lives are colored by such fear. In a culture such as ours that places emphasis on getting along, being a team player, our best energies are often devoted to figuring out what others want from us, to divining the impact of what we say and do on others whose opinions of us are more important than our own. At the end of a social occasion, the people-pleasers among us will leave the scene with one question in mind, "What did they think of *me*," but hardly ever address, "What did I think of *them*?"

Needless to say, fears of rejection can be sexually crippling. Under such circumstances, we make sexual advances only very tentatively, when our partner's positive response is assured. Indeed, if not met with entirely open arms, we may doubly hesitate to try again:

> I'm usually not the initiator. I usually wait for my partner to make the first move. I wait until my partner makes it patently clear that it's time we did it.

*

It's like, "Oh, God, is this person gonna accept me?" I'd like to get over that.

*

Once the contact has been made, I'm fine. I'll do all sorts of things, not wait for cues. I'll have oral sex before he does. I just need to get past the fear of being rejected. Even though we've been married thirteen years, and he's told me, "Margaret, when you get into bed, just reach over and grab me. You won't be rejected," I still can't make myself do that. There's still that fear.

*

When I ask her directly, she gets tense and frozen, and it doesn't work, and I feel rejected. And then it's worse. The joking I do is like testing the waters without exposing myself.

Leaving the sexual moment up to our partner out of fear that acting on our own impulses will lead to rejection is not the best of solutions either. It can often result in having to decide what to do about one's *partner's* sexual advances. In addition to the fear of rejection can be the fear of rejecting which, for some people, is even worse:

I generally leave it up to him, and then when he does initiate, I'll occasionally get annoyed and want to say, "No, I don't want to." Nowadays, if I'm real dead set against it, then I won't do it. I'm getting better about that. I don't feel as obligated.

Of all human transactions, a sexual exchange probably carries the greatest risk of rejecting or being rejected, of hurting or being hurt. The underlying conviction that we or our partner may not be robust enough to withstand an honest response, that one or the other of us needs to be treated delicately, is more often responsible for deep-seated difficulties in a sexual partnership than anything else I can think of. Concerns about our own or another's vulnerability makes it close to impossible to be spontaneous in our exchanges, to communicate our needs or to act in ways that are congruent with them, or to disclose enough about ourselves to maintain a truly viable relationship. Such concerns are responsible for the deceits and the lack of wholeheartedness that characterize many sexual partnerships. And if we suppose that our partner is tiptoeing as carefully around us as we are with him or her, how can we ever believe that the other is acting honestly? A powerful remedy for a deteriorating sexual relationship is, no doubt, a solid dose of real talk, real communication, mincing no words, speaking the truth (if we can find it) from the heart (if it is still there). But this is easier said than done.

Congratulations to couples who are able with fine incaution to make their desires known, who reveal themselves, bluntly or indirectly but in no uncertain terms:

> She plays with me. She kisses me. She whines. I can tell! She comes on to me. She touches me. She hangs on me. She drapes herself toward me.

*

> Sometimes we'll say, "Hey, let's fuck!"

*

> Either one of us might say, "It'd be nice if we could make love tonight," or "I'm horny."

*

> We'll usually start with one or both of us feeling horny. We'll start flirting in the morning, and he'll say, "Doing anything later this evening?" And maybe he'll whisper in my ear something naughty he'd like to do. He can be very gross. I like that in a man. We just sort of flirt off and on all day, and we have our little jokes. One of them is, "Do you like oranges?" That's because I once told him that in a prior relationship I had we'd start off having sex by asking, "Do you like oranges? OK, so do I; let's fuck!"

*

> I'm a "C'mon!" man. I don't mince words. I just say it. If we're going to do, let's do it.

Some, if not most, people find it easier to request sexual contact openly the more urgency they feel:

> **The more important it is to me at the time, the more likely I am to make it clear.**

THIS IS HOW IT IS

How sex is initiated and by whom and under what conditions tells us a great deal about sexual partners and their relationship. For example, there are couples set in their gender-related ways who, not in for surprises, have a firmly set pattern. They always know ahead of time that *he* and not *she* has the responsibility for "getting it on":

He's the one who usually initiates sex. Basically, he'll do things, and I'll respond.

*

He always initiates it, about 99.9 percent of the time. He complains that before we were married and right after, I wanted to more than I do now. True! I didn't have a 12-hour-a-day job, a huge house, laundry for three and a child in daycare. It feels like I'm always worn out.

WILL YOU JUST WAIT A SECOND!!

Many females explain their lack of initiation simply: their male partner does not give them a chance to make the first move. They feel crowded out by his zeal, his unrelenting pressure for sexual contact:

Sometimes he complains I'm not more forward, and I say, "Why should I be?" I know it's going to happen regardless, just like night follows day. It's no wonder I can't be forward or sexy. There's no incentive!

*

When he asks me why I haven't initiated, I just tell him that he didn't wait long enough. But it didn't change anything.

*

He just doesn't wait long enough for me to get around to it!

*

He was so interested when we started that there was no room for me. You can't have a lot of cooks in the kitchen. You can only have one leader. Now that his interest has come down a little bit, there's more room for me to express how and when I like it.

A woman in these circumstances never gets to know the measure of her sexual drive and interest, never gets a chance to experience sex as a function of her will, of her decision, never gets an opportunity to feel responsible for what occurs. She may well engage in sex half-heartedly. The male's impatience, combined with the female's more or less grudging accommodation, is probably as responsible as anything else for the sexual malaise that characterizes so many relationships. A great many men suspect at some level that their female partners would not engage in sex with them at all but for their insistence, and that thinking leads to behaviors that then sustain the pattern:

> I just feel if I don't initiate it, maybe it won't happen.

*

> She just assumes I'll do the initiating.

*

> At first it was, "Whenever you feel like it, just let me know." But that ends up making me the initiator more than half the time.

If all the men in America suddenly decided to back off for the next six months in order to allow their female partners to initiate sex on their own, to act in accordance with their own and not the male's sexual drive and interest, not only would sexual relationships miraculously improve, but the men themselves would be given a chance to experience sex without needing to be coercive.

Some men, weary of the aggressive role, realize that it does no good to the relationship or to themselves to be seen as a sexual tyrant:

> I don't want it to be like I'm nagging her all the time.

*

> I knew she'd always be there for me, but I really didn't want to bother her. I wanted to give her a break.

*

> I don't want to impose on her. I don't like to demand satisfaction.

I'VE GOT MY REASONS

There are, of course, less charitable reasons people (usually men, sometimes women) give for not being the sexual pursuer. Often it is a matter of feeling thwarted by one's partner, of being rejected outright:

> A couple of times when I've snuggled up to her and started kissing her neck, she's said, "Why don't you just get off me?" I feel bitter a lot of the time.

Some people quit initiating sexual contact not because they expect rejection but because the partner has become indifferent. What used to be a hearty welcome has given way to the countless excuses stereotyped in jokes we all have heard. In real life, though, there is no laughter, only pain and loneliness:

> I get tired of hearing, "No, I don't want it," so I quit asking him. Usually when we have sex it's because he initiates it. He falls asleep before I do, and if I wake him up, he's grouchy and doesn't want sex. He's tired. He doesn't feel good. He's got to get up early. I'm sick of his excuses.

In the face of a partner's indifference, there are those who give it up, who refuse to take the first step ever again:

> Sometimes I think, "If I have to initiate all this stuff, I'm just not going to do it!"
>
> *
>
> We'd get into bed at night, and he'd roll over and go to sleep. Sometimes, I'd make a few attempts to touch him, to get cozy, and he wouldn't respond. I wouldn't persist then any longer at all.
>
> *
>
> I get tired of hearing him say, "No, I don't want it" when I approach him sexually. I've just quit asking him.

As with every other aspect of a sexual exchange, which partner initiates it, and in what way, or how often does not, in and of itself, affect the quality of the relationship. Far more emotionally consequential is the meaning assigned to what takes place, the conclusions one reaches about oneself or one's partner or about the relationship itself. Regardless of how initiation takes place, we reach conclusions about ourselves that are relatively benign or malignant, self-congratulatory or demeaning. Some people feel good about themselves because they initiate, others because they do not:

> I usually do the initiating. I'm more important than she. If I want something, I go after it.
>
> *
>
> If I don't remind her, then it's going to be forgotten.
>
> *
>
> As a wife, I think I should want to have sex with him sometimes. That's about as far as it goes.

Some label their tendency to initiate sex as "self-expressive," others as "self-indulgent," some as testimony to their normal and healthy sexual drive, others as a surrender to their basic impulses and an inability to control themselves; some ascribe it to their general assertiveness, others to their need to accommodate their partners. The self-attributions people make in this regard are practically infinite. So, too, is the variety of explanations for not initiating sex. Some connect it to their greater interest in more important matters, others to their sexual inhibitions, some to their regard for their partners, others to their *lack* of regard. Needless to say, what we conclude about ourselves on the basis of our inclination or disinclination to initiate sexual activities can either raise or lower our self-esteem and our view of ourselves as sexual partners.

PARTNER ATTRIBUTIONS

A major question involves the extent to which we explain our participation in "getting it on" according to who *we* are vis-a-vis who our *partner* is. Often an individual is averse to interpreting experiences of any kind as a function of his or her own needs, interests, or conflicts, taking no responsibility for the events in his or her life.

Everything that happens comes about through others' quirks, hang-ups, histories, or inclinations. In the sexual domain, the partner's needs and behaviors explain what occurs. Sometimes these attributions to the partner can be benign, more often quite the opposite, all having a telling effect upon the relationship:

> I'm not sure why she doesn't initiate more. The main thing, I think, is that she's shy. She's just a shy person and doesn't feel comfortable doing that. It doesn't have anything to do with our relationship.

*

> She's not the aggressive type.

Some feel that their partner fails to encourage their initiatives:

> There was a time early in the relationship where my initiating sexual contact didn't seem to work very well. She felt I was pressuring her if I initiated, so I got the message real early on that it wasn't a good thing for me to initiate.

*

> The odds are much better when she's the aggressor.

There is no question but that how we expect our partner to respond can profoundly affect our interest in initiating sexual contact. Controlled by the fear of being turned down, we keep our requests to a minimum and, finally, make them unknown even to ourselves:

> It usually begins with me being kind of aggressive, trying to get her to have any type of sexual interest at all. When I start cuddling or flirting or kissing, she'll usually say, "No, I'm tired," or "My stomach hurts," and if she gives in, it's like she's doing it out of duty.

*

> If I don't initiate it, it will never happen. I can get in a sexy nightgown, start to undress in front of him, and toss my clothes at him so that he notices that I'm undressing, and for a while I get his attention. If I couldn't at least get that from him, I'd probably never initiate *anything*!

While for some people taking the sexual initiative seems to be fraught with danger, for others it involves no daring at all:

> She's never complained once. I've awakened her at 3:00 in the morning to make love, and there's never been a "Honey, I've got a headache, don't do that, don't touch me." She's always willing and able and ready to please.

*

> Rarely does either one of us not want to do it. It's more like who can jumpstart the other one. We both expect the other one to initiate and carry it to a certain point where the other one's turned on enough to carry on.

Some explanations for why we are inclined or not to initiate sexual contact have less to do with how we view ourselves or our partners or our relationships than with other extraneous factors, such as the presence or absence of opportunity:

> I initiate more often when I know we'll have an opportunity to carry through with it in a relaxed way. Like when I know we're going to have time for a long lunch or I know it's morning, and we still could have time. I tend to do it a lot more on the weekends when I know there are more opportunities.

*

> I don't usually initiate unless he hasn't in a long time. Then I finally start letting him know that I want him to fuck my brains out!

*

> If we've had a lot of sex lately, I'm more interested. It's more on my mind, and so I may be more likely to run up and grab his butt, or run up and put my arms around him from the back and give him a kiss on the neck to let him know.

There are others, however, who explain what occurs as the result of whatever else is going on in the partnership:

> She's more likely to initiate sex after a really good evening or a really good day, if we've had a good time together and we've been communicating and getting along.

Perhaps this last comment provides us with an important clue as to why couples bedding down for the night are not at all certain about how to proceed, how to connect sexually, if at all. For too many couples, sex does not develop in a mood of satisfaction with each other whose outgrowth is an interest in reaching out to one another, in knowing and being known. Too often it is just another of the nighttime rituals already mentioned, a thing one does; it may be entirely discordant with conflicts the two people may be having, a form of connectedness that does not fit, an affront to what has actually been happening in their relationship, perhaps just another "should" whose potential is dishonored by what is going on between them. Some people compartmentalize sex, keeping it separate from the rest of their relationship, but they are in the minority. The majority find it exceedingly difficult, no matter how hard they try, to keep this ultimate of human acts separate from their monumental failure to connect in any emotional way outside the bedroom. And if one or the other tries, the transaction and its consequence is all too predictable:

Usually he'll just say, "Let's go in the bedroom." No touching, no kissing me. No nuzzling. No passion at all.

AT AN IMPASSE?

The matter of who will make the first move in a sexual exchange, who will first show interest in drawing close, has to do with far more than bed. It displays a couple's established style of relating to each other and determines as much as anything else whether they can progress towards fulfillment together. In the wake of countless times when one's expectations of the other were not fulfilled, when tentative attempts to draw close were rebuffed, when individual efforts to enhance the relationship availed nothing, all that remains will be a partner's vow: "Never again! Never again will I make myself so vulnerable, never again bother with a saving gesture for the sake of our relationship. From now on, if he/she cares about me, he/she's got to make it clear that I'm not the only one who cares where this relationship is going." People who make such resolves can be viewed as trying to salvage a modicum of self-respect after years of forfeiting themselves in behalf of the relationship, keeping quiet about their needs when they might have spoken up in order to preserve some form of harmony. By the time they can no longer stand to sacrifice so much of their own truth, the only step that seems left to take is to protect themselves from further pain.

Thus, for many couples who seek professional help for a fast-deteriorating relationship, one principal issue will be: Who will take primary responsibility for rehabilitating the relationship? Who will see to it that we both work on our problems? More correctly, who will make sure that we find the time to share our thoughts and feelings in the new ways we have learned? Who has to do the reminding about all the tasks we've been assigned—read this, discuss that, write it down, share it later—when heaven knows these exercises are risky business and pretty easy to avoid.

A first task for the therapist, then, is to find out whether and how much either partner seems to feel that the ball is in the other's court. If one partner believes that the other is chiefly responsible for their sexual misfortunes or has taken very little action in behalf of the relationship until now, or if one partner is convinced that he or she has had a far greater investment in the relationship than the other, chances are good that this "forever-giving" partner will want to wait for evidence that the "getting" partner truly cares about the relationship, such as diligence in working towards a remedy. Unless this state of affairs is dealt with from the beginning, the wait will be a long one.

This sort of impasse will never be overcome until partners learn enough about themselves and about each other to forgive their mutual failures and to give reasons for them. It is out of such understanding that the question of who takes the initiative will no longer matter. Perhaps an agreement will be reached in which, for a week, one of them will lead and the other submit, with a reversal of roles in the following week. Or this format could change daily instead of weekly, in cases where unaccustomed initiative or passivity would be too hard to sustain very long. Whatever is worked out, there can be nothing quite so important as the couple's coming to see that the ball is in "our" court and not in "his" or "hers."

7 Warming Up: FOREPLAY

While it's true that the sexual act itself is the climax to our encounter, I'm more concerned about what leads up to it. I want to be sure our relationship is right, that our hearts are in harmony, that the sex act simply becomes the culmination of what's preceded it.

How much time couples spend in non-genital contact with each other, if they do not skip the preliminaries entirely and get right down to the "main event," and how they feel about each other during foreplay, will inevitably depend upon what they believe about why they are having sex, in the given instance or as a general rule.

Ideational trails in the sexual domain invariably begin with what we believe sex is all about. Many sex therapists disdain the term "foreplay" because "fore" implies that penis-vagina contact must necessarily follow. But most couples do regard non-genital contact as an appetizer. Those of us who hold that sex is primarily for

"Foreplay is inevitable. This is where we negotiate the levels of intimacy, eroticism, meaning, and emotional connection in what follows next."
(Schnarch 1997, p. 190).

closeness regard foreplay as a major element that must not be skimped or rushed through. On the other hand, those of us for whom sex is about physical release may measure the time (figuratively speaking, but not always!) until we can get to our orgasm and its aftermath of relaxed comfort. If our sexual motivations are heavily spiced with visions of excitement and pleasure, we expect foreplay to provide both of us with the required buildup of sexual energy.

What takes place at the beginning of a sexual exchange—no matter the value we place on foreplay—our gestures, our communications, what we think is happening and why, are all determined by our individual recipes for the sexual feast. The ingredients and their proportions are always diverse: perhaps a dash of sexual relief versus an entire clove of relationship-enhancement, a half teaspoon of accommodation to one's partner versus a tablespoon of control and power over our bedmate, or a cup of effort to escape the worries of the outside world versus a pint of pride in our worldly accomplishments. Whatever the mix, it will determine what goes on after a sexual exchange is initiated, the spirit of the proceedings, and the direction they take.

For some couples, foreplay does not begin in bed. Rather, from the moment they get up, their day includes an assortment of caring and loving exchanges that establish erotic interest and fuel their desire for ever deeper intimacy:

> We don't have to have a lot of foreplay. I think the affection that goes on between us every day sort of fulfills that function.

> *

> I consider just going shopping or to a show as part of foreplay.

> *

> It might happen slowly. Maybe we'll go to the movies and be caressing each other. I need a buildup. I don't feel it starts just in bed.

THE BEGINNING OF THE BEGINNING

Many couples would be hard-pressed to report exactly when foreplay does start since it is hardly distinguishable from their other relations, in or out of bed. How they say hello and goodbye to each other, how they talk to and look at each other at the dinner table, the tones of voice they use, their gestures, their expressions (concern, delight, empathy) are all cut from the same cloth as their sexuality. Their sexual relationship is not a thing apart; it is part of their experience when *"listening to a particular song on the radio," "talking about the things we've done or we're planning on doing," "sitting on his lap and just being close,"* or *"looking into each other's eyes."* Again and again throughout the day, little or big connections are made as these couples make time for each other to hear and to be heard, and this intimacy is not left at the bedroom door. It follows the couple to bed, often in the form of pillow talk, sometimes in friendly teasing and joking:

> We have a little funny game that we'll play. She'll ask, "Do you love me?" and I'll say, "Yes, Yes." Then I'll say, "Oh, you're so pretty!" and she'll say, "Oh, you're so ugly." Every time she looks at me and admires me, she tells me, "Oh, you're so ugly."

*

> It's not really genitally focused. It's more like kissing and teasing and maybe rolling around. More like playing.

*

> It's nice to take a whole day, just hang out in bed, talk and be goofy and play with each other.

Gradually, the desire for connection can take other forms as well:

> We like to eat food off of various parts of our bodies. It's kind of kinky but exciting. The last time we had intercourse after we ran out of M & Ms!

*

> We both like to receive massages, so we might do something like that, not so much geared toward getting the other aroused.

*

> Usually we light candles, and then we sit down and meditate together. We feel like it helps to align our energy.

*

We almost always talk for a while, even if it's clear that we're going to have sex at some point. We turn off the light 'cause neither of us wants the light on. Privacy is very important.

A LITTLE HERE, A LITTLE THERE, A LITTLE MORE

Sooner or later there comes body contact, the kind of touching that does not involve genitals:

We usually get undressed, almost always in bed, and hold each other for a while. I sort of feel good. We touch, joke. A period of intimacy.

*

We're very into touching, so we like to touch each other and just hug.

*

We call it "advanced snuggling."

*

Often, we'll roll our t-shirts up around our necks or else take them off if it's warm enough so we can just be two naked bodies touching each other. That always feels wonderful, just soft and gentle.

*

Foreplay, for me, is lots of skin, lots of contact with skin. I like to be able to see a lot of skin and touch a lot of skin.

Notice that these comments have to do less with sexual arousal than with unhurried time together, with cuddling, and nurturance.

In time, the partners begin to kiss each other. Kissing, seldom a part of prostitutes's or sex attackers's repertoires, may be the strongest token of genuine intimacy:

"Loveplay includes all the talking, touching, rolling around, playing, resting, and fantasizing that comprise lovemaking."
(Castleman 1983, p. 61).

We'll kiss and hold each other for ten minutes or so.

*

There's a lot of kissing and licking and that kind of stuff.

*

We do a lot of French kissing, and there's a lot of tongue stimulation over the body. We both enjoy that. It's fun to kiss or lick him all over and he does the same for me. He likes me to lick his genital area, and I don't mind doing that.

When genital contact finally is introduced, it is often as an extension of the kissing and stroking that have been going on:

We'll take our clothes off. We might play and do some genital touching, teasing. Sometimes I'll get massage oil out, and we do stuff like that.

*

I like him to perform oral sex and to suck my breasts.

*

We just stroke each other, and he touches my genitals, and I play with his. I've been more interested in stimulating him orally, licking his penis and stimulating his nipples.

CONNECTING

The general tone of these remarks, references to playing and laughing and touching and snuggling, to mouthing each other in various ways, captures very well what is the essence of foreplay for many couples. Foreplay is an opportunity to reclaim the child within us, to experience the safety and security not often found or permitted in adulthood, to own the vulnerable state that we too often deny in other contexts. Such trustful foreplay amounts to an important statement of who we are at the very core.

Born into the world alone, knowing that we shall die alone as well and that we cannot control more than an insignificant corner of the universe, we are seldom able to do anything about our existential loneliness. But in foreplay, our sense of isolation can be overcome, however briefly; our reaching out and connecting is reciprocated, and we can sink into a fully welcoming embrace. Barriers that keep us separated from others and from our inner selves are broken down; an array of defenses that keep us from feeling really alive can be set aside. We know and are known as in no other way. This knowledge can be so powerful that death itself seems less threatening.

> You insult the whole process when you don't have caring or communication before the actual sex itself. You have to kind of bond as people first, and as a man and a woman second. Foreplay is people caring about each other.

*

> How much foreplay people engage in depends on how long it takes to let down their defenses toward the other person. A long time of foreplay lets people know each other. It can really be an ultimate experience.

JUMPSTARTING

Most people, however, do not acknowledge that foreplay provides an opportunity for self-subsuming merger with the other. Instead, they tend to view it in strategic terms, as preliminary activities designed to ensure a successful sexual exchange. Men may be concerned that coitus will be painful to their female partner if she is not properly prepared, or that she will not have an orgasm if she has not been properly stimulated, or sometimes it is a matter of the man's having to be stimulated enough to achieve erection:

> I guess there is some degree of foreplay. It doesn't start with, "Yeah, let's screw," so bingo, I'm in her. The vagina has to be ready or else it's going to hurt. I don't want it to hurt.

*

> Usually there is some working up to the point where she's wet enough for me to really enter her. So we don't have me enter right away. Usually, I do a lot of licking and a lot of cunnilingus. This is real stimulating for me, too.

*

I like to kiss and touch until she gets to the point where she's pretty excited, and then we have intercourse.

Likewise, women are likely to note that they need enough stimulation for pleasurable intercourse, and may complain about the male's failure to take this into account:

If he seems like he's really ready and kind of in a hurry, I'll just say, "I'm not ready yet," and then we'll spend a little more time on the preliminaries.

*

The more foreplay I have, the easier it is. I don't have an orgasm if there hasn't been any foreplay.

*

Sometimes I get dry. He'll want to go inside me right away even though he hasn't done anything to warm me up.

*

I need a buildup.

In addition to this major distinction between those who view foreplay as interpersonal communion and those who view it primarily as jumpstarting the partner, reasons for omitting, shortening, or prolonging it differ widely:

If we're both really horny, then there's a lot more. Then there'll be a lot of caressing and a lot of hugging.

*

If I'm really horny, I just really want to get right to it, skip all the preliminaries and get to the main event. When I'm kind of in the mood but not really turned on, I want to spend a lot of time on preliminaries. On the other hand, if I'm tired, I don't want to spend the time on preliminaries, and I'll say, "I'm just too tired for that. Let's just go straight to it and go to bed."

*

One of the things that changes most in a long-term relationship is the kissing. It's just not as passionate.

*

I won't usually do it unless he asks. Part of the problem is I haven't mastered how to have an erect penis in my mouth without the feeling of choking. I can have his penis in there for a length of time, and the gag reflex comes up, and I think, "Hmmm," that part is not as much fun for me. I do it because he seems to like it.

*

If it's time for my period, and my breasts are sensitive, I don't want him caressing them. That's when I'd just as soon get on with it.

*

My husband's typical foreplay probably lasts five minutes, but that depends on how many times we've had sex. If we're having sex every single night, the foreplay is longer. If it's spread out more, he wants to poke it in just as fast as he can, which is understandable.

READY, SET . . . NOT READY?

Like everything else in a sexual exchange, a person's enthusiasm for the experience will depend in large measure upon how interested in it the partner seems to be, what we believe motivates our partner, our partner's actions, reactions, and preferences, and the extent to which our partner calls the shots during sexual contact.

Many women would need a lot of persuasion to believe that their male partners are really interested in spending much time on foreplay. Such men often seem anxious to get down to business, wanting to press on, compelled by their sexual excitement, eager to ejaculate. As mentioned earlier, in ancient times there was survival value in quick coitions. Some experts in the field (beginning with Kinsey et al.) believed that the answer to a woman's need to become sufficiently aroused for painless intercourse should not be found in extensive foreplay but, rather, in creating a society that did not inhibit female sexuality. In our real and present world, many women regard foreplay as a male's capitulation to their special needs and circumstances:

I'll think, "Well, he's tired. I'm not going to ask for all these preliminaries."

*

Sometimes I think maybe he is really hot and heavy to go and wants to arouse me as quickly as he can. He ends up moving in that direction a little faster than I do.

*

Sometimes I think, "Darn it, you're going to kiss me or else nothing is going to happen here!"

*

He cares to do it because I love it, not because he does.

*

Maybe he doesn't like it so much because body fluids really gross him out.

If a woman considers it a problem or a deficiency in herself that she needs more foreplay, she may be embarrassed to ask for it and sound apologetic if she does ask. Instead of persisting, she may begin to feel growing resentment, to detach from the proceedings, and to view her partner with bitterness or disdain. As her mind stores up criticisms, her heart loses warmth. Her chief complaint may be that her partner is oblivious to her needs, her tastes, and her slower tempo:

He usually starts kissing my genitals sooner than I want him to. I don't mind it, but I usually need more upper body touching and body touching all over before I'm ready for that.

*

When we're in a nonsexual situation, he knows how to share intimacies. But he doesn't know how to do it in a non-genital sexual contact. I have trouble categorizing sex as a purely animal act. He doesn't.

*

He doesn't kiss me for a long time. He doesn't, you know, kind of warm me up. He's very direct. His cock gets hard, and he wants to go inside me right away. He likes to eat me out, but I wish he'd do some other things as well.

*

Sometimes he'll use the power thing. He'll invade me, not let me become well lubricated through foreplay. He'll get real into it when I'm not there yet.

Some women characterize their partners as too clumsy or ignorant for skillful foreplay:

He'll stimulate my clitoris, but he does it awkwardly and does it too hard. I tell him it doesn't feel good.

*

Last night, I said to him, "Hugging is really nice. We should try just hugging more." He said, "Yeah," kind of half-heartedly. And I said, "Note the enthusiasm." And he said, "No, it's all right." Fact is, he doesn't really know how to go about it, to touch or to hug for a long time.

*

He has a tendency to rub my nipples or clitoris in a hard way. It seems that he can only do one thing at a time. I don't know if it's a male thing or not, but if he's rubbing his belly, he can't pat his head. If he's getting pleasure, he's not good at giving it. If he's touching my genitals, he leaves my breasts alone. If he's playing with my breasts, he doesn't bother to kiss me. Maybe he's not well coordinated. No wonder we never practice 69!

THERE'S MORE TO IT

When foreplay is unsatisfactory for a woman, or tedious for a man, the partner is inevitably affected by these negative feelings, and may indeed—through reacting to them—contribute to them. In addition, both partners may at some level accept the notion that males are eager for coitus only, and thus unconsciously encourage what consciously they see as the partner's ineptitude. A number of respondents specified complaints, sometimes concerning what they or their partners do or will not do with their mouths:

Foreplay is pretty minimal, because once she's ready, she's ready for penetration. She doesn't want to extend foreplay. She doesn't want oral sex. She really doesn't want to receive it or give it.

*

I kiss his penis. He likes that very much, but he'd also like to kiss my puss. I like it more when I'm kissing him.

*

It's probably just within the last four or five years that I've allowed him to have oral sex with me. I felt it was dirty. I always had oral sex with him, but I never allowed him to touch me.

*

He likes me to lick his genital area, and I don't mind doing that, at least not as much as holding his penis in my mouth. That's uncomfortable. I haven't learned how to do that in a way that would maximize his pleasure and minimize my displeasure.

*

Touching is one thing. Using the mouth is something else. You worry, "Is he going to enjoy my smell?" "Is he going to enjoy how wet I get?"

*

I'm not big on kissing. I don't like someone's tongue slithering around in mine. Sometimes I'll say, "Please don't kiss me." And so we don't kiss, because I just can't stand it. It varies with my mood.

Sometimes a partner's disinterest or inhibitions can have a telling effect:

As far as I'm concerned, foreplay starts when she starts responding to me. Up until then, it's been work!

*

I get to feeling that I don't want to put forth the effort just to be rebuffed most of the time. I get to feeling that even though she's responding, she's still holding back.

*

We usually have probably a longer period of foreplay than I would like. He doesn't like to kiss, but he likes to fondle a lot and be stroked and that sort of thing, longer than what I would like.

Sometimes a hesitation about engaging in foreplay is attributed to a lack of skill:

> I'm not sure how to touch his penis. I'm learning, but it's still hard for me to get it all coordinated. It's something we have to work on some more.

In some instances, the effects of sexual abuse in childhood make it all but impossible for a woman to engage in any behaviors that remind her of her past:

> There was not much foreplay because I couldn't tolerate it. My father would rub my chest, so when my husband played with my breasts, I just felt helpless. It wouldn't make me feel excited, just extremely helpless and manipulated. I suspect that my father didn't really put his penis in my genital area, because that's a real turn-on for me. I just didn't want him to put his hands on me.

*

> There was sexual abuse but also physical and emotional abuse. Her emotional garbage has her turned off before I've even started trying to turn her on.

*

> I want sex to be comfortable, but right now I'm just more comfortable without sex. If sex starts, I'd rather just have intercourse and not fool around or do anything orally. I'm very uncomfortable with touching. I think what happened most with my stepfather was touching. That's why I'm really uncomfortable with long foreplay. I get sick to my stomach. I can't concentrate. I'd rather stop altogether or just hurry up and have sex and get it over with and go to sleep.

BEYOND BODY PARTS

For those who can give themselves wholeheartedly to the sexual moment—for whom pleasure, delight in one's partner, closeness and contact are every bit as important as procreation or even orgasms; who are able to own their needs to touch and be touched; whose sense of self is not threatened by close contact with another human being—reports of foreplay are altogether positive:

> The whole time we are making love, we kiss. That means closeness to me, that I'm special to him, that I love him.

*

> He just feels like a sweetie when he's kissing my back or playing with my breasts. Foreplay has always been a real nice thing with us.

*

> It's fun to stimulate his body. I usually kiss or lick him, over the expanse of his body, and he does the same for me.

*

> It's great, always great! It's really good for both of us. We're not in a hurry to get into that penetration thing. We try to take our time and enjoy all the things that lead up to it.

*

> We're both excited during foreplay just because it's exciting. It's fun. Sometimes, though, it's just happiness.

*

> I think there's a real high just in foreplay. People who discover that can do a lot more things, communicatively and sexually and everything else.

In a society that has traditionally endorsed sex for procreation over recreation, and emphasized males's sexual prowess rather than their capacity for intimacy, that values work over play and equates sensual pleasure with self-indulgence, that stresses speed, knowhow, and efficiency both in and out of bed, it is no wonder that many people see little point in foreplay. Some are too busy or too tired to take the time. Others can tolerate only a very brief brush with genuine intimacy. For still others (like prostitutes who give blow jobs and engage in intercourse but never kiss), intimacy is not even the point and is assiduously avoided.

Failing to note, much less share, the impact of a partner's choices and behaviors, a couple may proceed with sex and be left to wonder why it does not feel like love. Making love consists of displaying more than a casual interest in one's partner at the end of a working day, of getting a feverish partner a glass of juice from downstairs instead of just water from the bathroom, of surprising one's partner with a compliment, of taking the time to listen to a partner's complaints instead of deflecting or topping them. And until a couple gets this point, fair and square, they will continue to limit the reasons for their sexual lethargy to a loss of physical attractiveness or to sexual incompetence or to the aging process or even to what goes on (or not) in foreplay. The impact of all these is *minuscule* compared to everything stored up in the couple's hearts and minds—fashioned of gestures made moment by moment or day by day, of what has been said or left unsaid, of signs of caring or neglect.

8

Going, Going, Gone:
ORGASM

As a sexual exchange proceeds through stages of arousal, partners usually begin to focus on orgasm. They choose activities geared toward both their own and the other's needs and expectations. When and how and by what means to achieve orgasmic relief often guides both partners, especially if they regard such relief as the whole idea of their encounter. They are apt to see the outcome as incontrovertible evidence of their sexual capacities and of the worth of their sexual partnership.

Males may be preoccupied with maintaining intercourse long enough for, as they suppose, their partner to reach her own orgasm. They may recall, with some embarrassment, their adolescent sexual excursions, when "wham" hardly ever got to "bam" before there was nothing left of their passion except semen in the wrong place. They may remember sexual occasions in which too much alcohol had led to little more than a shamefaced apology. Not many males are strangers to the concern over "getting it up," "keeping it up," and being able to ejaculate exactly when they want to and not a moment before.

Females, for their part, may remember occasions (even recently) when orgasm eluded them because foreplay or coitus ended when they were lubricated but not strongly aroused. If so they are more likely to be concerned whether they will reach orgasm at all, and by what means. Women who do not easily reach orgasm may resort to what they consider extraordinary means toward their goal or wait patiently, for years, for the magic moment to arrive. Some, with profound regret, will relinquish hope.

For many of us, when and how and if orgasm is reached is the barometer for our own and our partner's sexual interest, arousal, and gratification. Especially when things seem to go wrong, our concerns can be pressing:

- If I don't bring her off, does it mean I'm no good as a lover, or just that she wasn't interested?
- Why wasn't she interested?
- What else should I be doing?
- Is it true that I can't tell if she comes or not?
- Is she lying sometimes to make me feel better?
- How important is it for her to reach orgasm?
- How long will it be before she finds someone who can do it better?
- Should we get into therapy, or should we just wait and see . . . ?
- Why must he always come before I'm ready?
- Can he tell I wanted to get this over with as soon as possible?
- Has he given up on me, convinced that I'll never reach orgasm?
- Is he tired of trying? Is he going to find someone else? Am I really cold?
- Is he only concerned about *his* needs and could care less about mine?
- How much do I matter?
- Am I too worried about all this?

Any kind of misfire can unleash scores of fears about ourselves, questions about our partner, and concerns about the sexual partnership. The conclusions we reach, the attributions we make, will have a telling effect upon the life we live in the sexual domain.

POP! GOES THE WEASEL?

Contrary to popular notions, an orgasm is not a true, perfect, unique exaltation. Orgasms are not the same from one time to the next in a single individual, let alone for one individual compared to another. Orgasms differ in their physical and emotional intensity. They differ in what is required to reach them. They differ in how important they are to a person and in how interested a partner is in the other having them. They differ in whether or not they are mutual. They differ in whether or not they are multiple. They differ in how individuals account for them and, thus, in how they affect an individual's self-esteem and in what partners think they reveal about the relationship.

The same, of course, can be said about the lack of orgasmic response during a sexual exchange. Its impact can depend on whether it is the male or the female partner who does not reach orgasm, whether an individual has ever been orgasmic with any partner, or on whether an orgasm is anticipated. Some of us suppose that we should be able to reach orgasm by almost any means whatsoever and regardless of the conditions. For others of us it may come as a pleasant surprise or an almost miraculous achievement. Some of us resent our partner's pressuring us to reach orgasm, while others of us are repelled or hurt by our partner's apparent indifference to the matter. Some of us rely on our own efforts to reach orgasm, while others of us resent our partner's failure to "give" us one. Some of us, if given a choice, would much prefer that our partner and not we reach orgasm, and sometimes the partner, sensing how important this is, will feign the preferred outcome. Whether or not one occurs, nothing can be inferred about the individuals concerned or about the quality of their sexual relationship.

Typical manuals and textbooks dealing with orgasms may give a person the impression that orgasms are an either-or proposition, that on a particular sexual occasion we either reach one (or more) or we do not. Both plain and subtle differences are ignored in statistical tables ill-prepared to deal with the highly subjective experiences of sexual release. Indeed, many sexologists have been so intent upon refuting Freudian notions about women's clitoral versus vaginal orgasms that they tend to dismiss any discussions at all about differences in a person's orgasmic response. That dismissal may be prompted by the concern that ambiguity about orgasm might lead some of us to question the quality of our orgasmic response and thus our self-worth or the value of our sexual partnership. And yet, there are people who continue to insist that not all orgasms are the same:

> Just because a man ejaculates doesn't mean that he's completely satisfied. When it comes to orgasms, there are so many different degrees that you can go to. Sometimes it's a release, sometimes it's a little more, sometimes it's just like an explosion. I see that with her, too. Sometimes she shakes.

> *

> She describes her orgasms differently, depending upon whether she's making love or having sex. Having sex seems to involve a real sharp orgasm. When she makes love the orgasm is real deep and involved.

> *

> Sometimes it's just pleasurable. It's warm. It's good. Sometimes it about blows your head off. It takes you over the top of a mountain and drags you off. I don't know, sometimes it's stronger, it's better, it's longer. But it's always good.

> *

> Sometimes it will be like a total head trip. Other times it's totally physical, just a burst of color I can feel. The last guy I was in love with couldn't tell by watching me, so he'd always ask me afterwards if it was physical or if it was one of those head trips.

> *

> I have two kinds of orgasms, one in the vagina and the other in the pussy. (Clitoris?) Yes, the clitoris. It's more easy in the clitoris than in the vagina. I like it when my partner touches all the time my clitoris.

For most of us there is no mistaking the physical pleasure that accompanies orgasm. The myriad of simultaneous sensations can be profoundly gratifying if we can be fearless enough to submit to them. Nowhere else is the ability (or the inability) to let go more deeply evident, nor the body's capacity to make one forget life's woes more pronounced. For those of us whose intellectual or emotional detachment preoccupies us with the life of the mind or spirit, an orgasm serves as a powerful reminder that this is just not so. Orgasm joins with physical illness and finally death in proclaiming that we are never entirely removed from our bodies' pronouncements:

> There comes a point where I throw out my head and let my penis take over.

*

> I have hallucinations whenever I have an orgasm. Once, during an orgasm, I was a violin, and when I reached the top and began to climax, there were soft pink rose petals that floated down all over the violin. I really felt that I was the violin! Once I had one where I was an eagle, and I was flying across this beautiful, beautiful valley.

*

> The intensity of my orgasms is borderline psychedelic. It's like my whole body ejaculates, not just the penis with the sperm, but everything, the whole me. I can sometimes feel my whole self ejaculating into her, just incredibly intense and utterly pleasurable.

*

> At the point of orgasm, there's a release, from my belly button all the way to my clitoris. Sometimes it's just like it's never enough.

*

> An orgasm for me is my whole system coming out of the head of my penis at the time of ejaculation. It's like the head of my penis becomes as big as the world when I ejaculate. Everything in me and everything I am, will have been, or will be about, is found in that moment.

*

> It's like my whole being takes on meaning right then, and it's just exploded into the universe, and I have a whole sense of oneness with myself and my partner.

WATCH YOUR STEP!

Differences in orgasmic intensity can depend on how long it has been since we last had sex or on how much erotic stimulation has been applied, but perhaps most of all on the extent to which we can abandon ourselves to sexual pleasure. Some of us are dedicated to remaining calm, and cannot tolerate upset with ourselves or others. People who are trained to suppress their feelings come to distrust them and to fear embarrassment if others should discover them. They look away when tears come to their eyes, and clothe rage or disappointment in a cool demeanor. In their sexual exchanges they muffle sounds and may insist on darkness to cover any facial and other physical convulsions that bespeak a lack of control. If their overcaution is severe, the chances of reaching orgasm at all may be slim:

> It was hard for me to reach orgasm for a long time because I'm a very controlled person. I try to control my feelings. I try to control my life to avoid the pain.

> *

> I definitely think that the reason I was able to reach orgasm and able to feel really good is trust. I started to trust that he loves me and cares about me. That's really tied into it.

> *

> Having an orgasm is a big exposure. You've been out of control. Afterwards I feel really shy, like I might cover my face. I feel real exposed.

Sometimes such cautious persons feel unwilling to explore means of enhancing sexual arousal, especially in a woman. If a man's partner does not reach orgasm by penile intromission alone, he often surmises that he is not man enough or not sufficiently endowed, while the woman, unaware that her reaching orgasm will depend in part on the proper stimulation of her clitoris, may conclude that there must be something wrong with her if she requires more than what they both believe is normal. Both partners are not only under-informed and over-anxious but also averse to forms of stimulation at odds with their ideas of what is "proper." If they do adopt these techniques, which the majority of couples actually employ, it may be with the feeling that there is something not quite right about themselves or their sexual partnership.

The fact of the matter is that most couples, through hit or miss or through extensive communication, sometimes over a considerable length of time, can develop satisfying solutions unique to themselves:

> He has to stimulate me or else I have to do it manually. I can't have orgasms with him in me. Sometimes we both have orgasms without having intercourse. Intercourse to us is almost incidental. We probably have more oral sex than intercourse.

> *

> I don't have any difficulty reaching orgasm, though not through intercourse. I can't even think of times when I've made love that I haven't had an orgasm.

> *

> The vibrator was sort of a thing that we played with. When she couldn't be orgasmic because of fatigue or stress or whatever, it brought her pleasure.

> *

> He knows that I like to be on top because that's a great way for me to get off really quick, so he'll roll me over on top of him, and then we have intercourse.

> *

> I have more orgasms with him than I have ever had in my life because he takes the time to make sure that he can be in a position to reach and stimulate me in different areas at the same time.

> *

> She has the strongest orgasms when we're on the floor. She likes me to be really forceful, and I guess the floor doesn't give.

ON A SCALE OF ONE TO TEN . . .

It does not take much for a person to feel like a sexual cripple. Once a woman came to me complaining that she had no problem reaching orgasm with her partner as long as they were alone, but that during group sex she was virtually anorgasmic! Another, orgasmic on most sexual occasions, was worried that it took her too long to climax, and she did not seem particularly impressed by my observation that some women would go out and hire a marching band if their sexual circumstances were as fortunate as hers. Before Masters and Johnson reported their findings, there were women who looked askance at their multiple orgasmic responses. Now the situation is reversed, with many women seriously questioning their sexual competence if they are not multiply orgasmic. Women who are so fortunate often are openly delighted:

> I tend to come several times before he ever does. And instead of stuffing a pillow in my mouth for fear of the neighbors, I just kind of let things go and enjoy the moment because it's so pleasurable. I scream not because it hurts but because it feels so damn good.

*

> She'll have several, at least three orgasms if we've had oral sex. Sometimes she'll have up to four. One night we hit the big five, and she couldn't believe it!

*

> Whenever she's had several orgasms, she gets a "cat that ate the cream" smile at the end.

Some of us put less emphasis on the intensity of orgasms than on whether partners have them at the same time; having mutual orgasms can be the sine qua non of successful sex:

> I think she's probably the first woman I ever had sex with or made love to with whom I had an orgasm at exactly the same time and felt the buildup coming and felt the plateau and felt everything about it at exactly the same time.

*

> I always had in my head that mutual orgasm during coitus would be perfect.

*

Having your orgasm and her orgasm simultaneously is like the sum of the parts is greater than the whole. It adds to the intensity. There's something about simultaneous peaks that are definitely better than separate.

Whose orgasm occurs first, and how much earlier, can become a concern:

It feels much more natural, I guess, when we orgasm closer together. If I orgasm quite a bit sooner than he does, he may think that I'm just waiting for him to.

*

I either like to have mine first or at the same time, because I kind of feel that after he's had his orgasm it's not comfortable for him to continue, although he says he doesn't mind.

In order to ensure simultaneous orgasm, some couples repeatedly modify the pace and nature of their stimulations so that one partner does not get too far ahead of the other:

I try to maintain control if I know she's not ready for orgasm. There have been very few times when we haven't had orgasms at the same time. That's something that's always been important.

On the other hand, some couples see drawbacks in simultaneous orgasms, and many sex therapists would agree. They sometimes recommend that couples abandon a quest for mutual orgasm, and that when possible the female might reach orgasm first. It may happen that she then has another orgasm at the same time as her partner's, but if not, there are benefits that some respondents mentioned:

I don't even try to pace us to come at the same time. In the first place, I actually prefer that we don't because I like to feel him when he comes, and I like to feel my own. When it mixes in, it's hard to concentrate on the feelings if you're doing it at the same time.

*

I'm not sure I like mutual orgasm all that much. One reason is I like knowing what his pleasure is, and I also like the attention that he focuses on mine. If we're doing it at the same time, it's a little hard to give that same attention to each other.

DID I STRIKE OUT?

For too many couples, the big question after sexual intercourse is, "Did you have one? Did I?" It is as though reaching orgasm is the litmus test of the worth and validity of their sexual exchange. Regardless of whether the female partner is concerned about having an orgasm, the male partner will often become concerned if she does not. He may suppose that his partner was not particularly aroused or did not enjoy the sexual exchange, and that the next time he approaches her she will refuse him; perhaps she disdains his sexual prowess or is growing tired of him or does not find him physically attractive, or perhaps she is deliberately withholding so that he (or she) will not be satisfied.

Female partners will often feel pressed to prove that their sexual exchange has been gratifying, and they try hard to present the male with the gift of a bona fide—or failing that—an ersatz orgasm:

> "[The male is] extremely sensitive to fears of sexual performance [in a culture that] has placed the responsibility for the outcome of the sexual encounter squarely on him . . . [His sexual prowess] has also been tied to competence and masculinity in general."
> (Gottman 1976, p. 110).

Sometimes I feel a little guilty that I fake it, but men get real uptight if you're not having orgasms.

Many men believe that they should be able to bring about their female partner's orgasm through their own ministrations. When the female appears not to orgasm, men can be deeply distressed by feelings of sexual incompetence:

I went through the stage where if she didn't get off, I was really hurt and felt really inferior.

*

When I learned that she wasn't having orgasms, I felt inadequate for a long time. At some point I think I realized that it wasn't something I had sole control over.

*

When I'm inside her and she hasn't come, I may start thinking, "My God, maybe my penis is not large enough!"

*

I'll think to myself, "Well, that's not as large as her last one. I didn't rip her shirt off like that last time. Was that as good as the other one? Did she really have one?"

When a man feels these concerns, his disquietude is seldom lost on his partner:

He worries about whether or not I've orgasmed, It makes him feel that he didn't do something right.

*

If he had an orgasm and I didn't, he'd feel bad, so I felt like I had to, quick!

*

Once I told him that I wasn't having orgasms, and he became pretty upset about that. I was too. It was a real wedge between us for quite a long time. For several years we scarcely even approached each other.

Sometimes, if infrequently, a man's dismay over his female partner's lack of orgasm has little to do with self-evaluation. It is rather that he wishes she could enjoy sex as much as he does, and is concerned that attention be paid to her needs:

I always try to make certain that she has hers.

*

I orgasm every single time, and sometimes I think I shouldn't because sometimes she doesn't, and I'll think to myself, "Oh, she's so much better than I am. She gets me off all the time."

*

I just want her to reach a state where she's really out of her mind because it would be really fun and enjoyable for her. I'm not sure if we've reached that point.

*

Most men are pretty glad to have sex. He's extra glad when I reach orgasm. He'll tell me, "I want you to enjoy it too. If you don't enjoy it, it's not that good for me either."

One respondent described with a chuckle her partner's resolute efforts in this regard:

I remember one time, and this was after we'd been married for like three years, after the sex act he said, "Was that it?" meaning, was that my orgasm, and I said, "No," and he said, "OK," and slowed down. I asked him, "What are you doing?" and he replied, "I'm thinking about baseball scores!"

Most typically the male is more concerned about his female partner's orgasm than she is herself. Sometimes this concern is based upon a monumental ignorance of female sexual response and on his projection of his own circumstances. A man is likely to suppose that the woman who does not reach orgasm has not found the sexual encounter arousing or satisfying; insofar as he engages in sex in order to discharge tension that can only be relieved by ejaculation, he assumes that the same must be true for his partner. The fact is that there are anorgasmic women who become at least as sexually aroused during a sexual exchange as do multiorgasmic women. (The latter, like males who ejaculate prematurely, may reach orgasm easily, *too easily*, without reaching a very high peak of sexual arousal.) A key misconception involves the notion that it is the male's responsibility to *give* his partner an orgasm, ideally though penile intromission. What he does not understand is that when all is said and done, the responsibility for his partner's orgasm remains in her hands (sometimes quite literally), and that his penis is not usually the most effective instrument for carrying out the kind of stimulation that is required.

Most women are more concerned about why they participate in sex to begin with than whether they reach orgasm with every sexual exchange:

If he wants to come, that's fine. I don't have to come every time. If I have to come every time, then we end up making love less often because it becomes too much work. Sometimes I don't feel like coming. I just want the contact.

*

A lot of times he keeps trying to make me come, and I'll just say, "I don't really feel like it." I really enjoy fucking and him going inside me, whether or not I have an orgasm.

*

It's not a matter of do or die. If I don't reach an orgasm it doesn't mean that everything else is a failure. There are other parts of lovemaking that I enjoy.

*

He knows now that I'm not a scorekeeper. It doesn't make any difference to me. I'm enjoying myself or I wouldn't be there.

*

For many people, having an orgasm is the aim of sex, but not for me necessarily. Just the pleasure is an end in itself.

Nevertheless, it is wrong to conclude from all this that women have little interest in orgasm, compared with males or not compared with males. Women whose emotions and arousal state are fully engaged expect, or at least hope for, orgasm and are painfully uncomfortable if it is thwarted. It follows that partners must try to foster those circumstances that most favor the woman's reaching orgasm.

"Whoever said orgasm wasn't important for a woman was undoubtedly a man." (Hite 1976, p. 57).[1]

WHO'S COUNTING?

A word of warning to those whose preoccupation with orgasms, our own or our partner's, has become something of an obsession.

---

1. *The Hite Report: A Nationwide Study of Female Sexuality*. New York: Macmillan.

Concerns about how often orgasms occur or how intensely, about how they are brought about and how expressed, can lead to a self-absorption antithetical to making love. It is truly difficult to express deep affection when we are busy thinking about the various physical and mental machinations that are supposed to promote an exquisitely pleasurable outcome. This particular quest is fraught with danger for a partnership. It can lead to feelings of failure and blame, to guilt over manipulating the other for our own gain, and to deep resentment over being used for another person's physical or psychological gratification.

Throughout history, in certain cultures, there have been those who maintain that sexual exchanges that aim for and result in orgasms are perverse, and contrary to the deepest purpose of sex. One author, J. William Lloyd, describes a method of intercourse (termed *The Karezza Method*) in which there is no "orgasmal conclusion" and in which neither the man nor the woman even "desires to have the orgasm." Instead the goal is described as "soul-blending," in which "sexual passion is transmitted and sublimated . . . into tenderness and love . . . and orgasm is not desired or desirable." The author goes on, "Real Karezza . . . requires first the understanding and conviction that the spiritual, the caressive, the tender ends of the relation are much more important, much more productive of pleasure in fact, than the merely sexual. . . . Sex is indeed required to furnish all it has to the feast, but strictly under the leadership of and to the glory of love." Instead of "crude reckless appetite," sexual enjoyment should include "wonderful embraces . . . the hour-long, longer, indwelling of him within her . . . the infinite understanding of each by the other, the transcendent uplift of each by the other . . . harmony too sweet for violence, osmosis of soul within soul . . . singing without words . . . absolute peace, realized heaven . . . the joy of joys and truth of truths."

While the words of this author and others who share his views may betoken an unhealthy division between the "sacred" and the "profane"—a disdain for the body's needs and impulses and the relegation of them to an unworthy rank—they do provide a much-needed antidote to views of a quite different kind. The same sentiments surface in what some respondents had to say:

I've heard that one can reach the orgasm level and just stay there, a kind of Nirvana-like state. We haven't gotten there yet.

*

I like to stay in the preorgasmic state. When I come, I lose the sense of just being together. It's as though I come back to reality, and all my interest is gone. Having an orgasm, I lose all the energy it took to get there.

*

When I decide to stop and not have an orgasm, I feel more giving, more generous.

*

When I'm about to have an orgasm the feeling of closeness usually diminishes.

*

After reaching an orgasm, I start to cry. I don't know if it is guilt or what, but there is a feeling that I only wanted God instead.

While I am not about to endorse the Karezza method or others like it as the sole remedy for the hunger that may linger after physical release, I cannot think of a single couple who would not profit from sexual exchanges that occasionally include a respite from preoccupations with orgasm. Expanding our outlook and repertoire to engage in non-orgasmic intercourse by design, not because of emotional or physical incompetence, may lead to the discovery of a radically different sexual moment.

9

It's Not Over 'til It's Over: AFTERPLAY

I keep saying everything's my favorite, but I really like afterplay. I think that's important. It's just really nice, to hold on to each other.

*

We've rarely done the afterplay because both of us are rather self-conscious about it.

The business of orgasms is over; now what? All unconsciously, perhaps, the sexual partners are deciding—based on this latest exchange and on their past experiences—about how to bring closure to the episode. What happens next never just happens. It is the result of habits formed over the years, of how we make sense of our sexual transactions, of what we think may be expected of us, of what seems appropriate just now, of needs and impulses beyond our physical responses. Some of us count to ten and bolt. Others of us want to cling and cuddle. Some of us are like those who, bored at a party, wait for the earliest decent time to leave. Some of us wait quietly for our partner to bring down the curtain. Others of us, almost at once, yawn and gently pull away, or else our partner turns aside and falls asleep.

How long is long enough? What are we to think? We disengage

our partner's embrace. Is this all right to do? We continue to stroke our partner's damp face. What might this denote? We ask our partner what it was like for them. Is there any harm in that? We wait for a last embrace, long into the night, which never comes. What do we conclude from this? Clearly, what happens "next" is not a minor matter. It may be our clearest answer to what we have each been up to.

WHAT HAPPENS "NEXT"?

Sex manuals typically devote their entire attention to sexual desire and interest and how to enhance it, or to sexual arousal and what interferes with it, or to various features of sexual functioning that promote or deter the orgasmic response. If I am correct, these approaches omit one of the most important variables of all: what occurs when the sexual exchange comes to an end. Afterplay can reveal as much as any other aspect about what a sexual encounter means for those involved.

Sex manuals instead call it the "resolution phase," reducing the topic to the return of bodies to a prior state, yet nowhere else in a sexual exchange is the use of "technique" more beside the point. Afterplay *is* the end, not a means to a further end, a profound statement about what has occurred and what the sexual exchange has signified. This is not to say that all behavior comes to an end. After sexual excitement and interest has diminished, couples display revealing differences as to their capacities for intimate contact. Many are reluctant to let go of each other and bid goodbye to so profound a connectedness. Absorbed in their feelings of closeness, as if spellbound, they linger in an embrace that their previous activities did not permit:

> One of the things she likes to do is what she calls "snuggle." She literally wraps her body around me. She puts her leg over my leg and her crotch against me and lays against me real gently, her breasts against me, and her head on my shoulder. She can fall asleep like that, lay like that for hours with my arms around her. She likes to be stroked during this time.

*

We usually try to hug each other and be close. It's not like, "OK, let's get something to eat."

*

We hold one another and then he comes out of me, and we generally hold one another again, for quite some time. He is not one of those men who turns his head and goes to sleep. He's very sensitive about that.

*

He's always real cuddly, and he holds me. He's very affectionate. He's real still for about five minutes, real still. I feel closer to him. I can hold him, touch him.

*

She likes to cuddle up behind me like two spoons fitting together. Like two cashews.

*

We typically hold each other, just hold each other for a long time.

Sometimes, besides embraces, couples include kissing in these final intimacies:

I'll hold her for a while or we'll kiss a little bit, caress each other. Then there's time for us to kiss again.

*

We snuggle and have soft kisses while we lie on top of each other. We always hold each other, just cuddling.

*

I like to kiss and hug and laugh.

*

Usually we hold each other and kiss each other a long, long time afterwards. Sometimes I'll think, "Oh, I don't want it to be over, don't leave!"

Some couples stress the delicious relaxation that can follow sexual frenzy:

We usually lay there awhile. Maybe I'll scratch her back, which is relaxing to her.

*

It's relaxation time for us, when she relaxes against me, and I hold her.

Indeed, "afterplay" can function like a decompression chamber, easing couples back into the world's demands:

There's always a period with us after sex when we just tend to touch each other. A lot of times we'll lay on our sides, back to stomach. He's almost always behind me. It's a nice recovery period. A cooldown for us to just become more conscious of what's going on around us.

It can also happen that these closing moments are what makes this sexual exchange—or this partner—distinctive:

He always holds me, which no one ever took the time to do or that I allowed them to do. I used to never allow anybody to get that close to me.

For those who engage in sex in order to draw close to their partners, comments such as these are typical. For them, what occurs afterwards not only meets but extends their original aims. They no longer feel quite as alone in a lonely world. The boundaries have been broken. Two have safely become one. It is a time of profound rest, with no need to do anything but *be* with each other. Two lives are twined in each other and transformed by it.

For many of us the silence is too much to take, the closeness too close, and so we break it with chatter. Perhaps we appraise our experience:

We'll be asking each other how much we enjoyed it and standard stuff like that.

*

We talk and laugh, giggle about silly things that were happening while we were having sex. Sometimes we sit and read a funny book and laugh together.

*

We talk about how great it was and how good it feels and how something he did felt really nice. It's never just nothing said throughout the whole time. We're always talking about what we're doing.

Some couples find that after a sexual exchange, they can talk to each other more fully and freely. With their guard let down, they take the opportunity to mention what had been in their minds but, perhaps, avoided before:

I'll say to him, "Talk to me!" and he'll answer, "What do you want to talk about?" So we'll spend the next fifteen minutes talking about things. We'll make decisions. That's when I've got his full attention.

*

We might talk about the fight we had. That will often be a time when we'll work things out.

*

That's when the most intimate talks come. We do a lot of communicating in bed.

*

We just talk and talk about different things, things that need to be talked about.

BREAKING THE SPELL

Talk gets us into our heads and away from our hearts. Talk of any kind can be used as a defense against intimacy as well as a defense against feelings that well up and threaten to overwhelm us. There can be the fear that we might be swallowed up by nothingness and be left ungrounded. Perhaps the greatest challenge of our sexual exchanges is to rest in the moment, to suspend our usual preoccupations and observe a Sabbath in an effort to experience ourselves and another entirely, to replace the banal with the profound.

There are those whose momentary communion, if it occurred at all, is broken by leading or joining the cleanup brigade:

When it's over, it's over. We kind of lay there, and it's like, "O.K., who's going to be the first one to clean this mess up?" This is fine with me, because I can't stand all that goo around. It bugs me, so we get up and clean ourselves off.

*

It's kind of a weird time, a little uncomfortable. Instead of this postcoital full of togetherness, it's more like, "Well, what do we do with the stuff that's leaking out of your vagina now?" or "My dick's all wet, so let's get the Kleenex." She hops out to the toilet to go pee, and it's over. I don't have the feeling that we've just shared a wonderful experience.

*

He usually gets up, and he'll get me a towel, whatever I need. We almost always go in and take a shower. Maybe I'll wash him or he'll wash me.

*

She cleans herself off, and that's it. She goes to her work, and I go to mine.

Continuing merger with another human being, especially of the kind that can occur during sexual congress, is a terrifying state for all too many people. It may feel as if we are being smothered. We may feel as if we are losing our identity, and we want to rebel. If in addition to these claustrophobic reactions, we feel uncomfortable or embarrassed by the experience, it becomes more understandable that we force a premature conclusion:

> She gets up and pees. That's her first reaction. She has a jar right there.

> *

> He gets up and has a cigarette. By the time he comes back to bed, I am usually asleep.

> *

> I will always get up to get her a glass of water and a cigarette.

> *

> We never just lie there. When she goes to the bathroom, I turn on the light and read my gun magazine. I am almost embarrassed that it happened. It doesn't feel right.

*

When she goes back to bed, I like to read or do crossword puzzles for a half hour or watch the late show.

Some people are uncomfortable with doing nothing; they feel uneasy in the immobility of afterplay and may transform it into foreplay, with its more familiar sets of techniques, goals, and strategies:

When I have lingering feelings of closeness, I start thinking, "Could I do it again?" or "Do I want to do it again?"

*

We still may play with each other's genitals. It feels kind of neat. Sometimes we'll start having sex again.

While we may sometimes feel energized by sexual contact, ready to wash the floors or clean the refrigerator, much more commonly sexual satiation leads to sleep. This may begin in an embrace where the closeness lingers or, alternatively on opposite sides of the bed, where we can begin to reconstruct ourselves as separate individuals. Like everything else that takes place in the sexual domain, going to sleep may mean quite different things about what the individuals involved are up to:

There's still a lot of emotion and kissing after we orgasm, and we usually hold each other. I usually fall right asleep.

*

Even when I was pregnant, he would just lay down on top of me and fall asleep.

*

Eventually we might take a little nap, fall asleep in each other's arms, that kind of thing. It is really nice.

*

If she's in the mood, we'll just go to sleep naked and generally wake up later in the night and put our pajamas on.

*

He comes to a climax and then rolls over and goes to sleep while I read.

*

It's a peaceful state, we don't even talk sometimes. We end up drifting into sleep in each other's arms. It's just a peacefulness that occurs.

The elements of afterplay are all of one piece: how much time is devoted to it, how important it is to the partners, what feelings are elicited in the wake of the sexual rush, what each partner expects of the other and thinks the other expects during that time, how each partner would like that moment to be, and the emotional consequences of what takes place. Each factor helps shape the final stamp on the event that has now become a part of their sexual history.

Some people explain the manner of their afterplay by what they view as opportunity (or not) to prolong their contact:

If we're having sex during the middle of the day, there's maybe a little more afterplay, and we're a little bit slower to get up and clean ourselves off.

*

If it weren't for one of our children knocking on the door, it would be a longer period.

*

Sometimes we'll just lay there and sometimes doze a little. Other times we have to get up right away because we have things to do.

*

At night time it seems to go on forever until we fall asleep. During the day, we usually jump up and run around, scream and take a shower.

Afterplay habits may have physical explanations:

We like to snuggle and kiss but not if we're really tired.

*

It's hard for me to hug and stay close afterwards, because it seems like I expend myself so much that it's like I've passed out almost.

*

It takes so long for her to orgasm that she's at the point of exhaustion, just ready to go to sleep. There have been very few times that we're both alert enough to do much talking.

*

It depends on how much I have to do and on how antsy I am.

*

She'll fall asleep because she's exhausted, since we usually do it late.

NOTHING MORE THAN FEELINGS

Because of what has just happened in their sexual exchange or why they engaged in sex to begin with or their feelings toward their partner, people differ dramatically in their emotional reactions to afterplay. But every gesture communicates delight or disgust, desire or revulsion, closeness or detachment. A number of respondents mentioned feelings affirming their relationship with their partner:

How good it feels to lie next to each other and hold each other, to just feel close!

*

It's a reuniting type thing.

*

I like the contact at that point because we can be so close. I feel so close to him at that time.

*

I feel loved and cared about and very protected.

*

There's the feeling like we're finally one. It's the time when we feel the closest because there's really nothing that can separate us at that point.

*

Lovemaking is not just having sex. It's a whole process that carries into your sleep, how you are with each other when you are caressing each other and holding each other, being in a good mood with each other, and being happy with each other.

Some describe an utter bliss that recalls the repletion of infancy:

I feel real, real comfortable, real, real good and warm.

*

It's when there is a feeling of peace.

*

Secure is a good word for it, just kind of nice, calm, sort of floating. My mind just usually drifts. I don't usually think about anything in particular.

Unfortunately, there can be quite different feelings that are just as consequential:

I don't think it's so wonderful. I don't feel like I'm really lucky that my husband lies with me.

*

I sometimes want to pull away. I don't know why that is. A lot of times I don't want to be touched. Sometimes it's a relief when it comes to an end. I'm usually feeling relieved that this ordeal is over. I don't feel I've been a very satisfying sexual partner. I feel I've done my duty.

*

It's one of the more uncomfortable times. There's not that real feeling of togetherness. I don't have the feeling that we've just shared a wonderful experience. I'm not lying there afterwards saying, "This is the best sex I've ever had" or "I feel so close to you now," because I don't, and I don't think she does either.

*

I usually want to get to my reading. I need that time to myself.

*

When it's all over with, I'll think to myself, "OK, it's over with. Now I can get up," and then she wants me to stay here for a while. She may be thinking, "Ah, I can't get enough of you. I want to hold you and look at you." And I'm thinking, "Well, I don't want you to. I want to get up." So I have to make up an excuse for getting up and getting dressed. I just want to get out and be by myself sometimes, not because sex is bad or anything. It's just really hard to explain the feeling.

Our attitudes toward what occurs after sex, and the degree of importance we assign to it, are surely communicated to our partner as clearly as our emotions:

The afterplay, really, for me, is more important than the foreplay, because it doesn't take me very long to get interested or turned on, but I really like to linger afterwards and just be touched and kissed and caressed. That's real important to me.

*

It doesn't make it as much of a meaningful interaction if there's no closure to it. Just separating makes it seem cold and abrupt. The orgasm is not the only high. The sharing afterwards and cuddling, to me, is just as important.

*

It's kind of like putting a stamp on a letter. Without afterplay, it feels unfinished, incomplete, even though there's mutual orgasm. It's the communication between two people that puts the seal on it, the after stuff. But we've rarely done that after stuff.

*

I'm not ecstatic about it. I wouldn't say it's the highlight of my life. Not that I'd like it if he just rolled over and started snoring right away.

*

I could never stand anyone who rolled over and went to sleep or smoked a cigarette. He'd be out the door!

What we may not be able to tell, however, is whether our partner wishes for more postcoital contact:

Ideally, I'd like to have more time after sex to just be.

*

I would definitely like more afterplay. It's not something that really bothers me, but it would be nice to have, to just lie there together for a longer time.

*

I don't like to be left laying there while she goes off to the bathroom to pee.

*

I would rather he just lay there and hold me, cuddle each other, maybe talk a little bit. By the time he's had his cigarette and comes back to bed, I'm asleep.

*

I end up wanting to cuddle afterwards. I feel a hundred times more cuddly than before. I wish she'd reach out and tickle my balls.

*

I always like to lay next to the person I'm with. I don't like to just spring right out of bed and go on with my life. I like to lay and cuddle and rub her stomach and tell her how much I love her.

YOU DANCE WITH WHO BROUGHT YOU

In afterplay, as with other aspects of sex, what we believe pleases or displeases our partner will mightily influence what occurs. Between partners there is often agreement on what should happen in sex, or on boundaries beyond which any further contact would violate the other's sense of self. But, since afterplay involves such basic issues as revealing ourselves to another and our comfort with closeness, we are sometimes loath to make our wishes known. We leave our partners to second-guess, perhaps to feel guilt and shame over their inability to meet, our expectations. Whatever our reactions, we can be sure that they are steps in a dance that holds closeness and distance in fragile balance:

Maybe I read too much into how he feels, but I don't think he's very much into fondling.

*

She wants more contact, but I have this withdrawal thing.

*

The next day, I'm still in that space where I feel love for him and want to be with him. But he's like, "You mean every time we have sex, you're going to be like this? Let's get off it. Let's get on with the program!"

*

Afterplay is not part of her sexual structure. I don't know where that started from.

*

He's more interested in smoking a cigarette or in going to sleep. He's like a lot of men. They're afraid of opening their souls to somebody and becoming too close and intimate.

*

I'd say if there is anything I do wrong it probably has to do with afterwards. She likes to hug and stay close, and it's hard for me to do.

For those fortunate couples who can integrate sex and affection, for whom sex is no shame and closeness is not fearsome, afterplay can be celebrated quite as much as any other feature of their sexual encounters. In fact it can be the most treasured of all. Listen to some individuals' testimonies:

Being together in that way can give us a new perspective on some of our troubles. It gives us a different place to return to, a safe place from which we can emerge recharged.

*

The closeness stays. We're able to drop some of our worries and to talk about things with our mindsets less entrenched.

*

It opens us up to conversation, like a conduit. We're somehow free to talk about things we might not want to talk about otherwise.

There are too many couples, unfortunately, who for a variety of reasons have not reached the state that some of our respondents described, for whom the joys of afterplay are an emotional mystery.

They may have a history beginning with their parents that has never included deep emotional attachments and has not been marked by a real connection with anyone. They have become strangers to a longing that was snuffed out too long ago. Sometimes it will appear in a brief fantasy or in a dream, in a restlessness of the heart that is never eased. In the sexual domain such folk count their orgasms, if, indeed, they occur, and declare themselves satisfied.

Externally observable signs do not necessarily reveal our deepest dispositions and cannot always be used to judge one's capacity for intimacy. That can only be learned by becoming much better acquainted with our most secret selves, brushing aside nothing that we find there. Any effort to trace the origins of what actually happened during your last embrace is worth your while. Every acknowledgment of what was there in the farthest corners of your mind and heart when you finally disengaged from your sexual partner, either anxiously or reluctantly or somewhere in between, will grant you a new freedom at other times of contact.

There is a beginning and an end to every human contact, hellos and goodbyes that shape the nature of each and affect whether we want to repeat it. In fact, it is probably the inevitable final goodbye that most profoundly affects our daily lives; and, until we can come to terms with our own death and the deaths of those we have come to depend on, making and ending contact with others will continue to be troublesome, raising deep inside us the issue of abandoning and being abandoned. It takes uncommon courage to battle the terror of potential loss, to overcome the ambivalence that marks every human exchange. We must understand that these fears govern every one of us.

Interlude:
Carly and Ron

Ron and Carly report an unusually gratifying sexual partnership. They are both in their thirties, he a graduate student, she a professional who daily commutes an hour each way. They relish their sexual good fortune and account for it in numerous ways. Carly explains:

> We're both really open to sexuality. Wherever we are, it's always being hinted at. And if it happens, Yes!

She explains:

> I think we are both very committed to our sexual relationship. His sexual interest in me has made me more self-confident. He seems to delight in my body, and that really helps. I'm sexually attractive to him, no doubt about it.

She sees parallel attractions between them:

> We share commonalities. He's fit and healthy; I'm fit and healthy. We're so alike, in terms of what we like to do. It's just an amazing match.

There seems to be no end to her sexual joy:

He always likes to go to sleep, touching me. In the middle of the night he'll reach out and try to find me. It makes me feel completely loved, connected, wanted, yes, even adored!

Ron is equally enthusiastic, going on to describe the various ways in which they connect sexually:

We'll have the classic 'quickie,' or the long one, or the romantic one, or the 'tear off your clothes on the floor' one.

He has his own explanation for their sexual success:

Communication is the key. The joy of our marriage and the joy of our sexual experience is wrapped up in just becoming real to each other. We're committed to doing that with each other.

This is not to say that Carly and Ron, married six years, have no sexual concerns at all. As we shall see, Carly sometimes feels unattractive and lacking in confidence. It is not always easy for her to ask for what she wants. She has multiple orgasms but finds Ron uncomfortably preoccupied with whether she is satisfied. She is sometimes reminded of the negative sexual messages she was given by her parents. Ron is *"still working on being more comfortable with cunnilingus."* He's only too well aware that he can get anxious about Carly's orgasms. According to both of them, their greatest challenge is that of combining undiluted passion with deep intimacy. And they still have some way to go on that front.

―――――――

When asked what she thinks chiefly motivates Ron to engage in sex with her, Carly answers:

Part of it is the need for a physical release. Another is that he gets a lot from being touched. He likes to be touched all the time. I think that's a human need, but some people like to be touched more than others do. Ron is one of those people who likes to be touched and held and caressed, a lot! So he comes to me for that. Underneath is the need to bond on an emotional and physical level. Sometimes you just want to get into the head or under the skin of somebody else. I guess I'm only speaking for me, but that might be true of him as well.

Carly's own motivations vary, depending on the particular day:

Some days I want sex for emotional soothing. Sometimes because I feel 'horny' and want physical release. Other times I want to be as close to Ron as I can possibly be. I'll look over at him and think, "This person is amazing. How can I get as close as possible to this person? How can my soul touch his soul?"

Until fairly recently, Ron and Carly's sexual exchanges focused on his interest in her reaching orgasm as many times as she could (sometimes more often than she actually wanted to) and on her need to reassure him that he was the best of all possible sexual partners. They seldom lingered over "the necessary preliminaries." They kissed, of course, but not simply for the pleasure of kissing. They caressed each other in impatient prelude to "real"—that is, genital—contact. Neither of them felt at ease until Carly had achieved orgasm. Ron needed to feel that he was sexually effective and worked at ensuring her response. The point of foreplay was *"to get her excited, to make sure that she was moist."* He reports that even now, *"I'm still learning how to do that."*

Ron is currently concerned about his discomfort with cunnilingus, which he attributes to an unusual sensitivity to odor and taste and to what he terms his "clean phobia": *"If she has a bath the night before, it's not a problem."* This mild aversion troubles him on two counts. First, he feels a need to be the perfect lover, who can bring Carly to orgasm more than once during a single exchange, and because cunnilingus is so effective in that regard, he sees his sexual repertoire as flawed. Second, he views his "phobia" as a marked personal deficit:

I'm trying to develop a taste or a smell for it. I should be able to accept her for who she is and not insist on some sanitized version of her. But this still requires a conscious effort.

In addition, he is mindful of the fact that Carly has no difficulty performing fellatio on him:

She loves it! She even swallows my cum, which she never did with anyone else. This is a real turn-on for me. I'm the first partner she's ever fellated!

They are now having second thoughts about how they have connected sexually. As Carly puts it:

Up until now we've had pretty wild sex. There's not been a lot of foreplay. Now we're deliberately trying to not be so goal-oriented. We're taking our time before we actually start intercourse, just to see what it is like to relax and be more in tune with the moment, to let our senses be alive.

She expects this change to improve things:

We both want a more complete sexual relationship. For that to happen, we'll have to ease into it instead of saying, "O.K., let's load up and go at it, honey!"

From the very first moment of any sexual exchange, both Carly and Ron have their eyes on one goal—orgasm: getting one (or more), giving one (or more). So far in their sex lives, neither of them feels comfortable until Carly begins to moan and then shudder, two signals that she has reached the goal-line. According to Carly:

All during foreplay, I'm wondering what to do to reach orgasm.

According to Ron:

As soon as she asks if I want to "play" and I know that we're going to have sex, I'm thinking about how I'm going to get her aroused.

Much of the pressure Carly feels comes from her sense that Ron insists she be multiorgasmic:

He'll even ask, "Wow! How many was that?!" Or he'll say, "Why don't you come again?" I'm always afraid that he'll be disappointed if I have just one. He gets so much gratification from bringing me to orgasm! God forbid I have none at all!

As she explains, *"He needs to know that he's doing a fabulous job!"*
This preoccupation of Ron's leads to Carly's sometimes resenting the
need to reassure him:

> Sometimes I'll get aggravated. This isn't supposed to be a
> competition to see how many orgasms Carly can have! I want it
> to be mutual. I want him to focus as much on himself as on me,
> to stop counting mine. I love to see him reaching orgasm. When
> he's building up to orgasm, he can't look at me any more. What
> a relief!

Ron's concerns go far beyond wanting to hear that he is technically competent, although that surely is present. To him, Carly's
openness to the possibility of orgasms, regardless of their number, has
to do primarily with whether or not he thinks that she is really *there*
with him, connecting with him, flowing with him:

> If she says, "I'm not going to have an orgasm, I'm not into it,
> let's bring you to orgasm," I'll think, "If I'm going to be by
> myself, I might as well masturbate." She contends that it's O.K.
> for one of us not to be there, but I disagree: When she's not
> there, I feel as though I'm making love to a mannequin. If we're
> not there together, it's of no consequence!

Hence he feels relieved when she comes. The question of whether
or not she is really *there* with him gets answered in her obvious
responsiveness:

> As soon as I can feel she's ready to have an orgasm—and I can
> tell by her breathing, sometimes by a flush that appears on her
> skin—I feel wonderful, relieved. From that point on sex be-
> comes fun because I know that it's going to be O.K. The
> pressure is off. I can relax.

What happens *after* Ron and Carly have had and counted their
orgasms illustrates, as well as anything else that happens during their
sexual exchange, their major challenge: how to integrate passion with
intimacy. Carly notes:

As soon as he comes, he laughs. Can you imagine, he actually laughs! The first time it happened, I was like, "Wow, what is he laughing at?" And since then it's always taken me aback. Here we've been through a deep, intense emotional experience with each other and he responds with, "Ha, ha, ha! Wasn't that fun?" Our sex has probably been too recreational. "Wow! Look at this position. I'll bet nobody else does this!" I've wanted to develop a deeper, emotional element to it. That's what I've missed the most. Fast and furious sex may be fun but there is no big emotional bond involved. I'm hoping for very quiet sex where we can focus intensely on one another.

Ron's account is somewhat rueful:

I'm not sure what my laughing is all about. She thinks it has to do with all the partners I've had and my effort to detach myself from them over the years before Carly and I met. There was no emotional attachment involved, no commitment, just a fun, light-hearted thing. I had no idea that my laughter bothered her. I'm not laughing now because she doesn't want me to.

Both of them are hungry for more than fun. In addition to a "successful" sexual exchange involving enjoyable orgasms for each of them, they are intent upon making their encounters "meaningful." As Ron explains,

Sex becomes meaningful if we become connected again. When I'm inside of her, when she engulfs me, or whatever, that's one ultimate physical connection, but it goes beyond that. When we truly engage each other, our spirits connect. We can see and be seen beyond the walls of our flesh. This is the ultimate human experience. That's where we approach the divine in being fully human, in reaching our human potential.

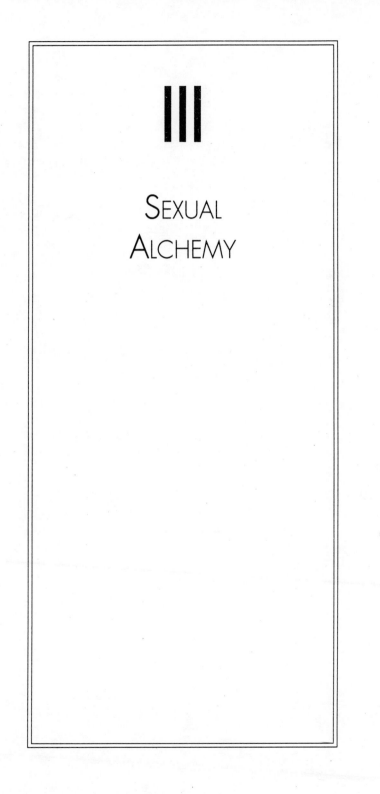

III

SEXUAL
ALCHEMY

10 It's All Your Imagination: FANTASY

I like to fantasize a lot when I'm making love. Sometimes I don't feel it's totally right, and it will make me feel uncomfortable, but usually it increases the pleasure and the intensity. At the same time it often makes me feel bad to think I had to think about somebody else to get off the way I wanted to get off. It can get pretty depressing. I'll begin to wonder if my partner is really fulfilling me sexually. They say it's natural to fantasize, but I'm not sure it's good for a relationship. What does it mean to fantasize being with someone else when you're with someone you care about enough to have sex with? Sometimes I wonder if it's normal. Why do I have to fantasize about someone else to really get fulfillment? Fantasizing may be healthy, but I also think you can get carried away with it!

*

Fantasies help me go over the brink, but it also makes me feel guilty. I don't want these people in my head. I don't like the idea of fantasizing while I'm making love. I try to keep those images out, but they just keep creeping in.

Perhaps no aspect of sexual experience causes more consternation than our sexual fantasies, whether we see them as our own concoc-

> "Sexual fantasy is regarded by some as a marriage rescuer and an enhancer of eroticism, by others as an escape from reality and politically undesirable."
> (Hooper 1992, p. 110).

tions or as unwelcome intrusions. Few of us can help making judgments about ourselves, our partners, and our partnerships based on the mental images that precede or accompany our sexual transactions, judgments that shape our emotional reactions to what occurs. Here is where the notion of sex going on primarily between the ears becomes most evident. In our sexual fantasies we think not only about sex itself but also about what we were thinking about:

- Are my fantasies abnormal?
- Do I rely on them too much?
- Do they reflect a shameful wish?
- Do I really want to try what they suggest?
- If I don't mind them, am I copping out, avoiding needs and issues?
- Do they mean I am dissatisfied with my present partner or my partnership?
- Should I regard them as welcome additions to my sexual experiences or as crutches I wouldn't need if I were sexually fit?

OUT OF MY MIND?

Despite a tradition respectful of rugged individualism, in our society much of what we do is compared with what others do and evaluated as to whether it is normal. This is especially true in the sexual domain, even though other people's practices—thoughts as well as deeds—are seldom known to us. We may secretly fear that our sexual proclivities are unshared, that we are quite alone in the kinds of things that trigger our sexual interest, in the images that emerge from our unique sexual histories and in the sexual gratifications that accompany them:

> I'm afraid of being thought of as some kind of freak! I can't imagine that anyone else could be as obsessed as I am with these erotic fantasies!

> *

> Maybe I should be classified as abnormal. I have fantasies of humiliating and restraining women where they're held against their will.

"The role of fantasy is to spice up your sex life. Fantasies are best thought of as an additional stimulation technique that builds a bridge to greater sexual arousal . . . give yourself permission to use a range of fantasies to enhance sexual desire." (McCarthy and McCarthy 1990, p. 107).

Many people seek reassurance that what transpires in their minds is pretty much the standard, evidence that there is nothing particularly unusual about what they do or think or aspire to. In the sexual domain they are relieved by the conviction that they do not stand alone in what they fantasize:

My fantasies are nothing out of the ordinary.

*

We all have fantasies. We all like to explore our fantasies and try to fulfill them.

*

I think everybody experiences times when they're fantasizing another partner. I know I do.

*

I can't get them out of my head, which is not uncommon from what I've read.

*

I think everyone has to have some type of fantasies. Sex gets to be the same old thing after a while.

Since it is popularly known that sexual fantasies generally accompany masturbation and, frequently, coitus as well, there are those who are discomfited by the fact that they seldom fantasize in either context. What is the matter with me? What am I missing? What does it mean that other people have fantasies and I don't?

> I wouldn't even know what to fantasize if I wanted to!

*

> There used to be random mental images floating through my head. Sometimes there were sounds or colors. Now they are gone and that worries me. I seem to have a very impoverished sexual fantasy life. Even when I'm masturbating, I don't seem to be able to work up any sexual fantasies that are very exciting.

PUTTING ON THE BRAKES

One of the reasons for a blank mind during coitus is not mysterious. Sexual engagements of any kind can easily become reminiscent of past sexual trauma, of moments when one was scarred irretrievably, betrayed beyond one's capacity to withstand the experience. Memories of those moments can be so unendurable that every effort is made to block them out, that one's best energies are employed in keeping them hidden. This defensive vigilance can begin with a lack of sexual interest and come to include a renunciation of whatever one associates with painful sexual transactions. The emphasis is on caution and control:

> I used to have rape fantasies, but I deliberately stopped them. I never think about that any more.

*

> Up until the last two years, I fantasized that he was a young man in high school and that we were strangers. It was too much for me to think of him as my husband. It smelled too much of incest.

*

> I don't fantasize about men who are older than adolescents.

The caution and control impressed on sexual fantasies, the need to restrict what is imagined, is not limited to those with unusual sexual histories. For example, an individual who has, for whatever reason, difficulty integrating sex with affection is apt to depersonalize his or her mental representations of the sexual act:

> I have fantasies of an abstract cunt that's exciting. I can't fantasize sex with a specific person. It has to be a body part.

> *

> Women whom I admire or fall in love with are never a part of my sexual fantasies. Those are reserved for imaginary women who exude some kind of sexuality that I don't identify with a woman I'd like to marry.

For the individual concerned about homosexual predilections, sexual fantasies about members of the same sex or excluding members of the opposite sex may confirm grave fears:

> I felt I was really getting somewhere, being able to have fantasies with women in them and have a good time. But I was never able to do it again after that.

> *

> All of a sudden I'll have flashes of being with another woman in a lesbian relationship. It just comes on me like a whirlwind almost. It's really scary.

Some of us may fear that if we were to fantasize too freely, we would somehow be compelled to act upon the impulse that created the image, and we can give ourselves fuller rein only when we understand that sexual fantasies need not represent an actual wish:

> Sometimes she has fantasies about being with another woman, but she says very clearly that it's not something she actually wants to act on.

> *

> Fantasies are fantasies. They are not something you really want to happen.

WHAT AM I TO THINK?

Many people make a major distinction between masturbatory and coital fantasies. Men whose sexual careers began on a toilet with a copy of a *Playboy* centerfold in one hand and their penis in the other do not consider fantasies during masturbation particularly remarkable, surprising, or upsetting:

I do that a lot while I'm masturbating.

*

The memory ones I like, when I can bring back a particular sexual experience with somebody and come to orgasm.

*

Fantasies are a big part of my sex life because I don't have a partner. I really think I've done myself a great service by allowing myself to fantasize whatever I like.

*

Recently, when I was masturbating, I remembered one of the recent times we made love together. She talked dirty, and that really excited me.

If we view the sexual fantasies that we have by ourselves as benefiting our sexual partnership, so much the better:

Most of my fantasizing is about my wife and our sexual encounters. Usually my wife is the sexual object. It helps me remain faithful to her and my family.

*

I'll have brief little fantasies about what I think it will be like when I get home and certain things I might like to do. It sort of gets the old juices flowing.

*

Sometimes I'll fantasize during the day, of what I want to happen or what I want her to do. It may involve some weird body positions.

*

I'll have a series of fantasies during the day to kind of build up my interest. The more I stimulate myself, the more prepared I'll be.

The use of fantasies during sex with our partner, on the other hand, we may view as anathema: What does it mean about my partnership if I have to rely on fantasies about someone else to pique my sexual interest or maintain my sexual arousal or reach orgasm? Am I being unfaithful to my actual partner if I have to resort to secret scenarios in which he or she cannot be found? For many people, sexual fantasies denote sexual infidelity, and they are either appalled by them or else relieved by their absence:

> I never fantasize. You can't be very happy with the person you're with if you're thinking he's somebody else. I want sex with *him*, not somebody else.

*

> I don't think I fantasize as much as others do. I'd feel guilty, like I was going outside our marriage, if I did.

*

> When I'm making love, it bothers me that I have to think of someone else to get aroused.

*

> The last thing I want to think about is anybody else but my wife. She takes precedence over any fantasy.

*

> One time she was doing a study for one of her art history courses on New Guinea tribesmen, so she imagined that I was one of them making love to her. In the back of my mind it was, "Why isn't she thinking about me? Why does it have to be someone else? What am I, chopped liver?"

Sometimes, those who may be threatened by sexual secrecy will make the sharing of their fantasies or even acting on them a part of their sexual repertoire. Rather like the swingers of old, nothing is, in this case, *thought* behind closed doors. Each is an open book to the other, and both share in the excitement of their joint productions:

We fantasize aloud at times about different scenarios. One time we're doing it next to a mountain brook. The next time we're doing it with someone else in bed. All sorts of different things.

*

I'll tell her fantasies, and she'll add to them as we're having sex. We are doing this much more than we ever did before.

*

When things were getting pretty monotonous we began talking more about our sexual fantasies. Or we'd talk about past sexual experiences. Some of the fantasies involved people in our current lives.

*

It's a 7 when the fantasies are in the head but a 10 when we actually *become* the fantasy. Sometimes she'll dress in a certain way or we'll act just like the people we've just seen in an X-rated movie.

Except for those times when fantasies are used to diminish sexual excitement (*"When I have to wait for her I'll think of flypaper or sand and gravel"*) or when they appear unexpectedly, most people seek a mental aphrodisiac to maximize the erotic potential of the present moment. They hope perhaps for more generous lubrication or a more robust erection or an urgency that will guarantee orgasm:

Sometimes I'll fantasize to see if that will increase my responsiveness to oral sex administered by my incredibly mechanically clumsy wife. It usually doesn't work!

*

Most of the time I don't have to fantasize, but when I do it's really good. My response is stronger.

*

I used to engage in my masturbatory fantasies during the sex act if I needed to pump myself up a little. Now it flows more easily.

*

If I was having difficulty reaching orgasm, I'd imagine people were watching, and I'd come faster.

*

I don't feel as turned on to him as I once was. He's picked this up in me, and he's right. I use a lot of fantasy to turn myself on.

A REAWAKENING

If our need for sexual fantasies and what they contain tells us anything, it speaks of what is dull or constrained in our lives, of the accommodations we make. Long ago we stopped defecating whenever we liked, and we gave up the wish for emotional nourishment from a mother whose breasts we could no longer claim. In the bosom of the family we were bent by rules of others' making, and in school we learned not to talk back, not to cry on the playground. Later we grew mindful of the rules for making friends and influencing people; on the job we learned to agree and keep quiet. We gave up one by one many of the liveliest aspects of ourselves and became barely recognizable for our lack of daring.

This self-forfeiture turns men and women into caricatures. Too often it surfaces in even the most intimate of relationships where, out of fears of abandonment (a good mate, after all, is hard to find), the principal aim is to please, to get along. If this makes us winners in the dating–mating game, we may be no more successful than the so-called losers for all that we have had to keep from our partners: our hurts, our disappointments, our rage, our guilt, our objections, our wishes for revenge, and, especially perhaps, our boredom. Rules and roles designed by couples to promote the safety of their relationship inevitably account for the sexual deserts they find themselves in.

At the same time, each of us has a dark side, the part of us that is tempted and intrigued by the forbidden.

In fantasy we can let the

> "The desire to know about something not yet experienced, forbidden, or seemingly unattainable is often a key feature of sexual fantasies." (Masters, Johnson, and Kolodny 1982, p. 246).

"Fantasies are part of your personal sexual expression. . . . Remember that as we were growing up and discovering what sexuality means, the whole idea of sex was taught to be something somewhat forbidden. So it's not surprising that some of us want to retain the element of intrigue." (Heiman and LoPiccolo 1976, p. 185).

imp on our left shoulder experiment with taboos, while the angel on our right shoulder guides our real life, everyday obedience. Somewhere in each partner there remains a dormant self anxious to be revived, a secret self that would remain unknown but for a dream or a fantasy, often shockingly at odds with whoever it is who prepares the family meal or takes out the garbage or sits in the office that has been assigned:

> I like to picture myself as a Greek warrior conquering a slave from an enemy kingdom. Once in a while I'll have thoughts like that. Maybe they help make up for my boring, white-bread, middle-class existence.

*

> A lot of my fantasies involve subjects I don't really approve of, like humiliating women or using bondage. Sometimes I imagine sex with children present. Sometimes I'll be the child watching or sometimes I'll be one of the adults participating in sex. These fantasies show me how complex our sexuality can be. There can be the child in us who's amazed and intrigued by the mystery of sex. There can also be a jaded adult in us who's out to get his rocks off, or the voyeur, or the masochist. All those elements are present in me.

The alchemy that is performed through sexual fantasies is not limited to refashioning oneself. It extends to the partner as well:

> I'll think about something he's done recently that I really liked or something that I'm proud of that he's accomplished or just that he wants me.

As if with the wave of a wand, the partner may be made to correspond to one's original image of him or her which had once so compelled us. Aspects of that image, worn away by closeness and familiarity, get revived. Everything about our partner that had once evoked our passion becomes restored, even enhanced. In this new image, the partner now combines what has intrigued us before: the forbidden parent we renounced during the Oedipal struggle, the old flame we never did seduce, the media stars we yearned for in adolescence, the embodiment of plain stark masculinity or femininity. The predictable partner becomes, for an instant, a mysterious composite of all those tantalizing missed opportunities that can still stir us:

I'll imagine I've been out on a ship for ten years and haven't had sex, and then all of a sudden I came across this beautiful woman.

*

All of a sudden she becomes a statuesque, Amazonian, voluptuous woman who doesn't have a hair out of place.

*

Sometimes I might fantasize that she's someone else, nobody in particular, just a fantasy woman. She may be a stranger I've just met or a female hitchhiker I've picked up. Sometimes motorcycles are involved.

In addition to awakening the muted self and to turning frogs into princes or hausfraus into strippers, sexual fantasies can be a way of exploding all the rules that govern most longstanding sexual partnerships. At least for a moment those rules are suspended, replaced by an unusual abandon in which all that was formerly taboo is defied. We may recall a time in the partnership when sexual transactions needed no uneasy negotiations or compromise, were not ground under by unresolved power issues, were not devices to reassure us of the other's interest. Whatever their content, most sexual fantasies typically reflect the need to revive or confound a dried-out partnership:

I sometimes think about the time we went to the State Forest, looking at the lake, and holding and hugging and touching. We used to have really nice, sweet lovemaking. It was really unexpected. Given our scheduled lives and our very scheduled sexual patterns, it's nice to think back to the time when we just wanted to make love and did.

*

It's just the two of us alone, away from people, enjoying each other. In actuality we don't spend much quality time together. We never see each other, and when we do, he's exhausted.

WE MAKE IT SO

It would be a mistake to suppose that fantasies in the sexual domain are a thing apart from how we conduct ourselves in other domains as well, or that they always have a chiefly sexual content. While the alchemy involved may be more apparent in explicitly sexual images of one kind or another, its magic is at play in every moment of our lives.

Experiences of any kind are shaped, sometimes created whole cloth, by what we mentally make of them. In the human enterprise, nothing is ever the same for any two of us, thanks to the magic of our mental alchemy. As one story goes, a pessimistic child distrusted impulse and hesitated to reach out in a roomful of toys, while an optimistic child, surrounded by manure, happily explored his surroundings

"Our mental life is experienced in the form of fantasies. These fantasies are present as scripts, stories whose content and function can be determined. And I want to emphasize that what we call thinking or experiencing or knowing is a tightly compacted, but nonetheless separable, weave of fantasies. What we consciously think or feel is actually the algebraic summing of many simultaneous fantasies." (Friday 1980, p. vi).[1]

---

1. *Men in Love: Men's Sexual Fantasies: The Triumph of Love over Rage.* New York: Delacorte Press.

convinced that there must be a pony somewhere. Our mental set, based upon past experience, designed to promote our safety and to make unfamiliar events more manageable, is what determines our perceptions and responses. How else are we to explain how agoraphobics can turn the aisle of a supermarket into a snake pit? Or why some would recoil while others are drawn to solo in a Karaoke bar?

"Beauty is in the eye of the beholder" approaches the truth of our personal reality, but it is the *mind* of the beholder that performs the tricks we play in our everyday encounters with others. It is what, at some level, we *want* to believe about ourselves and others that fashions our emotional responses to them. In bed during a sexual exchange, partners are *inevitably* transformed through sexual alchemy, from one episode to the next, into friends and lovers or strangers.

A man dying in a desert will often believe he sees an oasis. A person in solitary confinement will turn a cockroach into a beloved companion. People in bed with each other will turn the sexual occasion into a delectable feast or into bread and water, depending upon their needs and interests and moods. We refashion ourselves or our partners into desirable or undesirable sexual objects, whether or not we are even aware that we do so. What we make of a particular gesture, what we choose to focus on, what we imagine is happening, has the power to turn dust into gold, gold into dust. Our profound convictions about who and what can be trusted in intimate exchanges, based on memories held now in the body as well in the deepest recesses of the mind, cast their spell on sexual and nonsexual moments alike. The most fortunate among us are those who do not park our power to imagine at the bedroom door and who permit ourselves to turn the mundane into the extraordinary. In the words of one alchemist, probably unaware of the extent to which he has hit the nail on the head:

> It seems to me that sex, for most people, is based on one big fantasy.

Doing is not the same as thinking or feeling, over which we have far less conscious control. For instance, the true nature of a person's sexual orientation is not strongly related to his or her actual behaviors; what clearly tells the story are romantic attachments and sexual fan-

"For the average person (sexual fantasies) simply remain the necessary stimulus to the initiation of 'normal' sex activities, whether masturbatory or sociosexual . . . It is precisely this factor of sexual fantasy that distinguishes human sexuality from that of the lower species." (Kronhausen and Kronhausen 1969, p. xiv).

tasies during childhood, adolescence, and young adulthood. In fact, Saghir and Robbins (1973)[2] found that it was these mental events, and the age at which they occurred, that best distinguished adult homosexual and heterosexual males from each other, *not* their sexual behaviors prior to adulthood.

Another way to learn more about what a person is up to in the sexual domain is to mine the heart and mind for their treasures, with much less regard for any behaviors. It can be done all sorts of ways. A favorite of mine is to ask a couple each to write a description of ideal sex, to be shared at our next session. The last time I had a couple do this, the woman told me the assignment had stumped her. She did manage to fill a page and a half but was embarrassed at its saying so little. She did not know what she wanted. She took all her cues from her husband. With great pain she reported items from her sexual history that had made her a generic self, far more attuned and responsive to her husband's sexual needs and interests than to her own. The truth of the matter, she feared, was that she had no interest in sex at all, despite her expertise at fellatio, a source of pride to her. Her husband, whose own scenario could have passed for a novel in manuscript, heard her out with concentrated attention. What she was telling us he had already suspected; hence his retreat to a rich fantasy life, alone with a moodless and compliant penis. While the truths revealed in fantasies may be elusive, the search for them is enormously fruitful because they can be more real and far more dangerous than discussions of the so-called obvious.

---

2. *Male and Female Homosexuality: A Comprehensive Investigation.* Baltimore: Williams & Wilkins.

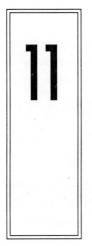

11 Me, Myself, and I: MASTURBATION

What do we think of ourselves when we supply our own relief and gratification? What does it mean that, although our partner would not refuse a request for sex, although we are very much dedicated to the partnership, we play with ourselves instead of our lover? How do we explain to ourselves that we have a good sexual partnership, including frequent and varied activity, and still we indulge in sexual solitaire? It might happen soon after a gratifying sexual exchange. It might happen only after a long period of abstinence. It can occur when our partner is far away and just as well when our partner is in the next room.

Any of numerous factors may seem to make sense of it. It can be attributed to boredom, an exigent sexual tension, an impulsive discharge of sexual energy; to being unable to ask our partner for what we want or to not wanting to wear out the sexual welcome mat; to problems we have with intimacy and closeness, to deliberately with-holding love and attention, or to generosity toward a partner not especially eager for frequent sexual exchanges.

Out of these attributions and out of those that follow them down the ideational trail will emerge meanings that brighten or darken every corner of the sexual domain we have fashioned from our minds

175

"Masturbation is the ongoing love affair that each of us has with ourselves throughout our lifetime . . . It's the way we discover our erotic feelings, the way we learn to like our genitals and to build self-esteem . . . Masturbation is a way for all of us to learn about sexual response. It's an opportunity for us to explore our bodies and minds for all those sexual secrets we've been taught to hide, even from ourselves."

(Dodson 1987, pp. 3–4).

and hearts, portraying ourselves and our partner as heroes or villains, our partnerships as palaces or dungeons.

THAT FIRST SURPRISE

Few of our sexual journeys begin in unalloyed joy. The discovery that manipulation, direct or indirect, of our genitalia can result in uniquely exquisite pleasure usually comes without warning:

> I didn't know what was going on. How could I? No one ever explains it to you.

Nothing our parents had ever talked about even hinted at what lay in store for us. In fact, as an enormously powerful but unmentioned event, our earliest self-stimulation cannot but violate the propriety that is expected of us. It is not something to be trumpeted around the breakfast table even in those families comfortable enough with bodily events to celebrate a daughter's first menstruation or to read sex education materials aloud in the living room:

> I remember touching myself but not for very long because I thought I wasn't supposed to. I thought it was bad even though I was never told that.

> *

> When I was a kid, I felt really ashamed. But after reading some books I realized it was completely normal.

It is hard to imagine that there are many families in which parents talk to their children about masturbation and what is in store for them, or suggest that their sons masturbate in bed instead of depositing their semen in the toilet, or remark that they too discovered sexual pleasure all by themselves when they were growing up. The very thought of any parents being so frankly encouraging of their children in this regard would revolt most people. Any comments or questions or extended conversations about masturbation are typically viewed as inappropriate, if not obscene, leaving such sexual experiences the most undiscussed event in the household.

A lack of openness about masturbation in early puberty is not the only reason why budding adolescents clothe sex in secrecy and feel uncomfortable with their sexual capacities. Not so long ago, a parent would explicitly admonish a child: "Don't touch yourself down there!" or "How can I get you to stop doing that?"

My mother used to tell me not to touch myself because it was dirty.

*

I can remember the first time I ever masturbated. I must have been about ten years old. I felt I must have been "possessed" to do something that terrible and I didn't do it again for years afterward.

*

One time I'd think, when I was a little kid, "Is God watching me? Is God going to pay this back?"

*

I never have. At one point I considered it but couldn't.

Beyond the insistence that one's child steer clear of his or her private parts, there may have been occasions in which a watchful parent ridiculed a child for seeking comfort in sucking his or her thumb or for taking too much time and pleasure in bowel movements or too much delight in sensual contacts of any kind. Many parents, themselves taught that bodily preoccupations can be dangerous, are sure it is not only appropriate but necessary to set up barriers against the enactment of sexual impulses. They may, in their own youth, have stood in line in front of a confessional to be forgiven for their sexual thoughts, words, or deeds; they may have sat through sermons vilifying "fornicators." Too often a sexually repressive culture produces young people who hang their heads, lower their eyes, and provide their own scoldings for having ever touched themselves on the way to sexual ecstasy:

> I don't remember the first time I discovered that I had this thing between my legs. I've always known it was there and that it was fun to play with. But since I was brought up in the Catholic Church, there was always guilt involved. Even now it's not something I talk about. For some reason I find it embarrassing.

*

> I would decide never to do it again, but then I'd do it again!

WHAT IS THIS BODY DOING AROUND ME?

Masturbation marks many people's entrance into the dread-filled community of those who will never be entirely at ease in their bodies, for whom the body becomes a battleground, spirit against flesh, where vows worthy of a monk or nun are continually, dismayingly, broken. Perhaps the wish to disavow one's own or another's body begins with—certainly it can be reflected in—a mother who exclaims in disgust at the sight and smell of soiled diapers, who never allowed herself pleasure in the genital sensations stirred up by her nursing infant, who could never delight in touching or being touched by her young child at play in the bathtub or on the living room floor. Somewhere, we can be sure, memories of others' reactions to our own bodies get stored up, form part of our very identities, and ultimately determine the extent to which our body is emotionally accessible, inviting or closed off.

There are those who are humiliated by reminders that they are flesh as well as spirit. They are put off by the body's claim on them and try to keep it a secret from themselves, as much as they can. It embarrasses them to raise their hands for permission to "be excused;" they are disgusted by any evidence that they have perspired under their arms; the women among them contrive to change tampons without touching fingers to body.

People who feel estranged from their bodies and are constantly at war with them are bound to view masturbation with alarm. And if they engage in it at all, either during their formative years or later on, it will not be to find a bright spot in a disenchanting life. Rather, recoiling at the necessity, they reach for their genitals much as they pick their noses or break wind, always in private. They masturbate in much the same way that they urinate or defecate, in resignation and sometimes in shame, looking resolutely away until the ordeal is over and the accommodation concluded. There is no immersion in the moment, no thriving on what occurs. Instead of using masturbation as an opportunity to let themselves go in flights of fantasy or in convulsions like fireworks that rival the sun, or as a way of being and acting that would be restricted or diluted by the presence of another human being, they will often masturbate behind glazed eyes, then go about their business as if nothing had happened at all.

> Sometimes I'll wonder if it still works down there, and so I resort to masturbation. I won't really get into it. I just want to see if I still have a sex drive.

*

> I've been in situations where I had to, when my sperm level got above my eyeballs.

*

> I'll masturbate about every day, whether we have sex the same day or not. A lot of times it's not even for sexual pleasure. It's a way of getting my sexual tension or energy or preoccupations out of the way.

Freud and his followers make much of the latency period in which libidinal issues, so prominent in the oral and anal periods of psychosexual development, are denied by repression and displaced by interests and activities associated with a young child's acculturation, to be reawakened during the genital stage. For many people, the reawakening is short-lived. From the first moment that they discover pleasure in their bodies, their every effort involves an attempt to contain themselves, to remain vigilant over impulses that, they feel, threaten to undo them. Such people prize caution above all, and doom the rest of their lives to a reverse alchemy in which gold is turned into lead. Underlying their monumental efforts is a profound terror that, were they ever to give in, their lives would disintegrate in uncontrol, that there is a dangerously low addiction threshold to pleasures unwisely sampled. The idea of pleasure conjures up the prospect of unremitting wantonness, and masturbation is perceived as a first step to opening up the floodgates.

Although guilt and shame over playing with ourselves—especially when it is termed self-abuse—may be attributed to moral remorse, they chiefly result from our dread that we may never be entirely in charge of our life, that our self-control may be far more tenuous than we need to believe. Along with the issue of self-control is the fear of being taken over by moments of pleasure, of being seduced by delights unearned. Accolades are reserved for those who go to work and don't complain, and certainly not for those who, on their toilet seats or in their beds or wherever else they choose to do it, gain pleasure and relief free of charge:

> I've done it at the library or in the car when I'm driving somewhere. Sometimes I do it when I'm bored, if I'm in the car for an hour or so. So why not masturbate? It's something to *do*, not because I'm particularly horny. Sometimes, of course, it can be a little dangerous. If you have an orgasm you can't drive as well!

DOING AND BEING DONE BY

As in every other area of sexual experience, how masturbation is viewed and, thus, the extent to which it is comfortable to us may well depend upon whether it is pursued by a man or a woman:

> I never knew women masturbated, only men.

> *

> Boys could talk about it and girls couldn't.

> *

> I just thought boys could do it but girls weren't supposed to.

There can be no doubt that everything about a male's physiology, socialization, and sexual development favors the practice of masturbation without as much distaste as is apt to be assigned to females. Whether it be a matter of hormonal differences—by age 14 most males have masturbated to ejaculation on virtually countless occasions—or of the fact that a boy can hardly fail to notice that he has a penis and remain forever preoccupied with its size and appearance, males are much more likely than females to engage in masturbation, to begin it at an earlier age, and to regard it more nonchalantly. Their shock or dismay over their initial ejaculation is subsequently replaced by keen delight and anticipation, most certainly by a preoccupation seldom rivaled by competing attractions.

I discovered my genitals when I was in the fourth grade and masturbated vigorously for years. If there's not any reason why I shouldn't, then I will.

During the stage of a boy's development when spitballs, pickup games, and relatively harmless acting-out behaviors hold sway and before he is much attracted to girls, masturbation may, like sliding into home plate, be regarded as evidence of male potency. It may stand as proof positive of that unquenchable sexual thirst which, later on, he will use to explain his predatory behaviors. However, once he has begun the mating–dating game, the male may begin to construe masturbation in quite different terms, as evidence of his failure to win the affections of a female partner, as a token of his unworthiness, as a distinctly less favorable alternative to sexual congress.

Among females, the sexual picture that emerges over time gets painted with quite different colors. Their introduction to the sexual domain, in comparison to the male's, is typically subtle, principally because they observe no bodily change so dramatic as an erection. Although they may learn early on to associate genital sensations with their pudenda, the clitoris, covered over by folds of flesh, can keep its presence a secret over all the female's formative years. Getting a look at it can be something of a challenge even for those women curious enough to employ a light and mirror under highly private circumstances. Even though the clitoris is the one human organ that serves no purpose other than that of providing sexual pleasure, the female may be slow in becoming accustomed to it, unlike the male who has held and handled and fretted over his double-duty penis. More often than not she discovers genital manipulation inadvertently, while climbing a pole or riding a horse, say, and sometimes her early orgasms are less compellingly explosive than males's. Furthermore, if she is encouraged to consider her new menstrual discharges as a challenge to fastidiousness, a female may hesitate to touch her genitals.

Not only do physiological differences help to account for differences in how young boys and girls develop sexually, but the whole of culture practically everywhere in the world seems to conspire to dampen a female's enthusiasm for sex, beginning with masturbation. While clitoridectomies, performed on millions of young girls by knife-wielding community leaders across Africa and the Near East, are the most extreme and reprehensible example of that conspiracy, their cultural counterpart exists wherever societies have a vested interest in inhibiting female sexual expression. We find universal insistence that sexual pleasure in the female serve a reproductive function, or, at the very least, be relationship-oriented, that the female's sexual experience be construed chiefly in terms of her need for or accommodation to a male. In any other terms, female sexuality is a threat to the community.

Males can be made uneasy in the extreme by a sexually autonomous female, who exults in her passion and warms herself by its fire, who reaches orgasm on her own beyond the reaches or supervision of a male partner, who does not use sex to service him and, in fact, can do quite well without him, who feels that sex is for herself and not for a relationship, who is not controlled by the prospect of her partner's applause or blame, whose sexuality is not prompted by fears of being abandoned and thus regarded as a failure as a woman. Perhaps, it is feared, sexually affirmative females who deliberately enhance their sexual potential by "getting it on" without men may have the audacity to leave their families if it occurs to them that facilitating the lives of husband and children conflicts with their own deepest needs and interests. Even if they remain, they may seek their sexual fortunes elsewhere. No longer constrained by outmoded views of what female sexuality is supposed to amount to, such women may no longer view their chief function as that of fostering "togetherness."

SOCIAL DUTY, PRIVATE NEEDS

Since in our culture, a life that is not marked by numerous interpersonal engagements is viewed as wasted and perhaps threatening, literally anti-social, it may be that, for many people, the very notion of *self*-pleasuring in any context, much less in the sexual domain, is a contradiction in terms. The Biblical tradition, be it Jewish, Christian, or Muslim, mandates the salience of community over individuality. One's seed is meant to sustain the community and not to be wasted on the ground without the prospect of progeny. Masturbation carries the threat of self-sufficiency, a first step in the direction of solitude and, ultimately, social exile. Many relationships are sustained by partners' fears that they could never make it on their own; fearful of being abandoned were they ever to enact themselves wholeheartedly, such people intuit that they are helpless and would be unfulfilled but for an interpersonal sexual experience, that sex, like going to the movies or eating out, *must* be shared.

THE IMPERFECT PARTNER

Ironically, it is this very need for another's involvement in their lives that may lead some people to *prefer* masturbation to sexual congress. Exhausted by their efforts to stem their fears of abandonment, first by accommodation and then by generous servings of rage, they leave the field and resort to themselves, trailing a host of unsolved relationship issues in their wake. Worn out by all the second-guessing they think relationships require of them, sometimes rebelling against another's sexual demands, they retire to a place where there is no insistence that they perform up to another's standard, where delicate negotiations are not required, where compromises need not be made, where interpersonal challenges for which they were never prepared need not be met:

> Sometimes I may be tired and not want intimacy. All I may need is a release. So it's easier to masturbate. That way I don't get his hopes up and then fall asleep on him.

*

He'll ask me for sex, and I'll turn him down. Then when he leaves, I'll masturbate. I guess I'm used to being independent.

*

When I masturbate, I can screw whoever I want to and do it any way I want.

*

When I masturbate I can grin from ear to ear. I can't seem to do that when I'm with a partner.

Free from the tyranny of interpersonal transactions, people can behave with abandon. Nothing must be hidden. If their stomachs bulge, so be it! If, on some occasions, they can't "get it up" or reach orgasm, no one else knows. And if they wish to fantasize a crowd of partners or the enticing neighbor or co-worker, they can do so without any sense of betrayal.

For some people, especially women, masturbation can represent an attempt to gain the independence that is not always apparent in the rest of their lives: "I'm in charge! I'll determine how and when I'll seek my sexual gratifications. My sense of power will come from self-reliance and not from my ability to stroke your ego! I refuse to perform on command. If I choose to reach orgasm, I shall only have *me* to thank. It will not become another debt I must pay elsewhere for my sexual pleasures." Claiming—regaining—control of her body through masturbation can mark for such a woman the beginning of a confident autonomy. When her body belongs to herself and is shared with her partner when she chooses, she is less likely to feel used and depersonalized in their sexual exchanges.

What matters most about masturbation is how it is viewed by the one who undertakes it. We may see it as a gift, a vacation, for a partner whose sexual appetite is less than ours. On the other hand, if we feel it is a last resort foisted upon us by our partner's indifference, we may engage in it with resentment or despair. It may imply questions about our capacity for closeness or the strength of our partnership, or in contrast it may express the individuality that makes our partnership healthy. It may show us that we have failed to ask our partner for what we want or, contrariwise, that we are uninhibited enough to act on our wishes.

We may regard our partner's masturbation in a variety of ways also. It may be a gesture of consideration when we are tired or ill. It may denote great sexual vitality or an unseemly regression. We may see our partner as experimenting in order to achieve a livelier sexuality or as announcing that sex with us has become tedious. All these perceptions, and not the actual habit patterns, are what shapes the effect that masturbation has on our partnership and our self-esteem.

What seems crucial to the consideration of masturbating is whether it reflects and promotes our sense of personal autonomy, of individuality. Both solitary and shared sexual experiences depend upon this sense if they are to be wholeheartedly gratifying. Those in whom it is weak are apt to be hindered by fears of being engulfed in merger with another, and also by fears of abandonment when they are not engaged with their partner. So the paradox seems to be that only those who can contentedly stand alone in the sexual domain, who can be by themselves from time to time, can ever fully connect with a sexual partner. All too often, those with shaky or tenuous identities will find themselves involved in aloof or grudging sexual transactions when, in fact, it would have been better had they felt free to masturbate.

If you truly want to uncover some deeply personal truths about what sex means to you and how you feel about your sexuality, to dismiss any arid intellectualizations about it, I would suggest that you imagine the prospect of doing three things. First, picture yourself calling a family meeting to discuss the place of masturbation in people's lives.

- How would you broach the subject?
- What do you suppose the reactions would be?
- What points would you want to make?
- What kind of feedback would you seek?
- How would masturbation fit into your family values?
- How strongly would you rather not discuss it at all?
- How would you judge the success of what transpired?

Spend time on this scene. Note what you would see and what you would feel. And if this is impossible, if the very idea is unthinkable or ludicrous, consider what this might mean about you. Try to get at the personal truths that are responsible.

The second thing is to imagine telling your partner that you had masturbated the night before.

- What response would you expect?
- How would you feel about making such a "confession"?
- What details might you add—what you were thinking, or feeling, or fantasizing?
- What message would you be trying to convey?
- Would you want it to appear that you had been pleased to enjoy yourself, that you were driven to this unlovely resort because of unfulfilled sexual needs, that you had given into a regrettable impulse?
- Would you expect your partner to be affronted, apologetic, disgusted, unconcerned, relieved, congratulatory?

Finally, imagine a scene in which you and your partner decide to forgo intercourse and masturbate in front of each other instead.

- Who is doing what and how?
- Would you look into each other's eyes or watch each other's hands?
- How would you feel about watching another person as you arouse yourself?
- How would your focus change as you each near orgasm?
- What kind of emotional contact would you maintain?
- What happens when you finally climax?
- How is this different from what happens when the two of you are in physical contact?
- Does "two feet away" make you feel alone? Does "two feet away" make you feel unnecessary?
- Does the distance bring any unaccustomed relief?
- Does it embarrass you or your partner to be observed?

These are all territories that you would do well to explore for what they tell you about yourself.

The author, George Fowler (1995)[1], in his autobiography, comments on the centrality of sexual events in our lives:

> A few times late at night I watched as I masturbated and I particularly remember the first time the experience left me feeling good and not guilty. I had experienced at last the upbeat feelings that "jerking off" had apparently been giving my buddies since grammar school.

Fowler goes on to describe how he felt compelled to share what was happening with his very best friend:

> Datus had never had to learn to like his body, but he seemed to understand me as I began learning to like mine. I wanted to share the feelings I was at last finding in solitary sex . . . it was my unrecognized final salute to the necessary guilt for genital pleasures that I'd been taught.

What story can *you* tell? Masturbation, like every other aspect of our sexual experience, involves far too much for us to dismiss it with a sneer or to mention it to others only when it is framed by a dirty joke. There is a glory, a purpose, an outcome in the most hidden aspects of our lives, and it becomes our chief challenge to discover what is there.

---

1. *Dance of a Fallen Monk*. New York: Anchor Books, Doubleday, p. 54.

12

The Sexual Dance:
ACCOMMODATIONS

Each of us carries somewhere in our head a portrait of ourselves and another of our partner, describing the people that we are and explaining every sexual gesture, every affinity or aversion, every act or omission in a sexual exchange. We attribute our sexual fortunes or misfortunes to the elements of these mental portraits, finding reasons to rejoice or complain in what we see as personal truths about the two of us.

Like dominoes lined up in an elaborate design, each collapsing on its neighbor when the first is tapped, so go our thoughts about our sexual lives—about ourselves and about our partner.

> I'm 46 years old and I still feel extremely sensual, extremely sexual. I have a strong need for sexual satisfaction. I don't think I've reached any kind of plateau sexually. Sex is a very important part of my well-being.
>
> *
>
> How can I consider myself a good lover? I've only been with one man, and he doesn't love it. I can't give myself a high score on that. I keep thinking maybe he wouldn't have his problem if he were with someone who's better than I am.

THE FRIEND, THE ENEMY IS ME

When it comes to understanding human behavior, at any age, in any context, there is probably nothing more important to take into account than our self-concept: how we view ourselves and what adjectives we would use to describe ourselves. Our beliefs about ourselves are among the most important convictions we possess. They are used to explain others' behaviors towards us as well as our own. They determine the nature and level of our aspirations. They reflect what we are told about ourselves throughout the course of our lives. They dictate our responses to success and failure. We rely on the concepts we have of ourselves in our search for the meaning of what befalls us.

Without a relatively clear, lasting sense of identity that colors every page of our lives, we are left with no sense of direction, no foundation for order and certainty. It would be terrifying if every morning we had to fashion ourselves anew because an ongoing sense of self is essential for personal confidence, and confidence is *the* basic requirement for normal functioning. All of human behavior can be understood as the effort to enact and to confirm whoever we suppose ourselves to be.

Whatever happens that is congruent with who we claim ourselves to be is deeply reassuring; whatever happens that is not consistent with our self-perceptions is deeply troublesome. Thus, a woman who has always viewed herself as kind and loving will only reluctantly come to realize that her generosity may have masked a need for control over others, and for as long as she can, she will cling to her former image of herself and try to bolster it with ever-increasing acts of kindness. In the same way, a man who has come to believe that he is fundamentally crusty and cantankerous has an investment in that image, and will resist evidence that his customary behaviors are a defense against tender feelings or potentially overwhelming hurt. The ideas we have of ourselves are not easily dislodged. The statements we make about ourselves to ourselves and others so strongly influence our behaviors that they are usually not even open to debate.

OUR SEXUAL SELF

Whether we find ourselves in the sexual doldrums or the sexual heights will be determined chiefly by the images we have of ourselves as sexual beings. Firmly grounded convictions about ourselves are enacted in our every sexual gesture and aspiration and in all that we allow ourselves to feel in a sexual embrace. If the environment in which we were raised was relatively sex-phobic, our sexual self-images may be highly constrained or, in dramatic opposition, daring and even reckless. If, on the other hand, our formative years included permission to ask questions about sex, tolerance of our sexual explorations, and acknowl-edgment of our growing sexual interests and capacities, chances are we shall be able to embrace our sexuality wholeheartedly.

Because behaviors in the sexual realm can have such thorough-going consequences, it follows that our involvement in who we claim to be sexually is especially tenacious. Those of us who were punished for childhood sexual impulses or frightened by warnings that God punishes sexual misconduct will, accordingly, construct views of our sexuality as impaired or nonexistent. Although we may complain about our circumstances, we will do whatever it takes to maintain them:

> It's so hard to think of myself as sexual. I've always felt it was for someone else's benefit.
>
> *
>
> I tend to ignore sexuality as a part of me.

Those of us with an image of innocence to protect are actually afraid of becoming sexually affirmative because it might change our basic identity, so it is reassuring to see ourselves as sexually naive and inexperienced, slow to arouse, a stranger to sexual fantasies or impulses:

> If I were to tell someone an interesting story it wouldn't have to do with my sexuality.
>
> *
>
> I don't think of myself as highly sexed.
>
> *
>
> I really don't have much of a sex drive. Most of the time there's nothing there.

*

I'm certainly not some kind of sex goddess.

*

I'm a zelig as a sexual partner. I'm not real expressive.

*

I'm asexual. The less sexual I am, the better.

One way to keep sex at arm's length is to maintain a very negative body image. People who are overweight may be distressed that their partner finds them unattractive or that it interferes with their own sexual interests, yet they may do nothing about it. Others may be preoccupied by characteristics beyond their control, such as breast or penis size, making it impossible for them to be fully erotic. That, of course, is the point. People who are mindful of bodily flaws experience themselves as not particularly sexual. They can have a vested interest in not making themselves too inviting to their partner; or perhaps they wish to protect themselves from the dangers of the sexual marketplace. They use such images of themselves to explain and to maintain their sexual retreat:

> "Self-acceptance at any level depends in part on accepting your body as it is . . . your body image has a tremendous impact on the quality of your sexuality. If you feel flawed on the outside, you will very likely feel undesirable sexually . . . and deep down inside you will suspect your lover of cataloging your body faults even as you are making love."
> (Engel 1995, p. 271).

If I was a guy in his shoes, I'd think I could find a heck of a lot better. . . . I can't understand anybody who'd be attracted to me physically.

*

I've always felt my penis isn't large enough. That's always bothered me. It makes me feel weak. It's almost humiliating.

*

Overweight is not attractive to him. Old is not attractive. Short hair is not attractive. It would help if I were slimmer and younger.

*

I don't look so great out of clothes.

*

"With all due respect to Freud, in my experience, women do not have penis envy. They have penis curiosity. It's *men* who have penis envy."
(Danoff 1993, p. 7).

I don't like the way I look at this point, but apparently I'm not doing anything about it.

Those on the sexual heights have quite different perceptions of themselves. Not only do they confidently view themselves as sexual creatures, but they do all they can to affirm this image. Either because of parental permission or example, or because they have been able to forge their own moral value system, sex holds no shame for them, nor do sexual idiosyncrasies alarm them. To be sexually affirming is to have a self-image that reflects and promotes an exuberance about sexual matters. This often includes a feeling of sensuous vivacity:

I love looking at bodies. They're great, so well-designed.

*

I enjoy physical contact. I'm pretty open about that. I like all kinds of physical contact. I just like to touch and be touched.

*

I'm very sensual. When I'm with my partner, I really focus on the moment. Nothing else occurs to me!

*

I feel really glad that I'm a woman and very much in touch with my body. I feel real connected to myself in that way. I know how to please myself when I'm not with a partner.

These people speak frankly, with no sense of shame, about their sexual needs and wants:

I accept a lot of aspects of my sexuality that others might have trouble with, like masturbation or attractions to members of the same sex.

*

I've always been a highly charged sexual person.

*

I've always enjoyed sex, ever since I got married. I'm pretty open about it.

*

I like to masturbate. I like sex. I like sexual feelings.

The positive image they have of themselves often extends to how they see themselves as sexual partners:

I think I'm a good lover. There's a good balance between pleasing my partner and seeking pleasure for myself.

*

I like to be very good in bed.

In sexually affirming people, feelings about their bodies are consistent with the positive views they have of themselves in the sexual arena. Whatever blemishes there may be do not bother them because they do not belittle themselves as sexual partners:

Little by little I'm seeing my body as more attractive. He makes me feel attractive. That's the biggest thrill for me. Now when he tells me I'm beautiful, I actually believe it!

*

I've always been happy with how I look physically.

*

My body image is getting better. I used to shave my pubic hair, but I don't worry about that any more.

*

I think I've got a decent body. It could be prettier and more muscular, but it's not ugly, and I'm not ashamed of it.

WHAT DO I SEE IN YOU?

Just as the images we have of ourselves profoundly affect our sexual experiences, so too do the perceptions we have of our partner. They are not always accurate, however. Sometimes they amount to sweeping projections onto our partner of sexual needs, attitudes, and wishes we cannot own in ourselves. Sometimes they are the result of mistaken identification with our partner, in which we suppose that what is true of us must surely be true of them. Sometimes, they are faulty because we do not distinguish our partner from other partners we have known or because we have stereotyped notions about our partner's gender or race or because we need to experience our partner in a certain way so that we can maintain certain views of ourselves. In any case, our images of our partners are not easily modified, since those images can be a function of our own entrenched needs.

Perceptions of partners often include what we surmise to be their reasons for engaging in sex. Our notions about our partner's motivations can then go on to influence our own sexual interest:

Whenever he wants to express love, it has to go through sex.

*

She wants to be loved.

*

It's her way of getting contact with me and feeling close.

*

For him the best expression of love is the sexual act, and he's very loving during it. When we have sex he becomes the most lovable person in the world!

*

He literally makes love to me, really enjoys satisfying me, making me happy and seeing me aroused. He doesn't worry about his needs all the time.

If our perceptions of our partner are unfavorable, they can quickly dampen our responses and squelch whatever sexual interest we might have begun with:

His self-esteem and enjoyment of sex seem to be based more on how often he gets that release as much as the quality. I believe he'd be satisfied with quantity alone. If he could have sexual release every night, his self-esteem would be awesome!

*

I think part of the reason she initiates is because she thinks I might stray.

*

I'm just there for him to get relief.

*

Nothing matters except his climax. Sometimes I don't even feel human.

*

He doesn't want to get close to me in a lot of ways, and he uses sex to not be close. He hardly ever shares much emotion with me during sex.

Besides what we see as our partner's sexual needs and motivations, our impressions of how much he or she enjoys sexual encounters are important to our own basic sexual circumstances. These impressions, too, may be positive or negative, accurate or erroneous, but inevitably they color the sexual exchange for us:

I don't think she's satisfied with our sexual relationship. When I ejaculate too soon, it bothers me. It makes me feel real bad for her. She's pretty understanding, but she can be understanding for only so long!

*

She'd never had an orgasm until we'd been sleeping together for some time. When she did it was, "Wow, geez!" It has a lot to do with why she's putting some effort into our sexual relationship.

*

He feels a lot of joy. He feels excitement. I think he feels a sense of empowerment. It's as profound for him as it is for me.

*

Appreciation, love, excitement, fun, pleasure: these are the things she's feeling.

OUR PARTNERSHIP, OUR SCULPTURE

It cannot be overemphasized that *both* sexual partners are deeply committed to maintaining not only their own, but also their partners' self-images. In every partnership there is unconscious agreement that neither will do anything to force a radical alteration in the other's sexual assessment of himself or herself. A partner's self-image is too important to tamper with.

The unique mixture of similarities and differences that we perceive is the very foundation of our sexual partnership. We need to view ourselves in certain ways and therefore we need to experience our partner in certain ways to make interactions predictable and their meanings clear. Whatever is said or left unsaid, whatever sexual gesture is made, whatever response is given, represent collusion by both partners designed to maintain the status quo, to keep intact their images of themselves and each other. Whether their transactions are positive or negative, both partners have a deep investment in them. Both, whether they know it or not, are involved in a sexual dance whose rhythm and tempo are determined by what they need to believe and by whatever interactions best sustain those beliefs:

> He has not had good experiences with physical contact. He was beat up a lot as a child. This makes it hard for me to be physical with him.

> *

> She's just a shy person and doesn't feel comfortable about initiating. Whenever she does she gets embarrassed.

> *

> Our sex life was definitely a "Wham, bam, thank you ma'am" kind of thing except I never got the "thank you." I had a lot of responsibility in that too, because I didn't ask for what I needed. I was so afraid of hurting his feelings. He seemed so fragile!

> *

She'll say, "I'm just someone for you to fuck!" Then she gets angry, pulls up her dress, and bends over so I can fuck her!

*

He's real attracted to a real feminine essence in me. He also really likes me as a person. I'm not just an object. It goes deeper than that. I get to share the deepest aspects of myself with him.

*

There's a barrier she erects that will not let her be sexual with me. It makes me pull back.

In these descriptions, we may find a woman who was raised to feel guilty or ashamed of her sexual needs, so that she distances herself from them. This allows her to view herself as a sexual victim at the hands of someone she can view as weak and selfish. We may find another woman who delights in her femininity and its appeal to her partner, so that sexual sharing is her opportunity for deep intimacy. We may find a third whose sexual aversions will not permit her to dignify her partner's sexual aims, so that she resentfully presents her body but withholds her affections. We may find a man whose childhood training for impassive masculinity included no vocabulary for expressing emotions, so that he "makes love" without tenderness. Or we may find a man frustrated because his partner moves her arms and legs as required but without really reaching out to him. We may find in both partners the need to erect barriers in order to accommodate their fears of intimacy. One or the other may consciously wish for more closeness but engage in behaviors that create the distance each needs to feel safe in a sexual embrace.

Whatever the dynamics, we can be sure that both partners's sexual responses are contrived to help them maintain consistent views of themselves as sexual beings. When it comes to sexual disappointments or delights, there is no passive partner. Each has a part to play that is far more serious than either may suspect. Each is acting on self-fulfilling prophecies born of convictions arrived at long ago that choreograph their sexual dance. In the well-rehearsed steps they execute they can make sense of what happens between them.

The sexual dance is based on the differences partners see between them and serves to reinforce their understanding of who they are as sexual beings. The differences thus highlighted may include sexual values, preferences, attitudes, aims, and a general style of relating. Again and again as couples enact themselves, they confirm their assumptions about each other. The person who needs to believe that sex is not his or her predominant interest is left with reassuring signs that the partner's interest is inordinate; similarly, the self-styled sexual liberal is comforted by the partner's customary prudish reactions. Like the diets of Jack Sprat and his wife, the sexual domain is notable for the ways in which partnerships come to depend upon differences:

> He's more openly passionate than I am. I'm not as open about affection as he is. I'm more reserved.

*

> I like to play sex around the house—on the couch or on the kitchen table or in the study—but she likes to have sex in bed.

*

> When he comes home from work he washes his hands real good before he eats, whereas I pick food up off the floor and eat it. That's why his sperm doesn't faze me at all, while he wouldn't dare put his mouth on my genitals.

*

> For me it's a physical release. It's fun and enjoyable. For her it's more of a personal, special type of thing.

*

> I'm more of an introvert than an extrovert when it comes to sex. She's much more extroverted. It's a good balance.

ROMANCE AND PASSION

Recognizing differences from our partner does more than just preserve our own identity. Couples who, over the years, have seemingly settled all their differences, who, their friends might observe, have even come to resemble each other physically as well as in their attitudes and values, will frequently report a lack of sexual passion. Battles over domestic turf, over who decides which issues, have long since ceased, leaving a steady calm that precludes fiery engagements. While a sense of similarity and mutual identification between partners can be pleasantly companionable, another result can be erotic indifference to each other.

Romantic attraction and sexual enthusiasm frequently depend on there being a sense of difference and distance between sexual partners. When partners are not clearly differentiated, there will be no quest for merger with the Other, with whom the prospect of sexual congress promises self-completion. Romantic literature is replete with stories of intoxicating relationships between utterly different partners, whose differences, along with the tensions they bring, continually threaten the stability of the relationship. It is just those differences and the accompanying sense of distance that seem to provoke the sexual excitement shared by lovers everywhere.

Identification with one's partner and a thoroughgoing familiarity can contribute to the tepidity of the sexual doldrums. Such partners are not distinct enough from each other. They have failed, for too long, to express what they want and contend with their differences. Their collusion, justified as keeping the peace, prevents them from experiencing the partner as the Other or forging a genuine sense of self, since doing so depends upon maintaining, even fighting for, a personal identity apart from a partner who is equally insistent upon claiming his or her own. There can be no sexual passion between those who have forfeited their identities in so-called service to the relationship. There can be no yearning for each other when we have not allowed there to be distance between us. Those who have stopped wrestling with their differences, who have stopped insisting upon their own time and space in the relationship, may end up with a treasured friendship sheltered in the sexual doldrums:

> **Sometimes I'm not eager for sex because the relationship feels more like a friendship.**

The major task of those who would have a vigorous and lasting partnership, sexual or otherwise, is to create conditions under which each partner can know and be known to the other as far as they can reciprocally identify and empathize. At the same time, they must be able to create boundaries in which each partner dares to be who he or

she really is without shame or apology or marked fear of abandonment. The paradox here is that only those who are not too fearful of
discovering and claiming their ever-emerging selves are able to
experience and provide the kind of trust that true friendship requires.
Without the certainty that comes from such self-acceptance, neither we
nor our partner will ever be sure that the love between us is genuine;
we will never know how much of what passes between us is contrived
to avert abandoning or being abandoned. Only the truly self-
confident individual can merge without fearing submersion and, at the
same time, tolerate the distance that a mature relationship requires.

Although sexual passion and enthusiasm are fed by a sense of
difference and distance, they also rely upon the uncommon trust that
emerges from a genuine friendship in a committed relationship:

> In our counseling, we talk more about emotional intimacy than
> physical or sexual intimacy, but it's really the same issue.

*

> There's no separation between just living together and our
> sexuality. There's a definite sensuality about the way we are
> together. It's all so intertwined for me.

*

> I think our sexual relationship is very much like our marriage.
> It's had its ups and downs. The times we haven't been getting
> along sexually coincided with the times we haven't been getting
> along very well in our marriage.

*

> They work hand in hand, a good overall relationship and a good
> sexual relationship.

SEX AND REAL LIFE

Some people view their sexual relationship as the inevitable
outcome of how they are relating to each other in other spheres. The
quality of their sexual exchanges serves as a barometer for determining
the quality of their overall relationship. Sexual well-being is an indication that the relationship is sound:

I find much of the success of our sexual encounters depends upon our attitude and the relationship that has developed between us most of that day. We can't fake it. We've got to be there totally, not only physically but mentally and emotionally. That plays a big role.

*

Our being good sexually is just an indication of how other parts of our lives have been coming together.

*

When I can be completely open with him, and things are warm and friendly between us, then sexually it's the same way.

*

Sex is a reflection of everything, of how we are emotionally with each other.

> "Our findings lead to the overwhelming conclusion that a good sex life is central to a good overall relationship." (Blumstein and Schwartz 1983, p. 201).

> "The more intimate your relationship, the better the sex." (McCarthy and McCarthy 1990, p. 82).

In the same vein, unsatisfying sexual exchanges reflect more general problems:

He would withdraw in general, and that extended into the bedroom, too. It didn't really start there.

*

My husband got to the point where he wouldn't sleep with me, which was a statement about our marriage.

*

If you're mad at somebody, it's hard to be in the mood for sex.

*

It's very much related to our relationship as a whole. Right now I'm feeling tense and insecure and distrustful. I'm not allowing myself to be too vulnerable with him, and that affects how I am sexually.

*

When a person is feeling really neglected in a lot of areas, they're not going to open themselves up sexually to someone.

For other couples, by contrast, the sexual relationship enhances the whole:

I know sex has kept us together. We have one of the most healthy sexual relationships of any two people I know. How many people, after this amount of time, still have sex a couple of times a day? We sure do, if there's the slightest inkling of the opportunity. It's definitely our bonding.

*

We're both investing more and more in being with each other in other ways, too. That's kind of the spillover effect.

*

Having finally gotten the good life in the bedroom has made the other parts easier than they were before. It works both ways. It's opened up communication in other areas of our life. That wasn't happening until we finally managed to get together about sex and really both enjoy it.

*

Sometimes sex is the one thing that seems to be going smoothly. If we're not getting along in other ways, it seems like we can always have good sex. Sometimes that helps bring us closer together.

*

Sex was the basis of our marriage to begin with, and it's remained the foundation of it. It has enabled us to overcome the differences between us.

"Although as a general rule of thumb the relationship comes first before sex can be enjoyed, sometimes having loving sex can dramatically improve the relationship."
(Gray 1995, p. 118).

*

Just as there are those who feel grateful for the affirmative power of sex on the partnership altogether, many emphasize its destructive impact when it is joyless:

> I needed exactly what he wasn't giving sexually, and it filtered down into every part of our relationship.

*

> We have a lot of friends whose marriages didn't work out. One of the reasons they gave for their problems was that sex had become very routine and monotonous.

Still others compartmentalize various aspects of their lives, and do not always associate sex with emotional or interpersonal expression. To such folk, sex may seem to have little bearing upon anything else that happens in their partnerships:

> I really think you can have a very warm and satisfying relationship and not have sex at all.

*

> We get to the point where we may have just been using each other for a release, and then, during the rest of the time, we'd be at odds in every other aspect. Being sexual with each other seemed so at variance with how we interacted outside the bedroom. This is what made it so painful.

*

> The sexuality just hasn't come along with the rest of our evolving relationship. We're close companions and now parents but not very enjoyable sexual partners. I still don't look forward to sex, and I don't enjoy it greatly.

*

> I had a bad marriage. We couldn't agree on anything except possibly sex.

Needless to say, how strongly couples connect sexual experience to the quality of the total relationship will determine the degree of importance they give to sexual issues. Some consider it virtually paramount:

When sex goes, there's no reason to be together.

*

We really put out a lot of effort in our sexual relationship. It's just as important as other things are in our life together.

*

It's a major part of our marriage.

Others believe that their interactions outside the bedroom are what is crucial and, accordingly, give less emphasis to sex:

> Our sex is a very small part of our relationship. If sex is a major component—highly sensual and enjoyable—but that's all there is, so what?

*

> If a lot of your other needs are not being met, I don't see how sex would make up for that.

Whatever else can be said about our sexual engagements with another, they clearly involve some of our life's most challenging assignments. We must be able to draw close enough to lose our wariness and our protective barriers, yet not lose our distinct identities. We need to choose a partner who is different enough from us to stimulate erotic passion, but similar enough to be a trusted friend. We must learn to reveal ourselves to another without

"Some couples with good overall relationships have poor sex, and, much more surprising to most people, some couples with poor relationships have excellent sex . . . All couples who have good sex have a good total relationship some of the time; some couples who have good sex have a good total relationship all the time; but other couples who have good sex do not always have a good relationship all the time. And, conversely, some couples who have poor sexual relationships are close and loving in other ways." (Sager and Hunt 1979, pp. 107–108).

shame, yet without dishonoring the ineffable mysteries of our person-hood, and to welcome the same capacity in our partner. How well we do in meeting these challenges will be plainly spelled out in all of our sexual transactions, and most of all in what goes on in the heart and between the ears.

Perhaps the most difficult thing for most couples to acknowledge or realize is that their sexual circumstances are related directly or indirectly to who each of them was before they ever met and to their individual, independent needs and issues. The reasons for their sexual health or poverty must be laid at both their doors regardless of any inclination to view one partner as benefactor and the other as beggar, one as inflictor and the other as victim.

If your personal truths seem to insist that you do not yourself color the relationships so vividly as your partner does, then you must explore further. You may ask yourself, for example, what part do I play in my partner's sexual indifference? Suppose that each of us, sepa-rately, accounts for it in terms of my partner's sexual abuse in childhood. In that case, how do I explain my initial attraction to a partner with this kind of history; what is there about me that benefits from such a disparity?

Whether it be an anorgasmic wife or a crudely insensitive husband, one partner's sexual infidelity or the other's painful inhibitions, the entire truth has not been discovered if one partner comes out the villain, the other aggrieved. That is simply not how human relation-ships work. The fact is, we do get what we are looking for, consciously or not, and are sure to contrive it by all we do or do not do. We do far more than occupy a front-row seat at every one of our sexual proceedings. We are both onstage throughout.

13 Sexual Doldrums/ Sexual Heights: COUPLING

It's become more a matter of having sex for the sake of having sex. There's not much passion any more.

*

The sex we have is just really incredible!

If you are one of those persons for whom sex has lost its delights, you are not alone. Many of us, with fading memories of more joyous times, find the prospect of going to bed with our partner somewhere between bearable and acutely intolerable. Our eventual disenchantment may have its roots in early experiences, such as the appalling discovery that we were born only because our father had stuck his penis into our mother's vagina, or our guilty dismay at our loss of innocence as we vowed over and over never to masturbate again. It may have arisen in the tense furtiveness of less-than-satisfying sexual pursuits in back seats; in disappointments after (if not during) the honeymoon; or later still, when our ardent desire for our partner gave way to fantasies that we thought made a pretense of our sexual conduct.

Only occasionally do we partake of nectar; more frequent is the taste of tap water or even vinegar, as sexual experience feels more like going to work than to a ball:

If 100 was the highest and 0 the lowest, I'd say we're at about 33.

DOWNHILL ALL THE WAY?

Perhaps the most frequent complaint is that our sexual relationship and encounters have too soon lost their passion. Gone are the days when sexual moments involved feeling most alive, when our excitement could barely be contained, when every gesture felt new, when we felt moved to the core of our being:

> I'd like more surprises, occasional passionate surprises, explosions.

> *

> I wish it were more of an adventure, like if we were on a train, and he just said, "Let's go fuck." I'd love that!

> *

> You'd like to think that every night is going to be like a honeymoon night, but it isn't. It's not as steamy or sultry as it used to be.

> *

> Things aren't what they used to be. I worry about that.

We sometimes take a lack of passion as a sign that, with memorable moments coming more rarely, our relationship itself may be in jeopardy:

> The relationship is going downhill. We keep doing the same things over and over. It gets pretty old. Sometimes I get real disgusted.

> *

> We used to be really into sex, but then the day-to-day stuff set in, and the sex flopped. We weren't doing it. I didn't want to do it. The relationship has begun to fizzle.

> *

> Our relationship is pretty rocky. There's not much excitement. When we make love it's wham, bam, thank you ma'am.

There are, on the other hand, those of us who expect the passage of time to have its effect. In fact, these people may believe that if years go by and a couple are still sexually enthralled with each other, it means the relationship has failed to mature:

> It's just natural that in the beginning there is more excitement and gusto.

> *

> It's not exactly routine, but the fact is we pretty much know each other's bodies and what's going to happen. It was definitely more exciting when we were younger.

In a sexual partnership there is no substitute for wanting and feeling wanted, nothing more gratifying than a genuine pursuit of each other by both partners; and when that is absent or begins to wane, we can be left with fearful assessments of our value to our partner and of the relationship. Instead of directly addressing these fears, most of us resolutely deny what is occurring. We persevere in the hope that our former passion will reassert itself so that we will no longer need to stimulate it. We try to keep our burnout secret and become frantic if a sexual dysfunction begins to develop, threatening to expose our indifference to our partner or forcing us to acknowledge our lack of sexual interest:

> Getting in the mood to have sex can be a real chore. It's been getting progressively worse.

> *

> I wish I were as enthusiastic as he is. I'm not always ready to go at the drop of a hat.

> *

> I used to be all over him. I'd try every which way to get him excited. Then I got bored! I'd like him to try new things with me! When I ask him if he's ever wanted to touch a woman's body in a certain way, he just goes, "I don't know." No wonder I've lost my desire!

Some of us hope that our lack of desire will be overcome through technique—by a hand here, a tongue there, a reliable fantasy, whatever has stirred the coals for us before. Occasionally, passion can be rekindled in this way, but more often our erotic apathy remains. The result will be low levels of arousal:

> Sometimes it's hard to get aroused, especially when I'm just sort of interested but not fully committed to it.

> *

> Sometimes I can't get aroused at all, and I just sit there and wait.

> *

> I have a problem getting wet enough. We try everything, and I still can't get aroused.

> *

> I keep wishing that something will trigger some kind of hidden response in me.

> *

> He can touch my clitoris for quite a while before it feels even remotely sexual. How come I'm like that? Why can't I come from him sticking his penis in me? How come I can't come when he comes? How come it takes me so long? It's got to be boring for him!

In addition to a lack of passion, with its attendant boredom and indifference, the doldrums of sexual partnership often include feeling little affection or intimacy in the connection with one's partner. The physical connection, if it occurs, may pass every test except, for some of us, the most important one of all: All the barriers and insincerities one needs in meeting the world stay put during what only *appears* to be a loving exchange. Often this particular lack is reflected in a disinclination to kiss or to be kissed. While genital displays may signify many different emotional meanings, a growing disenchantment may leave the prospect of kissing almost intolerable, may set a person's teeth on edge. How we feel about kissing our partner, how we do it, how we experience a partner's kiss reveal much about our capacity for intimacy and how much closeness we can now tolerate in a sexual partnership:

> He knows I like to kiss. I know he doesn't like to kiss, and it's OK with me. I can live without kissing.

*

I almost never kiss her. As a kid I never played spin the bottle or
kissed my dates goodnight. I always thought I was above that.

Whether or not these telltale signs are present, we may sense that
something is missing, has disappeared or was never there. For most
women, but also many men, expressing closeness is ideally the raison
d'être for sex between two people:

I don't feel close to him, not like before, when sometimes we felt
as one. That was a neat feeling.

*

I often feel rushed. Little things don't matter to him, but they
matter to me a lot. I miss being real sensual and close. My
emphasis is not on intercourse, but that's the way it seems to end
up. We've ended up less close emotionally than we were when we
were just friends!

*

I want to be connecting with him more, and this is not
happening.

A sexual partner may forbear to insist that his or her needs be
honored and, instead, drift along in acquiescence to the other's
interests. Such self-forfeiture inevitably leads to sadness, if not outright anger:

I was yearning for love and affection but didn't know it. I
wanted to be touched and loved and held, and when it didn't
come, I pushed for sex. I lost what I was really after.

*

Sometimes I don't feel good afterwards. I'll regret doing those
things when the feeling wasn't there, when my heart wasn't in it.

One way we can rebel against another's agenda for us, so as to
retain a modicum of self-respect, is to check our inner selves at the
bedroom door:

I'll be there in body but not in spirit. I get sucked back into my head.

*

Sometimes I won't feel very involved. I get distracted.

*

We'll be having sex and my mind will go off somewhere, probably because I'm not deeply involved.

SLIDING INTO THE DOLDRUMS

When sexual encounters lose their charge, either physically or emotionally, questions and concerns about our partners and partnership surface. Many couples are reluctant to give voice to their fears and instead begin to withdraw from each other, perhaps creating situations that are unlikely to lead to sexual exchanges, often questioning their interest in each other, and avoiding the pain induced by unenthusiastic sex. Many of us decide that we will never again risk the prospect of rejection so we wait in vain for our partners to initiate sexual contact, not knowing that our partner may fear the very same risk. Others of us seek to avoid the sadness or disappointment that has come to pervade our efforts to connect sexually. We will eschew being humiliated by any more sexual failures. The sexual doldrums resound with lamentations over our own incompetence or over partners who have let us down. Some of us take frequency of contact as the criterion of sexual health; no matter the fact that our sexual contacts are threadbare, we look for reassurance in just the fact that they have occurred at all. Given the quality of a great many sexual relationships, it could be argued that sexual contact occurs far more frequently than it deserves to:

> The only thing missing in my life right now is sex. We're not having the amount or the kind of sex that I'd like for us to be having.
>
> *
>
> Our marriage is pretty much on hold. There's been no sexual activity between us for a long time.

*

What I keep getting dissatisfied with is that when I want sex sometimes she doesn't, and I'll end up having to wait like an impatient kid.

*

I can get by without having a lot of sex. But, bottom line, I do want to have sex more often.

Instead of admitting that sexual contact is no longer very pleasurable or even that it has become grim, many of us give other reasons—to ourselves and to each other—for our lack of enthusiasm, for our failures to create opportunities. When we must explain why our sexual tempo has slowed to a stroll, what would we do without children?

After you've had a baby, you're always exhausted half the night.

*

I have a hard time getting started. We like to make love in the morning, but the baby is up by six so that pretty much shoots that.

*

We just never seem to find the time for it, what with the two kids.

*

I would prefer having sex more often first thing in the morning, but usually we have a kid in bed with us when morning comes.

Another convenient explanation blames the intrusive world beyond the bedroom:

With all the exams we have to prepare for, sexual relations have become very unimportant.

*

It's hard to leave all our problems at the bedroom door.

*

You can get so caught up in the day-to-day living of earning money and trying to raise a family that your sexual appetites are drained.

*

I just wish there were more hours in the day.

*

We're both really tired. We're burned out at our jobs and everywhere else.

OUR SEXUAL REPERTOIRE

The fact is, there are countless ways in which the prospect of a sexual encounter can repel one or both partners. There may be sexual issues screaming to be resolved, a lack of consensus that can lead to feelings of alienation, hidden resentments that sabotage our partner's appeal, concerns about ourselves as a sexual partner that we dread having exposed. A chief issue can be what takes place during a sexual exchange. We and our partner may have strikingly different expectations, interests, and needs. We may not have identified which activities are the most rewarding, physically and emotionally, for each of us. One result can be a sharply limited sexual repertoire:

Before, there was a great deal more variability and flexibility. We've lost that. What makes it bad is that I know it's not there.

*

We used to be real varied. We'd have sex at different times of the day and in different places. Now it's almost always in the bedroom and almost never in the middle of the day. I wish it were more on the spur of the moment.

*

Maybe it's not as wild as other people's. It's not as spicy as I think it could be. We pretty much stick to the missionary position—that's about it. It doesn't get any better than that. A month ago we tried front to rear, doggie style, but he feels it is too animal-like.

*

One of the things I miss sometimes is the real passionate type of kissing and licking.

A major issue for many couples is whether to include mouth–genital contact in their activities, if so, what form it should take, and the partners' overall emotional reactions to it. Some view it as plain wrong:

Oral sex never appealed to me. It seemed that the mouth was made for kissing, and the genitals went together like mouths go together. It didn't make a whole lot of sense to invert them. Also, you go to the bathroom with your genitals. Putting genitals in your mouth is not sanitary.

*

Our outlooks are both pretty wholesome. I'd say our feelings on sex are pretty biblical. Whatever the Bible says is the right thing to do pretty much dictates our behaviors.

*

I'm pretty mainstream when it comes to my sexuality, not much exciting to tell. There's no kinky sex.

*

Kinky sex is doing oral things.

Sometimes women who perform fellatio on their partners do not especially enjoy it, or else find it difficult:

He likes me to lick his genital area, and I don't mind that, at least not as much as I mind holding his penis in my mouth. That's uncomfortable. I haven't learned how to do that in a way that maximizes his pleasure and minimizes my displeasure in doing it.

*

He likes for me to give him a blow job. I can't really get into doing that.

*

She'll start doing it, and it will start feeling good, and then she'll gag. I guess if I had a really little dick, she wouldn't gag on it.

*

I don't know exactly how to explain what feels good when she's giving me head. Maybe she could watch a movie and learn a thing or two.

There are also women who prefer specific forms of oral-genital contact:

I don't like it when he kisses me in my pussy while I'm kissing his penis.

*

I like to kiss his penis. He wants to kiss my pussy, but I don't like that. I'd rather be the one doing it.

*

When we first met, there were no holds barred, but that's changed quite a bit. She doesn't like to perform oral sex like she used to. She says it chokes her. She can't do that any more. But she still likes to have it done to her, and that kind of bugs me sometimes.

It may be that oral-genital sex requires particular conditions for its enactment. Having nothing at all to do with procreation and being impossible to perform with decorum it violates the taboos that many of us grew up with. Some people, moreover, erroneously believe that a liking for such contact is a sign of latent homosexuality. In any case, it seems often to connote a brave triumph over our inhibitions, an extraordinary act of generosity to our partner, never so casual a matter as intercourse can sometimes be. To some of us it is a treat for special occasions:

Our relationship has to be going very well for us to have oral sex.

Another sign of sexual disenchantment is the failure to teach, learn, or display highly erotic sexual behaviors and techniques. Some people never get pleasuring and being pleasured quite right:

The one aspect of intercourse that he still hasn't quite got down yet is stimulating me with his hands. He doesn't quite have the rhythm down.

*

I think it would be arousing to me if he were more open instead of just grunting.

*

I like to be talked to dirty every once in a while, but he won't do that.

Some of us, though we may deny it, reduce our erotic potential by engineering with our partner a sexual routine that seems guaranteed to keep juices at a trickle. Our sexual lives come to be marked chiefly by a lack of spontaneity and excitement:

I hold back, especially in using different positions. Over the last couple of years it's been pretty much the same thing over and over again.

*

I wish there were a little more of everything: more foreplay, more kissing, more touching.

*

We don't try different positions. I'm fat, and I don't want him to catch a glimpse of my stomach.

*

When we were first married, we bought *The Joy of Sex* and tried some unusual positions. I found them very animalistic and unstimulating.

*

I sometimes worry that we are being too staid, using the missionary position so often: "Shouldn't we be doing something else?"

*

We start at one and get to ten with not a whole lot of variety.

Some of us put the brakes on our sensuality by censoring our sexual fantasies. Unfortunately, restricting ourselves in this way, often leads to a sexual lifelessness that only begs the very kind of stimulation we have renounced. As in other corners of our lives, to emphasize

caution and control only adds to the woes that instigated the problem
to begin with:

> I seem to have a very impoverished fantasy life.

> *

> Fantasies *used* to be real exciting.

> *

> Unfortunately I can't get certain thoughts out of my head. So
> even when I'm making love, more images will creep in, of people
> I don't even know. It's kind of annoying.

> *

> I don't know if my fantasies are healthy or not. Sometimes I
> wonder if it's normal. You have to be careful about getting
> carried away with them.

Self-preoccupations of one sort or another are another means by
which we can rob the sexual moment of its power. Instead of allowing
ourselves to be fully sexual, many of us erect barriers and take control
through a host of thoughts and feelings that inhibit sexual abandon.
There can be no end to worries about how we are doing, feelings of
guilt, uncomplimentary appraisals of ourselves, fears of rejection,
concerns about the relationship, and general disappointments in the
whole enterprise. All these very effectively check erotic experience
before it has a chance to surpass the power of a sneeze:

> If I'm having a hard time enjoying it, I'll begin to worry. Can he
> tell I'm not so turned on?

> *

> I started feeling unsexy when he actually came out and told me
> he didn't find me sexy. I'm still not over that one.

> *

> I'm often afraid I'll be rejected or that he'll be repulsed by me.

> *

> When she doesn't react, I wonder if she's not sexually attracted
> to me or if I don't stack up to her previous lovers.

> *

I hate being fat because it just hangs there. That's why I'd just as soon be on the bottom and not on the top.

*

Sometimes during sex I'll think, "Oh, gee, I didn't clean the bathroom!"

Some of us are preoccupied with our *partners*, reserving our animus for everything about them that we find unappealing, whether it has to do with their behaviors, their appearance, or the sexual motives we suppose them to have. Concentration on how much our partner lacks and on the ways he or she turns us off can make any sexual exchange highly unrewarding. As the list of complaints grows over time, no room is left for sexual enrichment:

I sure wish she were more joyful and enthusiastic about it!

*

It's hard for me to be attracted to him when he's gained weight. I hate to see people let themselves go like that.

*

When she looks sick and exhausted, she's no longer attractive to me.

*

I can't stand it when he tells jokes or says funny things when we're having sex.

*

Her coffee and cigarette breaks during sex are hardly a turn-on!

*

His bad breath is not very appealing.

The inevitable outcome is to take leave of sex altogether, to quit the playing field. If we are to make the sexual doldrums tolerable at all, we must downplay the importance of sex to ourselves and our partnership, make it a tired joke, trivialize its place in life, and perhaps snicker at the thought of how we once regarded it:

Sex is really not that big a priority to me any more. I'm just too tired for it. When I hit the sack I'd just as soon not have another person with me.

*

I don't seem to have the time for it any more.

*

Sex is more important to him than it is to me. I prefer reading or watching TV or taking a bath by myself.

*

Sex feels pretty good but it's not what it could be or should be. To tell you the truth, I'd rather stay up and drink.

What is most notable about those in the sexual doldrums is that even though they may have an idea about how they might improve their circumstances, they don't do it:

We were not getting a lot of satisfaction out of our sexual relationship, but for some reason, we never sought help.

*

I'm dissatisfied with our sexual relationship. It's an area we need to work on at some point, maybe now, maybe not now. There are a lot of other things that need working on right now.

*

I probably need to go to a therapist for help with the sexual kinks in my head. I know how to pick up a phone and dial, but I can't bring myself to do that yet. It will happen one of these days.

*

When we're having sex I often find myself preoccupied with other things. It might help to take time out of my week to spend time with him.

*

I think it would help if we had more time together with fewer distractions, maybe even go on a weekend together.

Instead of doing whatever it would take for them to operate sexually on all eight cylinders, those in the sexual doldrums remain gripped by inertia that can promise only more of the same. They are paralyzed by the very attitudes that got them there in the first place. To aim high sexually, to want more than our sex lives presently provide, and to try something that might get us off dead center, are not often considered worthwhile or acceptable pursuits. Many of us have yet to understand that true sexual success requires an uncommon emotional and interpersonal maturity. If we refuse to enlarge our sexual life we not only dishonor an absolutely basic human need but go far in promoting a diminished self. In settling for less in the sexual domain, we stop short of becoming a fully developed human being.

PULLING OUT THE STOPS

Given the history of most people's efforts to be sexual, it is hard to picture people who feel entirely free to live up to their erotic potential, to embrace their sexual impulses, to enact them without fear, to enjoy them without guilt, and to view them as a way to honor themselves as well as their sexual partners. Our culture has a peculiar fascination with sex in which, at the same time, we find horror over what we might do or equally might not do sexually, over what might become of us if our sexual fantasies and impulses were given free reign and not controlled by shame. Sexual difficulties are the inevitable result.

Parental silence about children's developing sexuality, occasional warnings not to play with one's private parts, and the admonitions often given to children old enough to date, are all eloquent reminders of the fears surrounding the dangers of sexuality and of its power:

> My parents never spoke about sex, didn't even joke about it. So I did very little questioning. I knew where babies came from, but even that was not real clear.

> *

> I feel only somewhat free sexually, because it was always a taboo subject. It's not only yucky to talk about, but it's not their business to talk about that stuff, the private, secrecy stuff. You're not supposed to talk about your body parts. You don't talk about your menstrual cramps. You hide your pads and throw them in the garbage so your father doesn't see them. My mother used to say she'd never have a husband with her during

the birthing process because that's a woman at her worst. She's dirty and sweats, and it's an ugly experience.

*

There was a big crisis when my sister told my mother she was sleeping with one of her high school boyfriends. Mom almost hit the roof! Her standard comeback was, "You realize, of course, that you'll be classified as a tramp!"

*

Sex was never discussed in my family. My parents must have had sex at least eight times but I don't know when or how, and I don't even *try* to imagine it!

*

My mom really got down on my sister for exploring her sexuality with a friend, just looking at each other and things like that. She grounded her for an entire summer and never let her play with that little girl again!

Beyond the family there is the school, where, in some circles at least, sex education of almost any kind is highly suspect, and free and open discussions about sexual needs, issues, and options are too often forbidden, lest students view such dialogues as permission for irresponsible behavior:

This teacher was appalled by the fact that I'd read Pearl Buck's *The Good Earth*. The book has to do with how people live, including their sexuality.

Likewise, some churches seem to be campaigning against sexual expressions of any kind:

I was pretty involved in the church when I was a teenager. Their idea of a good person was somebody who didn't have sex until marriage.

*

My father was a minister. I don't remember his ever sitting down with me and talking about sex. What I learned I learned from the kids at school.

*

My parents were very stead-fast and upright, very Christian and very proper.

The fact is, wherever in our society there are institutions that can impose control over people, every effort is made to minimize the likelihood of sexual contact. In prisons, conjugal visitations are the exception and not the rule. In nursing homes, privacy is kept to a minimum. In most hospitals, the authorities would look askance at a wife who crawls in bed with her dying husband. In the armed services, at least as recently as the 1970s, personnel engaging in masturbation ran the risk of receiving a dishonorable discharge! Again and again, wherever we look, sexuality is met with fiercely negative judgments and monumental controls. Is it any wonder that so many of us are ill at ease in the sexual domain? By the time we become adults we have learned in self-defense to be cautious in our sexual transactions, to keep our sexual secrets to ourselves, to be self-conscious in our sexual dealings with others, and to question our sexual normality. Self-doubt and ambivalence make poor sexual partners of us all.

"We are immersed in a culture that desperately wants to minimize and trivialize all things erotic and sexual, a culture that persistently tries to reduce the power and complexity of eros to something as simple as the physical release of sexual tension. We live in a culture that desperately wants to turn this profoundly deep and mysterious primal urge into something that can be easily understood, regulated, predicted, and controlled. And yet, whether we like it or not, the life force we call eros, the movement we feel as erotic impulse, again and again defeats our best efforts to control, tame, or confine it to our imposed boundaries of propriety."
(Steinberg 1992, pp. 3-4).

PERSONAL GROWTH AND SEXUAL FULFILLMENT

The sexual domain becomes highly charged for most of us not simply because of the sex-phobic culture in which we live. Sexual strivings necessarily involve the deepest elements and issues of human development: individuation from our parents and growth in personal autonomy, forging our own unique and authentic value systems, testing and shaping our sexual identities, and doing what we can to reach out beyond our families for love with relative strangers. How we manage these tasks can serve as the best indicators of how successful we are or shall ever be sexually. Nowhere can we find a greater ambivalence about changes and new adjustments than in the sexual ones forced upon us by physical and social unfamiliarities in our youth. We may feel on the one hand an eagerness to grow, to seek out new experiences, to fulfill our budding potential, but on the other hand an awkward discomfort with change of any kind, a tendency to cling to familiar images of ourselves and others, avoiding any opportunities there might be to learn new lessons about ourselves and others.

In order to be an unreservedly sexual adult, we need to have moved beyond the need for parental approval in sexual matters and to risk parental disapprobation. Masturbation in our youth can well represent such daring. Here we engage in an activity over which our parents have little control, which bids us delight in our own bodies, unsupervised, in which we act alone without parental permission while knowing how our parents would react if they discovered us. The sense of lost innocence that comes about when we engage in solitary sexual behavior, in secret places and unbeknownst to parents, is the sine qua non for the personal autonomy that will be required of us as adults. Later on, the same will be true of engaging in sexual fantasies that we experience as no one's business but our own. This is the stuff of which personal boundaries are made and from which the sense of self is fashioned. Again and again, it is defying the sexual impositions of our parents, tolerating the guilt that can be generated thereby, acting entirely alone without parental endorsement, that make sexual opportunities so compelling and, at the same time, so fearful:

> **Because of my upbringing, I had some negative feelings about sex. The first time I masturbated I felt as though I was possessed!**

*

I always felt furtive about sex, a lot of guilt.

*

I think my father didn't like it that I became a sexual person. It was the area in my life that he had the most difficulty with. It didn't stop me, but I know I felt very guilty about my sexuality when I was a teenager.

*

We never talked about sex. It was always under the rug. I knew there was a whole different side of everyone that we didn't talk about. My dad just had this warped concept of sex, like it was really bad. It wasn't until he died that I finally felt free of his pressures. It took me a long time to get past his puritan viewpoint. He's been gone two years now, and I finally felt like this huge burden has been lifted. Now I see that sex is good and wonderful!

In addition to our own needs and fears there are often parental needs that get thrown into the equation. Our effort to grow may be viewed, by them or by us, as an abandonment of them from which they will never recover. How much do parents' identities depend upon children remaining as children? Some parents become terrified of the prospect of their growing irrelevance and in effect forbid their children to function without them. Should they ever discover evidence of their children's sexual pursuits, such parents may display moral outrage, but, in fact, their reactions may have more to do with the sadness they feel over having to relinquish an accustomed role in their children's lives. Thus, to a greater or lesser extent, sexual pursuits in childhood and adolescence are inevitably accompanied by a sense of loss on the part of parent and child alike, which may induce lasting grief.

WHAT DO I BELIEVE? WHAT DO I VALUE?

Closely related to the need for an adolescent boy or girl to become increasingly free of parental control and influence is the need for a young person to shape his or her own moral value system. Too many adults I know differ hardly one whit from the values their parents held, moral and otherwise. As carbon copies of their parents, these so-called adults have never seriously questioned their parents' legacies and have never, even for a moment, tried others' on for size. In short, they fail to grow up in many essential ways. They are totally unaware that so long as they maintain their parents' views of things they cannot possibly achieve a mature morality. That can come only by fire and storm, by doubt and struggle with everything one has been told is so, until finally one is tempered like steel in a moral certainty that amounts to a deeply personal achievement.

Especially in the sexual domain, our opportunity to carry out this task is dramatic. To come to terms with our sexuality we must do far more than merely accept others' pronouncements. We must become increasingly honest with ourselves, in sure touch with our biological and emotional experience in sexual contexts. Only then can we learn to rely on who we *are* for direction in the sexual decisions we make. The failure to resolve sexual issues through the adoption of our own moral value system will spell trouble for those of us who would be sexual.

AM I BLUE? AM I PINK?

Another sexually-charged task of childhood and adolescence, which often beclouds adult sexual experience, is reaching some certainty about our sexual identities. Much has been said about androgyny, the possibility that in this day and age men and women should feel free to express both the masculine and feminine components of themselves. But in our society, as well as any other, the fact is that from the moment of birth boys and girls are socialized differently, in subtle and not so subtle ways. The blue world is filled with balls and bats and toy cars, the pink world with dolls and hopscotch and diaries. Young boys and girls are actually going about the business of finding out what people of their gender may or must do if they are to become bona fide males and females.

The task is probably harder for boys than for girls. They must come to learn to be ashamed of weakness in any form, to keep their feelings at bay, to pretend a confidence and an invulnerability which is not there. From their peers and older male role models they learn that real men are always eager for sex, must be sexually predatory, can perform on cue, and have a score of sexual conquests to their name. Even after they are assured enough in their sexual identities to become engrossed with females, their sexual repertoire seldom includes gentle passion, tenderness, permission to be a passive partner. As in other corners of their lives, *performance* defines their worth as males:

> I feel like I'm always supposed to be in the mood. It's a male thing. In our society it's okay for a woman to say No, but if a man says No, my God, what does that mean?

*

> The vast majority of men out there are assholes when it comes to personal relationships. They are unwilling to be intimate and sensitive to the way their partner feels.

*

> A man can just get turned on by looks.

*

> Men have to have it!

*

> Men are penis focused.

Girls likewise learn how to be pink and not blue, even though tomboys do not elicit the reactions of disgust and disdain that sissies do. In the pink world vulnerability is no shame, dependency can be overt, and the expression of feelings is typically allowed, if not encouraged, as long as they are the proper ones—not shouts of glee over coming out of a fight victorious or breaking the curve on a final exam. In the sexual domain, girls learn from their peers how to attract males and how, at the same time, to present the proper obstacles to the male's advances:

> I wasn't brought up to be the sexual aggressor. I was taught that men will do that, and that women who did that sort of thing were pushy, maybe not whores, but definitely too aggressive.

*

You were raised to please the male partner. This was just understood. You grew up, you got married, and you took care of your husband sexually. If you were good at it, he would stay home and not run around.

*

He'll complain, "All you do is lie there." And I'll say, "Yeah, but I grew up feeling like men were the ones who did more."

Although men may complain about their female partners' disinclination to make the first move, their disquietude typically emerges only after a considerable amount of time has passed in the sexual partnership. Initially, men tend to look with disfavor at women who do not adhere to their expected role:

Women who play hard to get definitely turn me on.

*

I find women who are upfront about wanting sex with me unattractive. I go for women who sit back and let me take the initiative.

*

It's important to me that she's a lady, reserved, not vulgar. I hate to see her in a vulgar position.

*

Any woman who's too loose or too forward can turn me off. I hate it when a woman's ready and willing for anything and everything. It makes her look cheap!

Above all, women are taught that the bona fide female is always capable of getting and keeping a male, and any lack of success in this regard can seriously shake their confidence. Sexual feelings, interests, and activities play a principal part in how males and females place themselves on the masculine-feminine continuum, and deviations from the norm can greatly affect how males and females see and value themselves. In every gesture in the sexual domain our core identity is at stake. Ironically, those of us who would be fully sexual must abandon stereotypically masculine or feminine roles, must disregard all we were ever taught about proper masculine or feminine behavior. Each sexual encounter includes the challenge of enlarging our sexual identities by shedding our accustomed selves and allowing ourselves to own up to the person we really are.

LOVE WITH THE PROPER STRANGER

Finally, complete sexuality requires us to love and be loved by another beyond the shelter of the family, a task which taps into the sexual dimensions of our personhood. The quality of welcome from our mothers long ago determined whether nurturance by another comforts or threatens us, which in turn permits us (or not) to own our needs for nurturance and to feel empathy towards another's needs. Any incapacities in this area can profoundly affect our sexual feelings, expectations, and conduct as adults. The quality of our early relationships with our parents spells the difference between experiencing others as competitors or friends and between viewing the world as boundless or highly limited in what it can offer us. It determines whether we become basically optimistic or pessimistic whenever we turn to others for care and comfort. If the love and welcome and respect we received as children were relatively unconditional, we are enabled to provide the same to others with whom we can now enjoy an intimate relationship. But if we sensed rejection or indifference in those past relationships, the chances are great that we shall remain forever wary in our dealings with others, in the sexual domain and elsewhere.

Beyond the family, our record of success and failure in love usually begins with a sense of belonging or not in a group of same-sex friends and with a best friend with whom we share loyalty and secrets. Such friendship lessens the loneliness we can feel as we venture farther out into the world. The process of developing love away from home goes on to include romantic attachments and fantasies, which ordinarily precede actual sexual experiences. These hold the promise of our never having to be alone despite our farewells to home and hearth, and even of the opportunity to receive what may have been withheld by our parents when we reached out to them; here we find the dream of fulfilling our longings, and embedded in the dream are sexual strivings.

In the sexual embrace we often feel the hope, rising up from deep within, that we shall finally be blessed to our core. All of us, to a greater or lesser degree, are casualties of a history that can make us question our own lovability and, therefore, our capacities to love. The sexual domain is where we can feel absolutely adored or utterly demeaned, depending on how we respond to or are responded to by our sexual partner. It is where the deepest and most important truths show themselves, in how love is meted out.

Sexual activity is inevitably accompanied by such profound and complex needs that it is unlikely there are any people with no sexual problems at all. In fact, I would suppose that anyone who reported otherwise is either too vain or too cowardly to tell the truth. Such a person has not gone far enough, has not paid the price required of those who would become increasingly autonomous, has not forged a value system that is truly his or her own, has faltered in the task of enlarging his or her sexual identity, and has chosen to remain remote from exchanges that might matter too much. Instead of welcoming sex as a crucible in which risks have the power to change their lives and advance their growth, such people maintain an only superficial ease in the sexual domain that too often represents an evasion and not an achievement.

UP AT THE SEXUAL HEIGHTS

Those persons, on the other hand, who truly inhabit the sexual heights to which all men and women are beckoned, have achieved far more than even they possibly realize. Although they may not have started out especially well-attuned, those on the heights have come to treasure their sexual partnership:

> I'm so glad we finally got it all together. We're now in a place we both like very much. I feel pretty joyful about it. It means a lot to me.

*

Our sex life is totally the way it should be. I wouldn't want it any different.

*

We both feel we've been fulfilled.

*

I'll have to get a pacemaker if it gets much better! There's no way to describe how intense it is.

*

Our sexual experiences have been sacred. We relate very well on a spiritual, mental, and emotional level.

*

Sometimes after orgasm it's like a "we" has been formed.

Those on the heights are candid about the passion they feel during a sexual exchange. They tend to revel in their sensuality; they are not secretive about their pleasure and do not recoil from it. They honor their need for the vitality they feel in a sexual exchange and proclaim being turned on as their right:

I just love feeling a penis inside me.

*

My whole skin becomes like a sensory organ.

*

I like to do special things for myself, like taking baths with wine and candles. Water really turns me on. I've had some pretty incredible experiences in a bathtub.

*

One day we tried to set a record for twenty-four hours. We had intercourse twelve times! I reached orgasm that many times, but by then my balls were falling off. She blew me four or five times that day. If I could, I'd have sex a hundred and fifty times a month!

On the sexual heights, turn-ons greatly outnumber turn-offs. Everywhere in the sexual domain, there are sensual delectations:

A great dick to hump . . . the way she wears jeans, her round butt . . . his power and strength . . . saying four letter words to each other . . . rubbing my cock over her teats . . . watching him reach orgasm . . . having her feel what she's never felt in her life . . . kissing her body, sucking on her breasts, kissing her earlobes, looking at her in the eyes . . . his youthful looks, his innocence . . . the sight and smell of his body . . . the sweat . . . calf muscles . . . being naked together . . . feeling cherished . . . being so close I can smell him . . .

Able to abandon themselves to the sexual moment, they seldom circumscribe their sexual repertoire. Their uncontained enthusiasm for exploration, disowning few impulses and disdaining the predictable, makes them excited by the prospect of new discoveries in the sexual domain:

It's been fun exploring oral sex.

*

He really thrives on having sex in different locations: in the moonlight on the patio, in the car driving down the highway, etc. Now he's wondering if he can do it on the treadmill!

*

I've always been big on variety. You name it: hanging from the chandelier, in the car, wherever. I'm not inhibited from that standpoint at all!

*

He thinks the vibrator is the neatest thing ever invented. I'll use it to bring him to orgasm. We joke about my getting it in the divorce settlement.

*

I really like semen. It's so exciting. It's so thick, it's just gorgeous. It smells good. To me, it's part of him.

Their lack of restriction extends to their fantasies as well:

Fantasizing is like permitting the wildest aspects of yourself to come out, that part of myself that is really free to be who I really am at the deepest level of my being. Just like intercourse is an opportunity to make sounds I wouldn't dream of making with anyone else.

Needless to say, those who allow themselves to be fully sexual put great importance on the sexual dimension of their lives:

> Sex seems to be a very important part of my well-being. If things aren't going well with my sex life, it puts a damper on just about everything else. When sex is good, I feel great.

> *

> Sex is central to my life right now. I certainly hope that will continue.

> *

> It means everything to me! Being able to achieve intimacy with someone you love through sexual union and mutual fulfillment is the most important thing in life other than eating, sleeping, and breathing. It ranks right up there with the basic human needs. It's one of the real imperatives in my life. We're working on our twenty-third year of marriage, and the prospects look brighter all the time.

> *

> I always say that in terms of the best things in life, sex comes first, in second place comes massage. Eating comes in third.

> *

> It's probably the most important part of our being together. It's the most "couple" thing we do.

Instead of sitting by as their sexual ardor begins to flicker, couples at the sexual heights take responsibility for their circumstances and actively pursue remedies to which those in the doldrums give only a passing glance:

> I think a woman has to be very responsible for keeping a little spice in a couple's sex life. Otherwise it gets very boring and very routine.

> *

> I decided two or three months ago that I was going to start sleeping in the nude from the waist up, because by husband is definitely a boob man. He loves boobs, mine mostly! If I'm in bed, he can't keep his hands off of them. I don't know what

made me do it. I guess I felt our sex life was really boring, that we were in a rut and that we needed to make some changes.

*

A lot of the inhibitions about oral sex have gone by the wayside on both our parts. We've done a lot of experiments with various sexual positions, have discussed our fantasies, have gone off on escape weekends. It's been a continually growing experience for us.

*

There are more times when I'm willing to try new things. We'll rent porno films and watch them and have a real good time. We'll dance with each other or I'll do a strip tease for him, or we'll put powder and lotion all over each other. We'll try all kinds of feeling and touching and doing things. We've had sex in the shower, in the woods, in a tub, in the caves, about anywhere. We'll try anything!

Two entirely different sorts of sexual lives have been portrayed here. There are the people, hesitant, passive, unimaginative, whose sexual lives on every count appear to have atrophied. Then there are those who insist on more and more from themselves and from their partnership, who respond with hope and confidence to the challenges of developing a vivacious relationship. How can we account for the contrast? Of course, some people have had unfortunate childhoods and some are better equipped than others to overcome intrapsychic obstacles. The nature of people's inner needs and conflicts may go far in determining quite different sexual outcomes. Nevertheless, the reasons why some people report a sexual abundance and others a sexual famine may also be found, as we shall see, in the nature of their partnerships, which can reflect and maintain, enhance or diminish, long-held convictions about the rightful place of sex in their lives.

Meanwhile, at the risk of proclaiming a cliche, I charge you to remember that human beings may be divided into two groups, no matter what context applies: those who make shift to keep going in the circumstances they find, and those who insist on looking for something better, something more; those who circumscribe them-selves ("I'm just not a warm person," "No, I don't like sailing, I've never been," "Learn French, at my age?"), and those who declare that they haven't yet had all the experiences they're going to; those who are resigned to life's penuries, and those who consider all setbacks temporary; those whose wishes and dreams are insurmountably barricaded, and those who are challenged by barricades; those who duck and those who dare.

Which person are you? Where in yourself can you detect the inclination to desert the dreams you once had and to then label yourself a realist? On the sexual realm, where have you given up? How fatalistically do you put up with your lot, settle for what is at least familiar, and congratulate yourself for nobly bearing it? There are other kinds of heroism. If you have the courage to risk changing your circumstances forever, you need to trust your vision of better times ahead even when they seem remote indeed. The bravery this requires may surprise you—not in how much it takes, but that you had it in you to muster.

Interlude:
Dorothea and Bill

Tearfully, Dorothea, the young, attractive woman seated on the couch, described, perhaps for the very first time, the darkness of her sexual domain. Over her ten-year marriage she had been humped on countless occasions, to her husband's delight but her own lonely despair. Despite her anguish over what was happening between herself and her husband, Bill, she had never sat with him as she was doing with me, had never even hinted at her daily disappointments and sense of isolation in their sexual forays. He had not had a clue as to her sexual whereabouts, nor had she ever given him a reason to care much about them. She was all too expert in suffering others' sexual predilections in silence, beginning with years of abuse by an uncle about whom she had complained in vain to a dismissive mother. Rescued from that household as a high school senior by Bill, who had even paid for her college and postgraduate education, she had been grateful for his intervention and, as it turned out, for his eagerness to take charge of her life.

The fact that she was now here, sharing deeply all her discontent, meant that something about her circumstances had begun to change. The fact that she sat ready to face the extent of her alienation from Bill and to express her grave dissatisfaction with what had become so predictable between them, in bed and elsewhere, was evidence of that change. To be sure, she was meeting with me in secret, so that he should get no idea that she was unhappy, but it was a start. She wanted more for herself than she had ever dared to hope for, with an insistence she would never have dreamed possible.

Her hunger for more was, it transpired, enacted in her growing enthrallment with Josh, a colleague of her husband's, whose attentiveness was a novelty to her. She'd begun to share feelings with him she had not even known were there. And he listened as if he were a trained counselor. There were telephone calls, and in the absence of contact, daydreams and irrepressible fantasies of him, fed by the goings-on of a husband not only oblivious to her needs and yearnings but a deliberate stranger to his own as well. There was no room for romance in his life. Sex, to Bill, was an itch you scratched, hand-holding a sexual-pursuit technique to be resorted to only when the quarry demanded it. The contrast between him and his attractive colleague was so marked, and Dorothea's unfulfilled needs were so pronounced, that she had begun to question the viability of her marriage and finally to share her doubts with her husband, who was both confused and amazed.

After our first meeting, she sent this letter:

Dr. Bell,
Enclosed please find payment for our meeting.

Thank you for all your help. I truly feel that our meeting went very well. I felt very comfortable talking with you. Your understanding and empathy were very reassuring.

I only wish I could continue to see you. However, when I told [Bill] I had met with you, he became quite upset because I had seen you without telling him. This is very uncharacteristic of our relationship. But I think he was even more disturbed that I'd consulted a marriage counselor at all.

This is a very complex situation. As I told you in our meeting, [Bill] holds very little respect for psychologists. He believes very strongly that psychologists "talk too much and put their own values, words, and ideas in your head." No matter what is said, he absolutely *REFUSES* to see a psychologist for any reason, and basically "forbids" me to see one, too.

So I asked him if he would be willing to consult a *psychiatrist* for counseling. He said he'd be more likely to do so, but he doesn't feel we need any counseling.

I sense that he is afraid to lose some sort of control if someone else were to "interfere" (as he puts it) in our marriage. [Bill] has always been very concerned with power and control in all aspects of his life.

The power he holds over me has become quite clear (and unsettling) lately. His refusal to see anyone to try to help our marriage is a prime example. He says we can "do it ourselves."

Recently when I brought something up that he found upsetting, he got very angry. He said if I was going to do things to make him angry, he would do the same to me. So he got on the phone to cancel my reservations for a trip I had planned with my cousin. At that point I was so hurt and couldn't quite believe what was going on (in the immediate situation and in my life in general) so I told him I was going for a walk.

I had barely gotten a block away when he pulled up and said I had to come home because he had to go to work and I had to stay home with the baby. I walked back home, and as I walked up the driveway I was horrified to see him with the hood of my car up, trying to disable it so I couldn't go anywhere while he was away.

I felt so angry and controlled at that point, I had no idea what to think or to say. He said he did it because he doesn't trust me lately, citing my meeting with you without telling him as a prime example of my "acting weird lately." I can understand that, in a way. I *have* been different lately. But I think he should take that as an indication that we *DO* need some help.

I even told him that I'm not so sure how much I love him anymore. He just reminded me that he loves me more than anything and that "things will be just fine."

Meanwhile, my feelings for [Josh] are becoming more intense as I become more unhappy with [Bill]. But that situation is very complicated, and I should end this letter now. It's really too long.

I appreciate all you've done. Perhaps I will get to see you again. Thank you.

[Dorothea]

Two weeks passed. Then Dorothea left a message on my voice mail, asking me to meet with Bill. He wanted to check me out before giving her permission to see me. He wanted to be sure that I had the proper credentials. Restraining an impulse to tell her that my credentials were impeccable but that such a meeting would probably come to naught, I arranged for an appointment time.

The man who greeted me, with his little daughter in tow, was a giant. I had resolved not to try to sell him on the idea of therapy and, in fact, to warn him away from it. Instead, we talked, or rather he did. I found myself surprised and strangely touched by his straightforwardness. He admitted to not being emotionally expressive. He was not one given to compliments. He was no expert at intimacy, he said, and he had a lot to learn. He described himself as a take-charge individual who needed to be in control. That is, he described himself just as his wife had described him, but without the antipathy toward counseling or toward me that she had related. In my notes I later described him as a "bear of a man but much more like a confused little puppy". He said he would okay my meeting with his wife and set up an appointment with her for the next week.

At the appointed time not only did she show up but he did as well, and the baby too. They had brought a video for her to watch, which completely absorbed her while her parents reported that they had done a lot of talking since I met with him. She had told him firmly that things needed changing, that there could no longer be sex for the sake of sex, that she needed more hugs from him outside the bedroom, and compliments besides. He, on the other hand, reported his jealousy and resentment over her tête-à-têtes at parties with Josh; he declared that she had never been direct with him, and that when she said they had "never made love," he didn't know what in the world she was *talking* about!

They returned the questionnaires they took home to fill out in record time. Their responses confirmed what they had said in my office. The Personality Research Form, one part of the questionnaire, showed him to be more outgoing than she, more autonomous, and more aggressive, while she appeared to be something of a pushover, passive and apologetic in her interactions with others. The Marital Satisfaction Inventory, also part of the questionnaire, showed her to be much less happy in the marriage than he was. They agreed that he should be head of the household and that her major role should be that of housekeeper and parent. In the sexual arena, I was not surprised to find, she reported that she engaged in sex with him primarily because he expected it, because he initiated it, and to meet his needs. For him sex meant primarily a relief from sexual and physical tension, *never* an opportunity to draw close to her, and hardly ever a way for him to express love. Each was well aware of the other's principal motivations and not at all pleased about it. Although he had already begun to change (making her wonder how to respond or what to believe), he reported finding foreplay boring and wanting even less afterplay—when it was almost nonexistent anyway.

In a letter that accompanied her questionnaire, Dorothea amplified the problems she was experiencing in her sexual partnership, in her marriage, and in Bill's changing behaviors:

> I found it difficult at times to fill out the answers to some of these questions. My answers to some questions would have been different before [Bill] and I really started discussing the issues between us. Although it is great that we are making the effort to improve our relationship, I tended to answer a lot of the questions based on how I was feeling in the last year or so rather than the present because all these changes are so recent. I haven't had time to adjust or fully accept them as "our relationship." Also, the feelings expressed in my responses seem to more adequately reflect how I arrived at the disappointment, neglect, and hurt I have experienced.
>
> The other issue for me was that I knew [Bill] would be looking at my answers. I told him I thought it was important that we not share our answers, but he can't stand not knowing. I was so pleased that he'd agreed to even fill the questionnaire out, I didn't want to "make waves" and risk his getting so angry that he wouldn't fill out the questionnaire. I knew he'd get tremendously hurt and/or angry if I answered some of these questionnaires honestly. As a matter of fact, when he saw my answer indicating I may have *considered* having an affair at some point in our relationship, it really confused and hurt him. He really grilled me!
>
> Finally, many of the questions regarding *SEX* were difficult

to answer because I felt there is a vast difference between simply engaging in intercourse for physical pleasure and actually "making love," which involves sharing intimacy between two people. For the majority of our relationship, [Bill] and I have experienced a mutually enjoyable *physical* relationship. We have been very much in tune to what turns each other on in order to achieve orgasm. In fact, it had become so mechanical to me that if I was given proper "warning" I could almost always insure our reaching mutual orgasm.

But so much more would have helped me feel closer to [Bill] . . . if we'd had any kind of emotional intimacy. I wasn't sure how these questions should be answered. If I rated our *physical* sex on a 1–10 scale, I would easily give it an 8+. But there has been absolutely 0 in the emotional scale until now.

I look forward to meeting with you to discuss your findings and ideas. I hope to hear from you very soon to schedule our next meeting.

Thanks!

[Dorothea]

Ten days later he called and came in by himself. He was in a state of shock upon discovering a cache of love poems, fantasies, and unmailed letters to Josh. What could he do? Could he ever trust her again? Two days later, when we met again, his mood had not changed. She should be punished! She does not find me special! She has started pointing out all my inadequacies! I've been betrayed! I want revenge! On the same day, when I saw her alone, she reported relief that her feelings were now out in the open but distress that she had been so careless in leaving her notes and journals around for him to see. She went on to discuss other issues: her undue dependency on Bill, how she has held in her dissatisfactions, her dislike of his using withdrawal for birth control, her failure to express her needs for emotional contact during sexual exchanges, how she has felt like a sperm receptacle, how sex had become so routine—"ten minutes from beginning to end"—and how disgusting she found it when "he'd spit on his hand to provide a lubricant and just push his penis in." Their need for better communication was, as she put it, a "no brainer".

Before leaving, she reported what was an additional source of stress: she was pregnant.

The next day I had another individual session with Bill. We went over some of the answers he had given to the questionnaire, and he reported that in the past he had had many negative experiences with women, all of them devoid of intimacy. Why did he use withdrawal for birth control? "Because I like it. I got that idea from all the pornography I watched. I like to see how far I can ejaculate, and I like her to see it too." As far as his sex drive was concerned, he would have liked sex three or four times a day plus occasional masturbation: "She doesn't like it when I masturbate. It makes her feel inadequate, so I do it on the sly. Sometimes she'll catch me doing it like my mother did!" Fantasies? "Of women who wear leather. They are strong and dominant and talk dirty." Intimacy? "If I get too close to her, I lose sexual interest and eventually my erection. I've always made love with my eyes closed. There was never any kissing. Perhaps it was because otherwise I'd feel too vulnerable."

Slowly but surely their cards were being put on the table. Unpleasant truths were being shared. Her anger born of fear and his anger born of confusion were on full display. Out of this cauldron, six days later, came a big surprise: they had just gone to Las Vegas to renew their wedding vows, in a ceremony that felt more real and exhilarating than the original one. Less surprising were his complaints, continued from before their optimistic flight to Nevada, that she was hard to pin down and not given to expressing her sexual wants or feelings. He was still furious over her romantic designs, asking sometimes whether he was the father of the unborn child, and given to vengeful fantasies. Her sexual reticence, misgivings, and uncertainties remained on the front burner with her growing demand that he not be so accusatory in their frequent discussions. She was beginning to speak up. Setting out her feelings and reactions and her truest and clearest need of all, that sexual contact be continued with intimacy, was her permanent concern.

This is where things stood when I had them come in to process, individually, their last sexual exchange. The purpose of this was to identify their thoughts and feelings, their reactions to each other, what was figure versus ground every step along the way, from beginning to end. To what did they attribute their own and their partner's behavior? What were their expectations? What were their principal concerns? What motivations could be detected in their stories of what transpired? What issues needed to be addressed during our remaining sessions? How could their priorities and differences be summarized? On the basis of detailed questioning, I would now be in a far better position to help direct our focus and to recommend strategies that promise to clear the air and set a new direction for their sexual partnership. A lot of progress had been made in barely three months. Who would have thought that, given the gravity of their difficulties and history of deeply entrenched and bitterly destructive patterns, more than a little hope would finally emerge?

BILL'S VERSION

Did you have any idea that a sexual exchange would take place?

I thought there was a possibility, because earlier in the day we'd been talking a lot about things, said a couple of sexual things to each other. She was more receptive to touching, things like that.

How did you know she was more receptive?

I could tell by the expressions on her face. Sometimes I can tell when she's not feeling well. If I touch her back or her shoulders, she'll pull away a little bit. She wasn't doing that. In fact we were sitting on the couch together an hour earlier and she laid her legs up across me. Then she pulled my leg up and was touching it. I thought something could happen a little later.

Why did you think she might be up for it then?

I guess I was really *hoping* that was the case. We'd both been in a pretty positive mood all day. If there's any sort of disagreement during the day I know that sex is out of the question. She'll have no interest in sex or intimacy. If I approach her, she'll say, "Why do you want to *touch* me if you're upset with me?" I'll tell her we can have a disagreement, but that doesn't mean we don't still love each other. Yesterday it had been all very positive. Also, recently, most of our sex has taken place around noontime. She gets real tired in the evenings and wants to go to sleep. Right before noon she usually feels pretty good.

In the morning I'd complimented her on her breasts, and she was real happy about that. She said they were feeling really big. I was also rubbing her legs, and I told her they needed to be shaved. She said, "Would you like to shave them for me?" As we talked, I sensed there was a possibility.

She went up into the bedroom and I could tell she might want to take a nap or might want a sexual exchange. I wasn't quite sure. Then I went up there and I could tell she wasn't sure if she was going to or not.

How could you tell?

She talked to me directly with her eyes open. I think we kissed a couple of times. But then she said she was getting a little tired. I wasn't quite sure how to interpret that. Then I lay down next to her and asked her if I could kiss her, if she felt okay with that. She said, that's great! So I started kissing her, and she said, I don't know if I'm really in the mood right now. But she kept kissing and touching. Then she went into the bathroom a couple of minutes later, and I was thinking I guess she *does* want to, and she's going there to clean herself up or something. But I wasn't quite sure. She came back out and laid down next to me. She said, maybe we could try for you to come by me stroking you, you could come that way. I told her that would be okay.

Why is she saying that?

Maybe she didn't want a full sexual exchange. She was a little tired. She also might have been a little sore because we'd had full-fledged sex twice a day before.

How did her offer to stroke you make you feel?

I felt maybe she doesn't really want to do this, and I wasn't too excited about the whole thing. I kept kissing her a little bit, and then she told me she'd really tuned in! I'd been kissing her breasts. She also told me that all day she'd wanted me inside her!

A total turnaround! I thought this could be one of two things. It could be she was really hot or that she was just trying to satisfy me because she knows I want more than just her stroking me. But I tried to take it as she's just really hot. She seemed it, because when I went down to touch her she was really well lubricated. I know when she's not she could be lying to me. Then we might have to use lubrication or something.

If you think she might be lying to you because she wants to please you, how does that make you feel?

If I have the feeling she's putting on an act I have a hard time orgasming during intercourse and before we started I won't be so excited as I'd normally be. I still go for it, though. She usually gets into it some, or at least I *think* she gets into it some when we get going into the actual lovemaking session. I can tell at the beginning when she's not ready. Maybe I do a good job of turning her on. So I don't feel real good up front because I don't know if she's really into it or just trying to please me.

What do you do when you're really turned on?

I just keep working on her until she seems turned on. Usually if I touch her breasts or her neck or perform oral sex on her she'll usually start getting into it after a little while. She's usually excited by any type of oral sex and starts feeling okay with it.

What's the matter with her wanting to accommodate you? You're her husband. She loves you, wants to please you. Why is that a turn-off?

I want to be desired as much as I'm desiring her. Otherwise I just feel I'm being serviced by somebody, no different from an exchange with a prostitute. More a matter of obligation, just to make me happy, but it doesn't. During this exchange I feel okay, but afterwards it's not a positive thing. I can sense a lot of times when she does that. Sometimes maybe I can't. Maybe twenty percent of the time she's not really into it. I can't tell if she really gets into it *while* we're going on with it or just . . . That's one of the tough things with her. I don't know if it takes me touching her a lot to get her aroused and into the whole sexual exchange, or if it's that I keep going with it and she starts just *acting* like she's excited. So when she tells me, "I'm not sure if I want to or not," then I'm saying to myself, "Is that because she's not adequately aroused or does she flat out not want it?" It takes usually five or ten minutes for her to become aroused, with deep kissing, touching her breasts, oral sex.

On this particular occasion you find that she is moist.

I was surprised. Usually she wants a lot of foreplay.

Why?

I just recently found out from her that she needs more foreplay to become adequately aroused, then when we have intercourse she feels good about it. She hates it when I rush into it because she feels I'm just trying to get it over with and move on. I understand that. It doesn't bother me. I even *like* having a lot of foreplay. It just extends the whole time. But I really never knew that before. She never told me that. I don't require a lot of foreplay for arousal.

How about emotionally, to feel more in synch?

It was really good that last time. We talked at the beginning. At first I was just trying to figure out if she was really interested or not, but then when she said she was, I told her how good that made me feel. I hadn't realized it, but she really likes it when I express myself verbally during sex, when I say things I'm thinking. Now I'll tell her when I feel love for her. I tell her when she's looking beautiful. It really gets her aroused. It makes her feel *wonderful*. I can tell by her expressions. She'll moan louder. She'll climax very quickly after I say these kinds of things. For instance we were really talking a lot at the beginning, and she said, "I've got to get on top of you right now! But I better not because I'll orgasm right away if I do." So she wanted intercourse laying on our sides.

Why is she concerned about reaching orgasm right away?

Once she orgasms it starts to hurt her a little bit. Penetration starts to hurt after she's reached orgasm, not so much before.

Are you concerned about her feeling pain?

I really am. When she was pregnant the last time, I was always concerned about that. I never knew how fast I could go or how deep I could penetrate.

Why is she in pain?

I'm really not quite sure *what* it is. She says my penis hits against her cervix. My penis is of average size, but certain kinds of positions bother her. I'm never quite sure. She wants intercourse to be slow. If motions are too quick, she starts to get sore afterwards.

So she was concerned that if she jumped on top of you and reached orgasm, the rest might be painful for her?

I guess that was what it was. That's what I read into it. I told her we didn't want her reaching orgasm now, because I knew she wouldn't want to continue. So we both lay sideways facing each other. I left my penis inside her but didn't move back and forth, and we talked a little bit.

How aroused were *you* feeling at that point?

I was feeling pretty aroused. When there's penetration I start feeling very aroused.

That's changed.

Yes, because I found out that if I go really slowly, then it doesn't hurt her as bad. So I was going very slowly. Five years ago I couldn't control myself. After five minutes there was no way I could keep from ejaculating unless I had some drinks in me. *Now* I can go twenty, thirty minutes. I know when I need to slow down. I pay more attention to that than I did.

What do you think she's feeling as you lay there together, side by side?

I think she's feeling emotionally really good, because we are talking a lot to each other.

What are you talking about?

How good it feels. I tell her how I love her, how she makes me so happy. She's telling me the same kinds of things. We're holding each other, kissing, soft contact. She prefers gentle kissing to deep-kissing.

What do you think of that?

I wasn't sure what that was all about at first. I think she sees deep-kissing as intensely sexual. Before whenever I kissed her it was a hard kind of thing, more because it would arouse me. So she likes soft, gentle kissing, only light tongue touching.

And that's what you are doing: feeling close, talking, touching, a wonderful connection. Then what happens?

Then I rolled her over on top of me.

Why did you decide to do that?

I guess because the penetrations was not deep enough. I was getting tired of just laying there.

How do you think she feels about your pulling her on top of you?

I sort of sensed she was getting really aroused when we were talking. She'd already talked about wanting to be on top earlier. I really like seeing her on top of me, especially with the new big breasts. I can also see her face a lot better.

What do you see in her face?

I see her eyes, and I can tell if she's really excited or not. When her eyes are a little squinted, I can tell she's really enjoying herself. But when her eyes are wide open, she looks as though she's distracted and not really into it.

Are you always looking with your eyes open?

Yes, I like looking at her face, seeing that she's excited by it. Also looking at her breasts. I also like looking at the actual penetration.

And what is she doing?

She's usually holding my hips or my shoulders. She prefers going quickly back and forth with her clitoris brushing me. That makes her reach orgasm quickly. That doesn't excite me too much. I prefer the up and down motion. So we kind of go counter to each other on that. So she started back and forth, and I pushed her back a little bit by her hips. Then she started going up and down for me.

How concerned are you about doing it her way versus your way?

I get concerned about doing it her way because I think she'll reach orgasm real quickly.

What if she does?

I get concerned because then we'll stop. I'll have to orgasm very quickly. If I don't, it starts getting painful to her, and I'll worry if I'm hurting her, and it doesn't get exciting at all.

Who's supposed to reach orgasm first?

We usually do it at the same time. We generally coordinate it. About 99% of the time we reach it at the same time.

What was that like yesterday?

We rolled back over again, in the missionary position. I asked her if she'd like to do this, and she said she would. She'd reached a small orgasm. She generally has a series of small orgasms or else one big one. She had a small one because she didn't want to reach a big one. She was on her back. I got on top. There was a lot of kissing.

What do you anticipate happening?

If she lifted her legs up high enough I could get stimulated enough to reach orgasm. I wanted to see if I could reach orgasm without deep thrusting. I actually could this time. I could sense she was really into the exchange. When she's really into it, I can come really easily. I don't have to rely on deep penetration or on fantasies. Otherwise I have to.

So you were not fantasizing yesterday?

No, just about the two of us. We weren't talking too much at the time, but then she told me she loved me. I told her I was close to orgasm, and she reached down and started rubbing herself.

How did you feel about that?

I like that, actually. It turns me on sometimes.

What do you like about that?

She's being more aggressive. She's looking to please herself. She's not doing things just for my benefit! She's not doing it to excite me. She doesn't even know it does.

As I'm reaching orgasm I tell her I love her. We're looking at each other. Then she has another smaller orgasm, and I continue penetrating her really slowly, in and out. We talk about how fantastic it feels. Then I roll off to the side.

I can never tell how long I should stay inside her afterwards. She never communicates that to me. When I pull out, she'll moan, as if she's disappointed. I'm not sure if it's physical or if she just wanted me to stay inside her. I've never asked her.

Why would she be disappointed?

Not quite sure. I think that when I stay inside afterwards she feels I didn't have sex with her just because I wanted to ejaculate. The purpose was not just for me to get off. It was more for an intimate connection. I'm not sure if I'm right or not. I figure if I withdraw and just lay there and keep touching her she'll be okay with that. I've asked her, but she never gives me a direct answer. She'll say, "Well, you have to get off me sometime." She's great at giving the signals, but I can never be sure I'm interpreting them correctly.

What would be a signal?

Her moaning. Does it mean she didn't like my moving off her? I can't be sure.

Why are you concerned about her seeing you as using sex to get off?

I never knew it was so important to her until we starting coming here and talked about these things. Once I saw where she was coming from, it became a big concern to me. I want to make sure she's happy with our sexual exchanges. I really want to please her. I don't want to have sex for the sake of making *myself* happy. I want *both* of us to enjoy ourselves. I can't be happy unless *she's* happy. Now I'm sensing she is. So afterwards, even if a small displeasure creeps in for her, I can't be perfectly satisfied. I'll feel I've let her down. I'm the kind of person who wants people to think I'm a guy who does everything right. Not everybody. Only those people I care about.

If you disappointed her in some way, how do you think she'd view you? How unhappy would she be? How good does it have to be for her for you to feel good?

I have to feel it was an outstanding experience for her, not just an average kind of thing.

What criteria do you use to determine that?

Now I have different criteria. Before, it was her reaching orgasm and it was intense and we both reached orgasm at the same time. That was it! Now, I need to see by the expression on her face that she's really happy, not just a pleasure kind of thing, but that she's *emotionally* happy. I can tell if that's the case if she gets red in the face. That really makes me feel great, that flush or blush. Now I look for that kind of a signal. I don't put as much on the orgasm as I did before.

Before you get off you're not sure it's been special?

She tells me she used to feel like a prostitute. I don't want her to feel I'm just using her. I try to show her that *she's* the one who turns me on, not just some generic woman who could be in the room with me. I'm trying hard to convince her of that, even though she'll fight me on that. She'll say, "Physically you'll rate me as an 8, not a 10! If an 8 came into this room, she could substitute for me quite satisfactorily! Why would I be different from her?

How does that make you feel?

Really lousy. Like I haven't adequately expressed myself. She really requires a lot of me convincing her. If I give her a compliment, she'll say, "Oh, I'm still fat." And I have to keep trying to convince her. When she was sitting here with us the other day, I was saying to her, "Well you're only six pounds heavier than you were before." But she'll answer, "But I feel so fat!" She does that about everything.

Yesterday, when you moved off her, how did you know what she was feeling? How did you know if the exchange had been special?

I was nervous. When I withdrew, she moaned a little bit. But then as we lay next to each other, she said how fantastic it had been. Then she said something that surprised me: "Tonight I thought about acting out a fantasy with you." There are two things she wants to do. Number one, she wants to pretend that she's just this high school girl, and I'm this older man who will teach her the ways of sexuality. The other one is, we'll act as if it's the first time we ever met and we're nervous about things.

Will you do this?

Yeah. Whenever she tells me what she'd like to do, I'll really jump on that! That's a very rare event.

How was your sexual exchange concluded?

She usually gets up and goes to urinate right afterwards. It used to bother me a little bit. I wasn't sure if she was just cleaning herself out or what. I used to like it when we were first together to just sit there afterwards, and we'd talk. We weren't worried about how messy we were. But apparently her doctor told her to do it to avoid infections. She gets infections rather easily.

So were you bothered yesterday?

She *did* stay longer than she usually does. She stayed about ten minutes.

What would it have meant to you had she stayed even longer?

Ten minutes was a big step. Usually it is only a minute or two.

What's the difference between a minute or ten minutes?

I really like it if we lay there afterwards and talk about things. I like for her to tell me what she liked and didn't like. She likes kissing then and not so much talking. She usually doesn't like to go on record about what she liked and didn't like.

So when she gets up to go to the bathroom, is it over then?

Yeah, the whole thing is finished. She puts her panties on and gets dressed.

How did you feel yesterday when you knew it was finished?

I used to value the times when we'd wake up in the morning and be together in bed for an hour or two hours and just talk. That's when we were in college. It felt great to me. Now that we have a baby, it becomes impossible to do that, in the mornings especially. I felt this was a time we could do that kind of thing.

How are you feeling about yourself?

Pretty good. Actually, really good. She'd talked about acting out her fantasies. I figured this must have been pretty good for her to be excited about doing something else later on in the day. That's been *extremely* rare!

How do you think *she* was feeling?

Good about things. Probably not as good as I was feeling.

Why would you think that?

Not sure. I'm not perfect at reading her. I just felt when she got up to go to the bathroom she was not feeling as good as I. Otherwise she'd have wanted to stay there.

How were you feeling about your partnership?

I thought it is changing for the positive. That's really nice. I told her I feel fantastic when we make love that way now. She said, "Well maybe we shouldn't do my fantasy later. I don't think of it as intimate lovemaking." I told her it would be perfectly fine. It's like the roles have been reversed! I was the one who used to ask her to act out my fantasies while she would want intimacy!

How do you credit yourself for all the progress you've made?

Before, I didn't really know about intimacy. I'd never experienced it with sex. I'd thought of sex as a means to feel good, feeling good from ejaculating. Most of my impressions of sex came from talking with friends or from having sex with women I'd only known a day or two or from watching pornographic movies.

How could you make this transformation so rapidly?

I don't know. I'm doing a lot of reading. I'm asking her questions. She's not much help there since she's not sure about what she wants or needs. I have to find out what women in general report needing, what they want out of sex, and then try those kinds of things with her and see if she responds positively. That's the only way I've been able to do that. I keep a mental list of all the things I read. One of them was verbalizing what you're thinking. That seemed to work really well with her. Other things too. She never let me know. When I asked her to show me what she wanted in a sexual exchange, she said, "If I have to tell you, then it's not coming from you!" So I got frustrated with that. Part of it is she's not quite sure what she wants but is not confident enough to share that with me. I think she needs self-confidence more than anything else. No one in her family took pride in themselves.

You'll have a big part to play in that!

The new way is the way I want to have sex. When we have sex for the sake of sex, my mind wanders. It doesn't feel good. I picture her with others. Yesterday I felt a real strong connection between us.

DOROTHEA'S VERSION

I'll ask you to think about yesterday. When did you have an inkling that there would be a sexual exchange?

I'd say just a couple of minutes before it actually started. I'd not been feeling well that morning, and I was trying to take a nap. We were just lying in bed together, thinking we'd sleep. Then the phone rang. It woke me up. I was almost asleep. When I was fully awake, I thought, "I'm feeling pretty good." I wasn't feeling nauseous.

What had gone on downstairs? Had there been any contact?

No, he wasn't even home. I put the baby in bed for her nap and went to lay down. Just minutes after that he came home. I was already in bed, trying to take a nap.

Do you remember how you felt when you heard the key in the door?

I was happy he was home. One thing that popped into my mind was I hoped he wouldn't go in the baby's room and wake her up. He did, though. He was in a good mood and walked right into her room. She wasn't asleep yet and wanted him to stay and play with her.

At that point you wanted to sleep?

Yeah. I was half asleep. I'd been in bed for about ten minutes. He came into the room and lay down next to me and asked me how I was feeling. We just lay there. Then the telephone rang. He got the phone and came back to bed. By that time I was awake.

What were you thinking at that point?

I'm feeling okay. So let's do it.

Why?

The baby was asleep. We were alone. I was feeling okay. Lately that's been a time for us to get together for intercourse.

What were you thinking *he* was thinking?

I don't think he was thinking we were going to have sex, since I told him I'd not been feeling well. So when I suggested it, then he was surprised and happy. And he agreed to do it.

Why were you suggesting it just then?

I didn't want to take the chance that I wouldn't be feeling well later. He's made it pretty clear lately that he'd like to have sex every single day, and I might otherwise have blown a chance for that particular day. It's not that I didn't want to, so I said, "Let's do it." I wasn't nauseous anymore.

How did you feel about having that window of opportunity, that you could function again?

It felt great! I have fun too. It's not just for him. It wasn't that I was thinking to myself, "I'm excessively horny!", but rather that once I got into it, it would be fun.

Why did you think that?

That's how I *always* think about it. I don't sit there all day thinking how horny I am and that I have to have sex right now. I never think that. That's why it takes him to start things. It's not in my brain.

How did he initiate it?

I told him I was having a craving for something, for pizza but for something else too. And I laughed. He got happy. I think I took off my pants. This is so embarrassing! He told me lately he has a "foot thing," a fetish, so I told him, "Do you want to fool around with my feet?" So that's what it was gonna be, a first. I asked him if it would help to take off his clothes. He said it would help if I got totally naked. So I did. We started kissing, and then he took off his clothes.

What are you thinking about his foot fetish?

I think it's fun. So I offered that yesterday. We started kissing.

How does that feel?

It was just soft kissing, not a lot of tongue.

What is there about deep kissing?

Unless the sex is really intense, I'd rather just be soft. I'd rather it be gentle, not so involved, not so sexual when we're not into that yet. Later on it's okay. But I still don't like a lot of it. So we were kissing.

What were you feeling? Is he kissing you or are you kissing him?

Sort of mutual. He was kissing me more. We were lying side by side facing each other. It felt good. It was nice. It was close. One thing I remember through the exchange yesterday was that there was a *lot* of eye contact.

Is that atypical?

Not so much lately, but there seemed to be more.

What's good about that?

I like it because it sort of lets me see how he's feeling. We don't talk a whole lot during intercourse. I like to see if he's happy and enjoying it and having a good time.

What were you sensing yesterday?

I think he was happy that I had sort of initiated it. It made him feel good about himself and about us together.

I wonder what it was like for you to tell him that you craved sex.

I put it in sort of a joking way, and he laughed.

Does that mean he was a little uncomfortable?

Probably. I don't know I've ever come right out and said that kind of thing to him. As I said, that's not what I think, not a part of my thinking, that we have to do it now.

Are you saying you *could* crave? You're not really craving sex.

That's true. I was just feeling good and knew I'd enjoy it. But if we hadn't, I could have gone back to sleep. Which is not so good. He probably wouldn't have taken it in a positive way. He might think I didn't want sex with him, period! His feelings would have been hurt.

And how much would that have bothered you?

I don't *want* to hurt his feelings. But I know that sometimes when I don't want sex, I *do* hurt his feelings. He feels rejected. I don't do it for that reason.

Were you relieved that since you were feeling well, you had this opportunity?

I was happy.

What makes the noontime better?

The baby is in bed and asleep. At night I'm too tired. In the mornings she wakes *us* up.

So what happens next?

We're on our sides facing each other. I wrap my leg around him. We start rubbing our genitals together.

What are you thinking and feeling then?

I'm aroused.

What's arousing?

The closeness. I could tell he was really happy. It felt good to see him like that. Just to be kissing, nice and gently. The physical part was our rubbing our genitals together. That was arousing. We did that for a *while*. I'd say five minutes or so. There was no penetration. His penis was barely there.

What was nice about the closeness?

There was a lot of looking in his eyes. He was smiling. I could tell he was feeling good. When he's like that, it makes me feel good, especially now.

You say that with a lot of feeling!

I hurt him so much. I want to get beyond it and be good together. I know lately that the days we have intercourse, it's better. He usually comments after that he felt good, that he felt I really wanted him and no one else. It's a big ego thing. He needs reassurance.

So you proceeded.

After a while he sort of put me on top of him. We'd reached the point where we were ready to get on with something else.

What were you doing to arouse him and vice versa?

Just the kissing and rubbing our genitals together.

How aroused were you feeling?

Very. I might have been rubbing him too.

What does sexual arousal feel like to you?

I don't crave it, like I said, but once I experience it I *love* it! Physically there's an excited feeling. Emotionally, especially lately, it's reassuring, because I know he finds me attractive. He's said that a lot lately, thinks my breasts are great. It's really nice to hear.

Do you believe it?

Yeah, because I *know* my breasts are large, huge! I have a hard time believing when he says stuff like how beautiful my body is. I feel fat around the hips.

Any other compliments?

He compliments my mothering a lot. We don't talk too much during sex.

How come?

Probably because of the lack of intimacy we've had until now. It was just a physical thing: get in, get out, get it over with. We'd established that pattern over many years. So it's hard to get into talking. We never said, "I love you," over all those years. Now we do, which is *nice*. It seems to get him off when we say that kind of thing. He really gets aroused. I remember trying early on to say "I love you," when we were first dating. Nothing happened so I gave up.

So who started saying these things?

I think *he* did. I didn't want to try it again. I gave up and just let it be.

So now you're talking, but not as much as he. How do you explain that?

I'm still uncomfortable with the idea of talking during sex. Before, the only time we would talk during sex over all the years was when we'd say something dirty, to get the other person aroused. I wasn't truly comfortable with that but he'd get off on it!

Why would you be concerned about saying something that was gentle and endearing?

I'd be afraid he would not acknowledge it, that I'd get no response at all! That would make me feel stupid. I'd have said something that was meaningful to me but not to him. I'm trying to get more bold. It's been such a habit. I'm so afraid of getting squashed. Now I know he's more sensitive.

What was the boldest thing you said yesterday?

I'm not sure I said anything really bold. Probably how I liked his butt and enjoyed holding it. It was true. Usually I'll feel something but never say it.

How do you think he responded?

He sort of smiled. He's not used to this either. All we've said is dirty talk.

What is "dirty" like for you?

When sex is just physical that's how it was. Nothing to make me feel good about myself or what was going on or about him. I've always told Bill that sex for the sake of sex is fine every once in a while. A quickie. I'm not a total prude. But when it's the majority of your interaction, it's no good.

How did you want it to be yesterday?

Just somewhere in between: five minutes of foreplay, ten or fifteen minutes in intercourse, and some cuddling afterwards.

Why did you want somewhere in the middle?

I didn't want it to be long and involved because I was still tired. But I didn't want a quickie either. I wanted something more meaningful than that, not too rushed.

How do you think all those quickies affected you?

It made me feel it was just a pure physical thing. After a long time I sort of wondered, Why does he have to do it with *me*? He could do that with anybody. Nothing special about it, between *us*. But I figured the fact we were married legally, he should stay here with me. It was nothing that we shared, nothing beautiful. I would certainly never tell my girl friend about it. It was empty, but it was *fun*! I told him, physically it was *fine*. So I didn't complain. It was fun. And I figured that's the way he was and that it could not be changed.

No wonder you had your affair! You were desperate for more!

He doesn't want to hear me say that. He doesn't want me to justify what I did.

He knows he failed you emotionally.

But at the same time I should have communicated this to him. I did try to hint at it. When we'd see something in a movie, I'd say, "Oh, isn't that nice!" or "I wonder if people really do that!" He'd just laugh and say, "No."

So yesterday, how did that go? Were you orgasmic? Where did orgasms fit in?

I recently figured out how to have orgasms easily. When I'm on top. For a long time I didn't get it, because he would still control the pace even when I was on top. I'd read all kinds of articles about how this was the easiest way for a woman to reach orgasm because she was in control. I used to manipulate myself, but now I don't have to. I can reach orgasm at the same time as him. Part of me was afraid he felt inadequate because he couldn't bring me to orgasm. I still have to stimulate myself, but that's not so true lately. It's more of an emotional thing. In fact there have been times lately that he can put himself inside me with no movement at all and I'd reach orgasm! It's in my *mind*. So I find I have to stimulate myself less and less. Which I think is great. I hope it makes *him* feel better. Yesterday I was almost there, and I could tell he wasn't yet.

Was his penis erect?

Oh yeah. From the beginning.

What do you think of the size of his penis?

It's perfect for me.

I'd had a mini orgasm. I was almost there. But I knew he wasn't ready so I sort of stopped while I was on top of him.

How did that feel?

Sort of frustrating. I'd rather have one big one.

Why did you want to wait for him?

Because we almost always come together.

Did he know you'd had a mini-orgasm?

Not sure.

Then he asked if he could get on top, in the missionary position.

How do you feel about that?

Fine. I like it. It's easier for me to reach orgasm. Emotionally I like being on the bottom better. I feel safe. His chest is so big. I can let go 'cause he's in control. I like this arms near me. It's a comfortable feeling. Part of it is that for so long I was so concerned about sex being satisfying to *him*, but now I like the feeling of protection, of safety. Also, if we're going to kiss, when he's on top he has more control over it, he has to lean down to reach me, and so I know when he does he really *wants* to. It's not just *me* making the effort to do that.

What does *that* mean to you?

It means sex is an emotional thing for him, not just physical. Before, we'd *rarely* kiss. In fact, I'm not sure we ever did. Now we do. I look and see him smile. It's nice to know things are okay between us.

What do you think *he* sees?

He's trying to see if I'm happy.

How do you convey that?

I try to smile. I have a nice, comfortable feeling.

How important is that to you?

It's *very* important. I think I need a lot of stability. I've had a lot of unsettling things in my life, so it's nice to be able to count on some emotional stability.

So you are feeling this yesterday, with him on top of you. Then what?

I think he asked if he could go a little bit harder, so that he can reach orgasm. He knows I don't care so much for that, since that was all we'd ever done before. Now he asks if it's okay. I said, "Yes, sure." And so he did. I was close to orgasm again, but since I'd already had that little one, I was okay. I don't have to have a big one. It was an emotionally satisfying experience. Before, when it was just physical, if we'd go at it and I didn't have an orgasm I'd be disappointed. That was the whole goal. But it was really nice yesterday. After he had his orgasm he said, "Are you okay?" He meant, "Did you have an orgasm?" I said, "Yeah, I'm fine." And I was. He stayed there on top of me for a few minutes. I felt really close to him. It had been a positive exchange. He just rolled off and we lay there.

How did you feel when he came out of you?

Physically I felt fine. Sometimes it's disappointing because I want him to stay there longer. Yesterday it was fine. He lay on top and we kissed. Sometimes we're not sure. He usually doesn't jump off right away.

Do you ever tell him to stay longer?

No.

What do you think he's thinking about when he gets off?

I think he thinks he had a good time.

You say you *think*. What are you not sure about?

He may have been disappointed that I didn't have a big orgasm because he's told me he's very concerned about my satisfaction.

What is that like for you, his concern about that?

I was surprised when he first told me. It had always seemed to be mostly for him. It seemed like it was more for him. He knew I could take care of myself by stimulating myself. Now I know it *is* important to him.

So what kind of pressure do you feel to make sure he knows you were satisfied?

Oh, he knows I'm pretty loud.

You made a face when you said that. What is there about being loud?

Well, it's not very ladylike. But it's just the way I am. So he knows when I have one, which is almost every single time, and usually together. You lose control, and you're not yourself. Talking dirty would be the same thing, that's not ladylike. The whole experience leaves you pretty vulnerable.

What is that experience like?

I'm always so afraid of being judged, of being criticized. I want to make sure I'm doing an okay job.

What could be criticized?

I'm not sure. It could be *anything*!

Like what?

Being too loud is the only thing I can think of. But I think he likes that. He never complains about it.

We know you're concerned about being criticized for your physical appearance.

Yeah. That's true. And I avoid certain positions that make the extra fat too obvious. I've tried to work it off, but it's not gonna happen. I'm uncomfortable with my whole midsection.

When you get up now, are you talking and holding each other?

We lie next to each other. We're both lying on our backs. It was really warm. Part of my brain said we should be holding each other, but it was too hot. But then I reached over and grabbed his penis, and that made him very happy. Then I got up to take a shower. I said I was gonna take one, and he asked if he could join me. I told him he could but that there was only one pink towel left. He said that was okay, so he came in with me.

How was that?

It felt good.

Would you have preferred to be there by yourself?

At that point, yes. I wanted to hurry up and get on with what I had to do. It also gets cramped in there.

Why did you think he wanted to take a shower with you?

He still wanted to be close. He didn't want the whole experience to end.

More than you did?

Yeah. I just wanted to get in and get washed up and get going. I felt kinda bad for that. Usually I'm not like that. But I had so much to do. I was also mad that he took the big towel, and I had to wipe myself off with a hand towel.

Which of you do you think was more physically and emotionally fulfilled?

Maybe him, I guess. But I felt great too.

How did that make you feel, to see him as more fulfilled than you?

That was great. It was reassuring that maybe some day we'll get beyond all this garbage.

The issue of trust is written over everything reported here. Will he ever be convinced that she wants him and no one else? Will she ever be convinced that he wants her and not some generic female? Addressing this issue will be our challenge during the weeks to come. And perhaps the time will come when their two-year-old, now patiently watching her video, and the child not yet born, will grow to celebrate their parents' courage and fortitude.

. . . .

IV

THE
SEXUAL
CHALLENGE

14 Getting Unstuck: REMEDIES

WHAT WILL IT TAKE AND HOW MUCH?

In a nation of fast-food restaurants, microwave ovens, superhighways that stretch from coast to coast without a single stoplight, and planes that can cross the ocean at the speed of sound, it is not surprising to find that many people esteem speed and efficiency before all else. But some of these people are clinicians who evaluate human services on the basis of how quickly "successful" outcomes can be achieved and judge caregivers by how soon they are no longer needed. Too often thoughtful appraisals of what the client or patient truly requires, considerations of the *entire* predicament, are crowded out by insurance-industry ceilings that specify limited treatment.

Holistic medicine, which focuses on the patient's entire lifestyle and its contribution to pathology, is left standing at the gate in a field where professionals race to medicate, by rote, individuals they hardly know. In such a setting, it is body parts that get attended to and not the person of the patient whose entire life has brought about the symptoms that walk through the door: headaches get "cured"; lumps get removed; arteries get bypassed. Doctors whose abilities and achievements are chiefly technical define the problems in terms most easily remedied. Thanks to this limited vision of what is truly ailing the patient, both parties may toast the outcome even as the pathogenic circumstances responsible for their meeting in the first place remain essentially intact.

The same, sadly enough, is often just as true of both counselors and their clients, in sex therapy or elsewhere. The practitioners have been presumably trained to be alert to every aspect of an individual's psychological and social development and adjustment, and more often than not those who come for help declare themselves ready to examine every corner of their lives in an effort to remedy their circumstances. But all too frequently, neither practioner nor client has the capacity to face the truths that emerge from all but the most perfunctory encounters. With the support of third-party payers, brief counseling or psychotherapy has become the order of the day.

"Cures" reached in record time may be reassuring to those involved in them and, in the most optimistic light, prove to be temporarily helpful, but they are fraught with danger. However reluctantly clients may call for help, once they feel some relief of stress they can confidently proceed in their accustomed ways. In some instances, the counselor may even help the client invent *new* ways to enact neurotic needs more successfully, thus enabling the client to shore up the old convictions and beliefs that are still responsible for the longstanding logjam. For example, clients with an insatiable need for approval might be encouraged to gain more of it by enlarging their repertoire of appealing behaviors. Or, clients with a longstanding fear of not being in control might be taught more effective self-assertion techniques.

To understand how harmful such superficiality can be, consider the nationally renowned behavioral therapist who used to counsel gay men and lesbians to change their sexual orientations. For some time, he accepted their definition of the problem—it is not easy, after all, to be gay in a homophobic society such as ours—and did all he could to help his clients renounce and expunge their homosexual fantasies and impulses. He came to believe, however, that what he was doing was all wrong, and charged that therapists who engaged in "change" treatment with homosexual clients were abetting the oppressors in a homophobic culture. Instead, he began helping his clients to overcome their self-loathing, to come out of the closet, and to fashion a life free of apology for who they were and had been all their lives.

DEFINING THE PROBLEM

In sexual therapy, we can find exactly the same dangers: counselors and clients agree far too quickly on a definition of the problem and embark on a treatment plan that promises to dispose of it as efficiently as possible. Instead of welcoming the sexual crisis as an opportunity to address important issues of long standing, ones that go far beyond a loss of technical competence, client and therapist become joined in a conspiracy that actively supports minimal time, minimal expense, minimal treatment, and minimal outcomes. They thus submit to those elements in our society that view therapy of any kind as just another form of dramatizing or pitying oneself, contending that most human problems can be treated either by sage advice or stronger bootstraps, and scorning as childish any attempt to link current problems to one's past. Accordingly, client and counselor settle for modest aims and "realistic" goals, and pride themselves on their economical approach to containing the problem, ignoring the unique chance to do something important about their lives.

In the past, therapists were often accused of making mountains out of molehills. Now, many of them are only too quick to accommodate pressures about the pace and scope of sexual counseling by limiting their views of what needs fixing. Instead of encouraging clients to own and to share the full extent of their sexual discontent, instead of tracking down and bringing into focus all the elements responsible for the client's sexual lethargy and disinclinations, the counselor often seeks to help the client settle for as little as possible, usually the restoration of one or another technical function. Counselor and clients may develop a nodding acquaintance with other issues, but their chief preoccupations during the course of therapy will be with *sexual* questions and *sexual* answers and *sexual* outcomes, all of which form but a minute part of what occurs in the sexual domain.

At the heart of this matter is the question of how the sexual problem comes to be defined. Some sex counselors prefer to delegate relationship issues to marriage counselors and long-standing personal issues to psychotherapists; they will limit their concern to a particular *sexual* disorder. Treatment will be highly predictable, beginning with carefully specified exercises in touching one's partner and ultimately including a series of sexual tasks designed to help the couple overcome various inhibitions. Other issues matter to such practitioners only if they become too distracting or cause the clients to balk at their homework assignments.

In fact, some sex therapists, too narrowly trained, are stymied by anything that complicates sexual behavior. Even while recognizing that their clients' actions and attitudes do not reflect those of the majority in treatment at the nation's most prestigious sex clinics, these practitioners continue to work in their accustomed ways. They resemble the man in the story who was searching for a coin under a lamppost, although he knew it had been lost farther away in the darkness, because "This is where I have some light!" They define sexual problems according to their limited training and expertise.

Their narrow perspective, combined with their clients' limited vision, often leads toward goals and outcomes unbecoming to any of them. All that matters to both parties, intent on making the *least* of the opportunity that sexual difficulties of any kind present, is that the magic wand work, making it possible, perhaps, for a man to achieve "proper" erection and ejaculation or a woman to end up sexually gratified, with partners whose needs they may not understand or whom they may not even like very much. All too often a superficial appraisal of how well the partners' sexual equipment is working reduces sex to a feat having little to do with the mind or the heart, with what is truly gratifying or troublesome.

The fact of the matter is that although the majority of men and women are not technically dysfunctional, that although they may engage in sex with each other at demographically acceptable rates and be reasonably pleased with the outcomes, they have not begun to fulfill the potential of their sexual partnerships and continue to wish for more than what takes place between them. The truth is, difficulties in the sexual domain may be as prevalent and run just as deep among those who are sexually "functional" as among their dysfunctional counterparts. In fact, because their problems are *not* so obvious, they are apt to fester far longer and eventually spread far wider, like a lump that has metastasized or clogged arteries that cause no symptoms. Usually their difficulties—of the mind and heart—are not attended to until the resentments and dissatisfactions built up over the years have turned hearts cold and left the sexual partnership in shambles. Individuals whose sexual functioning is up to par but providing few dividends are apt to shrug off their disquietude, like people who have enough to eat and a roof over their heads and feel guilty to complain of dissatisfacton when others are worse off.

Since many problems in the sexual domain are so subtle, even difficult to put into words, they are not likely to be addressed, much less serve as a springboard for remedial action. Instead, he continues to blame himself for his failure to turn her on, she continues to deprecate her sexual reticence, he continues to conceal the fact that he needs fantasies to stay aroused, she continues to resent feeling that her orgasms are more for him than for her. Both continue to wonder why their sexual exchanges lack the spontaneity or tenderness and affection of their early days together. What they probably do not realize is that their very capacity to function sexually when their hearts and minds are not in it, when the state of the relationship really calls for either confrontation or distance, is only further testimony to the pathology of their partnership.

Far from being the occasion for cheer, their ability to keep separate what occurs in the bedroom from everything else that is happening between them should be viewed with alarm, as a monumental failure to integrate sex with deep affection or to fully enact themselves in either sexual or nonsexual domains. Unlike their technically dysfunc-tional brethren, whose sexual difficulties serve as wake-up calls for addressing issues that can no longer be avoided, those who are adept at foreplay, for instance, or can reach orgasm at the drop of a hat regardless of mood, may never have to acknowledge what is really going on until the consequences of their behaviors have crumbled their relationship. Only then will they discover that the absence of technical sexual problems allowed them to disregard too much too long.

TOUCHING ALL THE BASES

The remedies I propose are based on the general premise of this book: that our entire selves are inevitably involved in our sexual exchanges, that we do not leave our libraries of "shoulds" and "ought tos" or "musts" at the bedroom door, nor do we leave our perceptions and evaluations of ourselves or of others there. Our entire familial and cultural backgrounds present themselves in full array in what may appear to be only a perfunctory sexual gesture. If it appears to be otherwise, that a sexual exchange *can* be superficial and relatively insignificant, it will be because of our failure to trace far enough the threads of our experience, back to their origins and down through their consequences. Sex is less a matter of bodies than of the mind and heart; it encompasses the most important elements of our lives; sexual difficulties, therefore, are not easily or quickly remedied and cannot be remedied at all by those who insist on viewing sexuality in primarily physical terms.

The suggestions that follow are meant for those who are now convinced that their sexual difficulties have more to do with how they think and feel, and not only in the sexual domain, than with genitalia gone awry, and that the restoration of our sexual wholeheartedness may well require radical changes in how we go about living our entire life. Above all, the proposed remedies can only make sense to those who are courageous enough to *own* their discontent and who believe themselves to be deserving of more than what many others appear to settle for.

MOM AND DAD, WHERE ARE YOU?

Since the lack of freedom to be fully sexual tends to originate in our parents' attitudes and messages, it becomes incumbent on us to ferret out whatever it was that we learned from each of them about how to go about the business of being sexual. We must make every effort to recall each parent's verbal or nonverbal message, to imagine the look on each parent's face in response to any evidence of our sexuality.

- How did they react to our questions? our interest? our behavior?
- What example did they set for us about sex and affection and intimacy?
- Did they often or seldom touch each other? Did they avoid touching us?
- What did they say or do that made us comfortable or uneasy about our own or another's body?
- Were we welcome to climb into their arms or their laps? Until when?
- What did they have to say as we set out on our first date? on subsequent ones? when we started going steady?
- Could sexual issues be discussed in our household or were they unmentionable?
- How severely did our parents punish us for sexual and other infractions? What form did these punishments take? How did they affect our self-images?

We should leave no stone unturned in our search for clues about our parents' contributions to our sexual circumstances, and this could include discussing them with our siblings and addressing our parents directly, perhaps with another person present to facilitate the process. If our parents will not agree to such meetings or are no longer alive, we might try to role-play a dialogue with them in which we tell them the consequences of their sexual messages to us, complete with their effect upon our emotional reactions toward sex. Express your appreciations, your regrets, your resentments.

If your parental relationships include a history of abuse, sexual or otherwise, emotional or physical incest, a lack of respect for your boundaries, you owe it to yourself to get to a therapist who can help you sort through the layers of memories and images and feelings that may have made viable sexual partnerships virtually impossible. And when this is done—a task of no small order—you must then declare yourself in no uncertain terms to your parents, whether it be on their doorstep, living room carpet, or grave. This declaration of independence, spoken, written, or faxed, may turn out to be the occasion for a new birth of sorts, of a voice that now belongs to you alone, of a newly-found integrity that cannot help but spill over into the sexual domain. If you have a partner, confide in him or her about the efforts you are making to grow up in some very essential ways. Make it clear that your sexual training began long before your partnership did and that the sexual circumstances you share are not entirely of your own (or your joint) making.

MY TRUTH, YOUR TRUTH

Truths about the past, confronted squarely and shared with those in whose behaviors and attitudes they were displayed, must be accompanied by truths about the present—truths about ourselves, our partner, our partnership, and our sexual experience, our thoughts and feelings and wishes. No place here for secret diaries. No place here for self-censoring. In an ideal world we would be utterly transparent to ourselves and to others. In an ideal relationship, partners would each help the other sift through and articulate needs, impulses, motives, and feelings in an uncommon display of honesty. Imagine a relationship in which couples nourished each other's capacities for self-awareness, encouraged each other to keep a daily journal of their pains and pleasures, within and outside the relationship, and shared their contents with each other over cups of coffee in the morning or glasses of wine at the end of the day.

How many couples have ever systematically discussed their last sexual exchange? This would include careful accounts of all that transpired during that encounter: why one and not the other initiated sexual contact, how that made them feel about themselves and each other, how they accounted for their behaviors, what they thought this told them about the ways in which they relate; their concerns, their expectations and what they supposed were their partner's, what they supposed each of them had wished for and why, the feelings of pleasure or fear or dread or indifference they had had and how these might be explained. How many couples have gone on to discuss to any extent at all what it was like for them to engage in foreplay and what it meant to them, omitting not one thought or feeling, how the transition from foreplay to coitus happened and why, how aroused they were, how aware they were of the partner's needs, all the way through to afterplay and its emotional meaning to them?

It is exactly this kind of appraisal and openness between two people hoping to enrich their sexual moments together that must occur if their effort is to be fruitful. In such a discussion, unheard of in most circles, there would be no pointing of fingers, no defensive rebuttals, only an interest in gathering more and more data about themselves and their sexual partnership, suspending judgments of any kind. Those who are really earnest will try to acknowledge their sexual attributions, whether they be benign or malignant, will explore their self-images, will discuss their judgments no matter how irrational, their sexual motives no matter how shameful; will question their capacities for intimacy, their fears of isolation or rejection; will acknowledge issues of power and control if any, perhaps complain about their impoverished repertoire, and share regrets over their lack of passion. No topic, no reaction, would be considered out of bounds for those daring enough to engage in such a free exchange.

TAKING RISKS

Talk, no matter how honest, is not enough, however, for those truly intent upon remedial action in the sexual domain. Out of such conversations will come the discovery of what each must *do* if the partnership is ever to change, the identification of the first little steps that must be taken, the little risks that will be required of each of them. If you have become honest enough with yourself and your partner, chances are you will come to know exactly how you must change and what the first step will entail. Inevitably you will discover something—an attitude, an old conviction, a characteristic gesture, a familiar action or reaction—that keeps you and your partner from moving on to where you wish to be, that serves as an impediment to any further growth or development, that maintains you in a dance to nowhere.

The risk typically requires changes in your sexual routine, from something as mundane as if and when the lights are turned off to who holds back and who is more daring. How are sexual opportunities avoided? How are sexual moments sabotaged? What red flag behaviors have you and your partner identified that turn sexual promise into despair? What caring behaviors in or outside of the sexual domain have you identified that would make the prospect of a sexual exchange more inviting? The answers to these questions will provide clues as to how to proceed, usually in unaccustomed ways, never in absolute certainty but with the growing confidence that comes from knowing more and more about each other's minds and hearts.

Having freed yourself from the constraints imposed upon you in the past and from cultural dictates as to the kind of sexual person you "ought" to be, you will now be in a position to embrace, declare, and act upon your *unique* sexual circumstances, to acknowledge what you think and feel and need in the sexual domain without apology. No longer will your sexual encounters amount to guessing games. What each of you is about will have been made abundantly clear. Emboldened by your ability to be honest with yourself and another and to assert your rights in the sexual partnership, you will no longer feel so vulnerable, so fearful that your personal boundaries will be disregarded. Having become less self-preoccupied, you will now be in a position to reach out and to be reached out to in new ways. You will no longer measure sexual success or failure by how frequently you engage in sex or whether the male's erection was maintained or the female reached orgasm, but rather by the extent to which the sexual exchange was honest and intrinsically gratifying, with hearts and minds prepared for a profound celebration of what two people can find in the sexual domain. It is that easy. It is that difficult!

P.S. A FINAL WORD

Since change of any kind envisioned here is not easily accomplished and requires such important shifts from mental sets ingrained over an entire lifetime, it is of the utmost importance that above all you be *patient* with yourselves and with each other in this task. There will be setbacks, and inevitably, there will be frustrations along the way. If you are honest enough you will sometimes despair that your best efforts seem not to improve anything and sometimes seethe that your partner is doing too little. Dark moments such as these will require two things of you. First, somehow, probably by a leap of faith, you must remain optimistic, strong in your belief that your vision of the possible will not ultimately be buried under an avalanche of baggage from your pasts, that what you have set out to do will surely be done. And you must convey this conviction to your partner, which brings us to the second requirement.

Whenever, wherever, you see your partner doing anything in behalf of the relationship, express your appreciation for it. Point it out with praise. Bring up every little detail that you notice. Let your partner know that you are sure he or she has what it will take to bring about a successful outcome. Just as school children tend to perform only as well as their teachers believe they can, a sexual partner will grow in the capacity for intimacy, sensitivity, and sexual joy only so far as his or her partner shares that hope and that vision. Too often people give up on themselves, confirmed by the negative expectations of partners who remind them of their past and present failures. If your sexual circumstances are ever to change, there must be kindness and respect and mutual support along the way. Real empathy, not just sympathy, can go far in alleviating what ails us. It is what saves any relationship, just as it can save yours. Fully comprehending and sharing your partner's truths is what will carry you to the point where, with hearts and minds known and welcomed, you can rejoice in your accomplishment.

15 Owning and Sharing Our Truths: EXERCISES

Many books and articles about sexual improvement include tips or techniques on the order of Ten Steps to a Sexier Marriage. Typically these center on stimulating sexual arousal, as if clumsiness and jaded appetites are all that stand between the reader and sexual glory. In this book, however, we have seen that it is our thoughts and feelings, not our choreography, that shape our sexual exchanges. The convictions and attitudes we developed long ago, our reactions to our sexual awakening, the unfolding history of ourselves as sexual beings, all are present in every sexual event.

The activities that follow are designed to help you meet the challenge of exploring and discovering your own needs and interests and fundamentals, and also, perhaps, sharing them with a partner. But how exactly is this done? How do you start? What should you say, or do, or try, and how can you keep from hurting a loved one, and how can you dare risk being hurt yourself? There is no one right approach; in fact, there are several ways you might apply these activities, depending on what seems the most comfortable for you. You might like to read through them first, think for a while, and then pick one or two activities to try. You might want to read a single unit with your partner and proceed immediately to do the things that are suggested at the end of it. You might want simply to talk about what you read and save the actual activities for another time. There is no time limit, no prescribed order, no rule.

Remember, too, that you are the best judge of what topics might be painful for your partner to deal with, or for you to share. Even if you go only a little way with only a few of the activities, you are still making progress together. In fact, by discussing which of the activities seem most appealing or most distasteful, you may find yourselves in a much more candid and heartfelt conversation than many couples ever achieve. Just to become a little more open with each other may shift you out of whatever rut you have been in.

When you embark on one of the activities, you will find a list of questions. It will help to write down your answers so that later, in talking them over, you don't forget what you had in mind. You should take enough time to list details or explanations; on reflection, you may find there is much to add to the first impressions you jotted down.

Most of the time, you are next asked to share your responses with your partner, but this need not happen as soon as pencils are down. Nor should you simply read off to each other all that you have written: you will probably want to spare your partner stress by beginning with mild generalities, even if you have come up with a fairly plain statement of your own truths.

If you and your partner are not at all used to frank and peaceable discussions of serious matters, you may want first to review "Couple Communication" (p. 297). Then perhaps it will be easiest for you two to begin with one of the activities that emphasize what is positive, such as "Sexual Appreciations" (p. 331) or "Sexual Peaks" (p. 326). If your partner is bashful or reluctant, you might want to start with things that emphasize your own whereabouts, such as "Thoughts" (p. 289) or "Hidden Assumptions" (p. 328). The activities entitled "Sexual Difficulties" (p. 318) should be left until the two of you are more familiar with the whole process. Many of our couples found that addressing one question at a time from "Almost Everything You Ever Wanted to Ask" (p. 334) really broke the ground for productive discussion.

Regardless of how you proceed, you will find these activities demanding. You must focus your attention, search your mind, and get up your nerve. The goal of these activities is what I have called "transparency," but you are not meant to be utterly transparent to your partner. No one, however intimate, has the right to know every single scrap of your thoughts and feelings. Openness is important, but the respect for people's privacy comes first. It will not be easy, and you may doubt whether the risk is worthwhile. But in the end, you will achieve a clearer picture of yourself, your partner, and your relationship that could transform the nature and quality of your sexual partnership.

FOLLOWING THE TRAIL OF NOTIONS

Much of what goes on in our heads during sex does not register as conscious thought. But, as this book has made clear, it is necessary to attend to what we think and feel if we wish to enhance our own sexuality and strengthen our partnership.

When you think back over your most recent sexual experience, you can recall something that was in the forefront of your mind. It might be an *attribution*, a reason you gave for what was going on; an *expectation* about what would or ought to happen; or an *evaluation*, an idea about yourself or your partner or your sex life together, based on how it all went. Next, with the gentle patience of a midwife, you can tease forth the reason why you formed this particular attribution, expectation, or evaluation. You will find that it is connected to a belief or memory or thought that you have had, which in turn arises from an associated action. . . . Each of us has, in fact, many an interconnected trail of thoughts and feelings that, with careful concentration, we can trace back to its origin in our lives.

As you proceed, the answer to each question prompting another question, you will often uncover more than one trail. At various junctures, several notions branch; you can choose one or another to pursue, and later return to unexplored paths along the way. For an illustration of this process, let us follow one man's thinking.

First, he makes his opening observation, implicit in which are two questions for which he will need to unearth a chain of explanations.

I try to maintain control if I know she's not ready for orgasm. There have been a very few times when we haven't had orgasms at the same time. That's something that's always been important.

Why isn't his partner always ready to reach orgasm when he is? And why are simultaneous orgasms so important to him? He must decide which of these to tackle first. Suppose he chooses to focus on his partner's lack of readiness. He might think:

(a) **She's a woman, after all. It takes longer for a woman to become sexually aroused.**

Or he might think:

(b) **Obviously I have not been doing a very good job of stimulating her.**

Or he might not generalize at all:

(c) **We were out of sync that time. Maybe we got off to a wrong start.**

Underlying each of these explanations are further ones. Respectively they might be:

(d) **Women, unlike men, are not always ready to go. It could be a difference in their hormones or in how they're brought up.**
(e) **I have not been much aware of her sexual needs and responses. I've been focusing primarily on myself.**
(f) **Maybe I was so eager that I didn't notice she wasn't all that into it.**

In (d) above our respondent has come pretty much to a dead end. He has declared what he supposes is a fact of life to which he must accommodate. For further explanations along this particular trail, he would have to look in textbooks on differences between men and women. There is no such dead end along the trail leading from (e), however. This explanation might lead to:

(g) Sometimes I get taken over by my sexual needs and responses, and I am oblivious to my partner's. As a matter of fact, I sometimes wish I didn't have to pay so much attention to how far along she is.

In the same way, (f) might be followed by:

(h) I don't like to admit that she may not be interested. I need to believe my sexual overtures are always welcome.

Continuing down the trail, (g) might lead to:

(i) Taking responsibility for my partner's sexual well-being can be a burden.

While (h) might be followed up by:

(j) It is important to me to believe that she is as eager for sex as I am. Otherwise I feel like a predator.

In either case, the trail could be extended, winding its way back to fundamental truths about himself, his partner, and his partnership. The trail from (i) might lead to resentments over having to meet others' needs, concerns about how people-pleasing tendencies can make for strained relationships, and fears that his usual sexual pattern may do little to express feelings of love and closeness. The trail from (j), on the other hand, might involve, step by step, fears about his sexual appetite, about how his partner sees him, and whether he may be ultimately rejected.

This example shows how to move along ideational trails. First, identify a particular aspect of your sexual experience. Next, find a possible explanation: to what do I attribute it? Then, ask yourself whether that explanation requires still another. And so on. Follow the trail as far as you can or want to go in order to see what emerges; afterwards, ferret out the emotional consequences of your thinking and consider their impact on how you go about being sexual.

Consider another illustration:

I prefer initiating sexual encounters:

Otherwise, we might not have sex at all.

↓

My wife hardly ever initiates. That leaves it up to me.

↓

Her libido is a thing of the past.

↓

She's too involved with the kids to have energy left over for sex.

↓

Her mother role takes precedence over her lover role.

↓

That's the way her mother was, and she's following her example.

etc.

I like to be in charge of things in the sexual domain.

↓

That's the way a man is supposed to be.

↓

It makes me feel more manly when I am actively pursuing her.

↓

If I didn't, I'd end up feeling like a baby being attended to.

↓

It frightens me to feel possessive and helpless.

etc.

One of these trails leads to a focus on the man's partner, with explanations for her behaviors and priorities. The other leads to a self-examination with each explanation or attribution followed by a deeper and more encompassing one. Notice that neither trail includes feelings or wishes or remedies, *only interpretations/explanations/ attributions*, how the individual *accounts* for what is happening. Usually our sexual circumstances are accounted for by what we *think is true* about ourselves, our partner, and/or our relationship.

Now all you have to do is get a paper and pencil and jot down an opening sexual truth of your own. It may have to do with yourself ("Sometimes I feel like an onlooker, like I'm not really involved") or with your partner ("He seems so mechanical," or "she . . . seems so uninterested") or with your partnership ("We seem to be stuck in a rut, and we are doing very little to get out of it"). Next, consider why this observation is true of you. Now, what about that explanation requires further explanation?

Do not require yourself to come up, on a first attempt, with a detailed self-analysis. That may be far too ambitious. If you can only go one step further, so be it. If you can go beyond a simple explanation, so much the better. At the very least you will be discovering that there is something to explore in what you are doing sexually. You may or may not want to share your discoveries with your partner.

THOUGHTS

Part 1: The Ways People Think

Every one of our sexual actions, and every one of our partner's actions if we have one, produces a reaction in us. These reactions are emotional, sensory, and, above all, cognitive: what we *think* is happening. It is this last feature of every sexual experience that determines the feelings we are having from moment to moment, the conclusions we reach about ourselves, our partner, and our sexual partnership, and our evaluations of what is taking place.

In this activity, you are asked to take stock of the thoughts you have had during sex. Some may be habitual, others momentary. As you recall them, you may find some of them entirely reasonable, others startling ("Where did I get *that* idea?") or even irrational. You must, in any case, discover the interpretations you are making in order to learn how sex brings you the meanings that it has for you.

Take the case of a woman for whom having her partner's penis inside her does not in itself bring her to orgasm. Suppose that she thinks:

> **I must be frigid. This means I'm not much of a sexual partner. Everybody else seems to be able to do this but me. I must really be screwed up sexually! I'm really ashamed. And who wouldn't be? No wonder my partner has so little sexual interest in me. Sooner or later he'll go looking for somebody else, and I'll end up alone.**

Here are the kinds of cognitive distortion—mistakes in thinking—that this woman unfortunately has achieved:

All-or-nothing thinking

She views her sexual circumstances in absolute terms: either she responds as (so she believes) other women do, or else she is a total sexual failure. She lets only one aspect of her sexual experience, which she views as a deficit, determine that the entire experience was bad. She does not know, or else disregards, the fact that most women do not reach orgasm through penile intromission alone, and that those who do not can be as sexually aroused as those who do. As a result, her conclusions wreak havoc on her self-image.

Overgeneralization

She has not yet reached orgasm through penile intromission alone, and so concludes that it will *never* happen. In fact, patterns of sexual response can change over the course of a person's life, so that down the line, she could be in for a big surprise. That is not so likely, of course, if in her bending the future to the present she is creating a self-fulfilling prophecy.

Mental filtering

She sees fit to focus on only one aspect of her sexual experience, which then overshadows everything else that has happened. And just as one rotten apple spoils the others in the basket, her narrow attention to what she thinks is amiss discolors everything else. Never mind the love between them or the intoxication of sexual arousal; all that matters to her is that she did *not* reach orgasm as she thought she should, and in the end she felt unworthy and unlovable.

Discounting the positive

She lets what she sees as her failure define the entire episode. It well may be that her partner enjoys her kisses and her warm embrace, it might be important that the two of them have taken time out of busy schedules to meet in this way, her partner may feel especially valued and appreciated during sex, but none of these positive aspects matters to her.

Jumping to conclusions

She has no real evidence to support her negative interpretations. Instead of checking things out with her partner, she thinks she reads his mind that he is disgusted at her failure to reach orgasm "normally" and will ultimately reject her as a sexual partner. Thus she responds to her present circumstances in ways that are bound to sour them, but also to what she is sure will happen in the future if she does not improve. This double-whammy is what makes her plight so desperate.

Magnification

The distortions already described show this woman exaggerates the negative and minimizes the positive. Her lack of balance, her emphasis in the wrong direction, arise from not taking an objective view of what takes place from the beginning to the end of a sexual exchange. She is bound to feel disheartened when all that she can attend to is her so-called failure.

Emotional reasoning

This woman assumes that what she is feeling is the way things really are. That is, since she is so upset by her "failure," it therefore truly *is* a failure. Put another way, since she is frightened that her partner may abandon her, this must be a real possibility. Since she feels ashamed of her incapacities, they must be shameworthy.

"Should" statements

This woman, by comparing herself with (imagined) others, is telling herself that she *should* be able to reach orgasm in the way she wants. She may be used to attaining whatever she has her mind on; she may demand perfection of herself; she may on the other hand be used to criticism by comparison, perhaps from parents with unreasonable standards. In any case, her internal vocabulary scolds her with such words as "must," "ought," and "have to," leaving her annoyed, frustrated, or ashamed. She spends her energy berating herself instead of seeking a different perspective or possible remedies, and the imperative cast of her inner language only cements her in her convictions.

Labeling

Instead of considering which of her own (or her partner's) behaviors may account for the circumstances she describes, we find her labeling herself as frigid, as a sexual screwup, as not much of a sexual partner. What most of us never quite understand is that our behaviors, our performances, are *not* who we *are*. Our essence, our basic character, our worth as human beings never depends on what we *do* from one moment to the next. However, the woman in our example is flatly labeling herself a failure, regarding herself in static terms, and on that account is less willing to take new risks or meet new challenges. Her self-labeling has left her dead in the water.

Personalization and blame

Once this woman has given herself a stick-tight label, it becomes harder for her to consider other explanations for her circumstances or to seek solutions of any kind. The blatant glare from this label blinds her to other factors that might be involved. So she does not invite her partner to consider *his* behaviors and their effect on her. She will not join with him in considering what rules, conscious or not, govern their sexual partnership and might contribute to what occurs. She will sit inert holding the blame, perhaps as a way of maintaining the partnership's paralyzing but familiar status quo. New strategies will never be sought, nor new behaviors, on either one's part. There will be no experiments in how they go about being sexual with each other.

She is no hero in taking all the responsibility for their sexual plight, for both of them will suffer the consequences. Of course, she might eventually come to think that her partner's sins of commission and omission are what led to her failure, and end up feeling victimized by the man she would make love to.

Part 2: Discovering Your Own Thoughts

Now that you are acquainted with the ways that cognitive distortions will inevitably color your emotional responses, you are ready to look for them in yourself. First, pick some strong negative feeling you have had—once, often, now and then—during sex with your partner. Use this feeling as the title for a list with two columns labeled *Negative Thoughts* and *Cognitive Distortions*. See if you can come up with what you might be telling yourself that could account for the negative feeling you had. Write out this internal message in the first column, then write out beside it which of the distortions we have just reviewed seem to be involved. Repeat this for each negative thought, or internal message, that you associate with the given negative feeling. You may want next to make separate lists, one for each feeling, that generally describe sex with your partner. Or you may wish to limit your assessment to your most recent sexual exchange.

Finally, after you have reviewed your various negative emotional reactions and gone as far as you can go down the two columns in which you have listed your thoughts and the possible distortions in them, go back over the distortions you have identified and start a list of thoughts that are more realistic and could substitute for whatever erroneous conclusions you found. For example, the woman whose statements and cognitive distortions were considered above might substitute something like this:

Just because I don't reach orgasm through penile intromission alone, that doesn't mean that I am sex-phobic or incapable of sensual responses, so therefore I'm not frigid. The fact is, when I don't pay attention to how I'm doing on this score, I often enjoy our sexual exchanges and get really turned on. Sometimes

I am sexually reserved, and my orgasm doesn't always come easily under most circumstances. But that's true of lots of women. I am not alone in this, so I am not sexually screwed up, any more than most women are. Sometimes my partner has no sexual interest in me, but the fact is, sometimes I have no sexual interest in him. There are many reasons that enter into that, and it would probably be a good idea for us to share them. It's about time I started thinking more clearly about this matter. I'm tired of being terrified that he might leave me!

Part 3: Things Your Partner Does

During the exploration of your thoughts and feelings you may discover that your attention is not so much on yourself as on your partner. If that is the case, make another list for each action or behavior of your partner's that causes a negative feeling in you. What negative thoughts accompany those particular events? What cognitive distortions may be involved? What more sensible thoughts might you substitute for those that are weighing you down?

Part 4: All Right!

So far, you have been dealing with negative aspects of your sex life. The reason for starting out this way is that bringing negative thoughts and mistaken thinking to light can help you with whatever sexual problems may be bothering you. But it is important also to identify what is positive, gratifying, fulfilling, satisfactory, pleasant. Whatever seems to be contributing to your sexual delight is the right thing, so you should list and analyze enjoyable behaviors on both your parts, your perceptions of them, your positive thoughts, and your equally positive feelings. You are bound to learn as much from this task as from the others. You may even be surprised at how important and consequential and beneficial some small behavior or gesture has been to you or your partner. You will surely be reassured of ways in which the two of you can maintain or even expand your sexual good fortunes.

SEXUAL MOTIVATIONS

This activity really stayed with me.

Several years ago we'd have had to lie to get through it. We've come a long way!

We were both good at predicting each other's motivations.

It can be done quickly, like the quizzes in the back of women's magazines.

It opened up many new discoveries, especially in how we perceived the other's motivations. There were a few wide discrepancies.

Part 1: A Checklist

For this activity you will need a sheet of paper that you use like the answer sheet for a questionnaire. Make four columns, headed *Reasons*, *Myself*, *My Partner*, and *Acceptable*.

In the Reasons column, list the letters a to z. These refer to the reasons for engaging in sex that are listed below. You can copy the reason next to its letter, if you like, but this is not necessary. Be sure also to add any other reason that occurs to you.

In the other three columns you will mark each reason for sex, according to how you would answer the following questions:

Myself: How often is this a reason why you engage in sex with your partner? Write O for Often, S for Sometimes, R for Rarely, N for Never.

My Partner: How do you think your partner would mark these reasons? Write O, S, R, or N as you did for yourself. Remember, you are putting yourself in your partner's place, so when the reason (for instance, "To please my partner") says "my partner," it refers to your *partner's* partner, you.

Acceptable: How do you rate the given reason as a motive for sex? Write YES for Perfectly Acceptable, A for Acceptable, U for Unacceptable, NO for Not At All Acceptable.

a. For the pleasure it brings
b. For body contact
c. To get caught up in passionate feelings
d. To "let go"
e. To feel totally absorbed
f. For fun
g. To please my partner
h. To enjoy my partner
i. Out of duty
j. To keep the peace
k. To feel worthwhile
l. To assert myself in no uncertain terms
m. To improve my mood
n. To show how sexually competent I can be
o. Out of love
p. To share myself with another in a very deep way
q. To reduce feelings of sexual tension
r. Because my partner expects it
s. To assure myself that I have a normal sex drive
t. To keep myself from straying
u. Out of habit
v. To get my partner involved with me
w. To keep my partner from straying
x. To celebrate a special occasion
y. To feel less lonely
z. To reassure my partner that all is well in the relationship

Part 2: Thinking It Over

Look at your checklist answers to see how your "Often . . . Never" markings match up or contrast with what you predicted for your partner's answers and with your Acceptability ratings. Consider these questions:

1. What might your entries tell you about yourself as a sexual being?
2. How do you account for them?

3. How do they shape your sexual responses?
4. What things would have to change in your sexual partnership for your sexual motivations to be any different?

Write down your musings on a separate piece of paper. Next, use another sheet to reflect on how similar or different you think your motivations and your partner's seem to be. How has this affected the character of your sexual exchanges?

Part 3: Sharing Your Findings

1. Which findings, thoughts, impressions and feelings do you wish to share with each other?
2. What are your perceptions of each other?
3. How accurate are they?
4. What do you see in each other that the other acknowledges?
5. To what extent do you see in the other what you see in yourself?
6. What changes would you like to see?

This activity is as important as any that you and your partner might engage in. It will go far in increasing your transparency with each other, in clarifying your needs and interests, and in helping you to formulate goals that suit where you are coming from while freeing you of guilt or shame.

COUPLE COMMUNICATION

After she shared important information about herself which she had never discussed in four years of marriage, we started talking about all kinds of things. In the process, our passion was reignited and our bond was renewed.

Just talking about our sex life led to an increase in our love-making!

The activity helped us get out of our usual finger-pointing.

The most powerful part of the exercise was hearing the other person hear what you said and repeating it back. I never felt so understood.

We've been much more affectionate and loving with each other since we did this exercise.

To turn a static partnership dynamic, it is not enough to get in touch with your own sensations, behaviors, thoughts, feelings, and wishes. While such self-awareness is the cornerstone for any flourishing sexual relationship, it must be articulated, translated into sharing with your partner the information you have gathered about yourself. Sooner or later, indirect messages, stubborn silences, light banter, occasional sniping, intermittent outbursts over what is going on in the sexual domain must be replaced by open and honest communication between you and your partner. If it is conducted in ways that help both of you clarify your needs, you will be able to go on to devise plans for your sexual engagements that promise the most for your relationship.

The first thing to consider is how to go about sharing once you decide to improve your sexual communication. These are the four chief considerations:

Time.

You cannot wait for an impulse to communicate. After the two of you have agreed to make communication a top priority, you must decide when you can sit down and talk, and how much time to take for your discussions. Should it be once a week? more often? less? What time of day would be best? early in the morning, over coffee, while the rest of the household is asleep? the end of the day over drinks before dinner? at night after the children have been bedded down? And what is a reasonable amount of time to allow? a half hour, an hour? It is important that your plans be realistic. Nothing fails like failure, and in order for you to feel that you have been successful in your resolve, your plans should not be too ambitious. One modest success, followed later by another, is fine, whereas elaborate plans that are thwarted by your hectic schedules are no good at all. You should choose to talk at times when both of you are apt to be relaxed, attentive, and uninterrupted.

Place.

Where—in your house or elsewhere—can you meet in comfort and privacy? It is best to avoid places with unfavorable associations or special connotations: not a workroom that is ordinarily dedicated to just one of you, not your bedroom if it has been the scene of past distresses. If you choose to talk while walking, pick a route along which there are places to sit down. If you choose a café or lounge, make sure it is one where you can see and hear each other clearly without being overheard. A roomy public park might do, but not if you take the children along: occupied as they may be, they can still run up and interrupt you. Avoid the car, because driving is (or ought to be!) distracting.

Topic.

You must decide, together, what you would like (or need) to talk about. At the beginning it is probably best to limit your discussions to fairly neutral topics that will not greatly upset either of you. Probably you should start out talking about your partnership (rather than your *partner*) and the ways in which *both* of you might function more effectively. In these initial discussions you might bring up your concerns about yourself, attitudes or reactions that make sex difficult for you. Only after the two of you have mastered the techniques about to be described will you be able to discuss more highly-charged issues constructively.

Structure.

After you have decided what to talk about, flip a coin to determine who will begin your discussion. This first speaker then introduces your chosen topic from his or her point of view. He or she should directly face the listener and try to focus attention on the listener, keeping glances away to a minimum. The speaker should also "hold the floor"—tangibly. By this, I mean that an object (a coaster, a pencil, a box of Kleenex) should be designated "the floor" and held by whoever is speaking. It should be understood that the speaker who holds the floor will not be interrupted by the listener, who will not respond until "the floor" has been handed over. The speaker should make every effort to describe things fully. Using statements that begin with "I" and never "you," the speaker describes his/her *sensations,* his/her own *behavioral interactions, interpretations* of those behaviors, whatever *feelings* these interpretations elicit, and whatever *wishes* the speaker may have that things be different from what they are at present.

That is quite long enough for an opening statement; much longer, and it is apt to wander off in more than one direction, too much for the listener to take in. It should be a statement of fact—the fact of the speaker's experience—over which there can be no argument even when it does not coincide with the listener's experience or point of view. The goal is not to reach a consensus about what speaker and listener suppose really is happening. Rather, it is to show both partners that each one's experience is highly subjective. Understanding this, we come to understand and be understood by our sexual partner. There is nothing quite so important as that.

An opening statement might take this form: "When I see you (or myself) doing X, I think to myself Y, and end up feeling Z. I wish that you (I, we) could ABC. That would mean a lot to me." A communication is only complete when it includes your sensations, a mention of specific behaviors, your interpretations of them, and a wish that some sequence of actions be different. Alternatively, the statement might not include a wish for any change at all. In that case, the opening statement might end, "That's one thing I really like," or "That's one thing I hope we'll always have."

After the first speaker has finished his or her opening statement, the listener is given "the floor." It is now the listener's turn to demonstrate an understanding of what the speaker has said, *regardless* of whether he/she agrees with it. What the listener does is repeat, by paraphrase or even word for word, the speaker's statement: "I hear you saying that when you do . . . you think to yourself that . . .

and this makes you feel . . . and that you wish. . . . Does that capture what you have tried to tell me?" Receiving the floor again, the speaker more often than not has to explain that there were certain parts the listener missed or misunderstood, and tries to fill them in. On his or her next turn, the listener then tries again to recapitulate the speaker's message. These two steps are repeated until the speaker finally says something like, "You've got it! That's exactly what I was getting at." The listener now becomes the speaker. With "the floor" in hand, he or she addresses the matter from his/her own point of view, and they go through the same process of speaking—listening—feeding back. "The floor" shifts back and forth, with either partner asking for clarification as necessary.

Finally the point is reached where each understands the other's point of view. They may decide to go ahead and negotiate their differences immediately. Or they may decide to postpone such efforts until they have been able to think about it further. Or they may discover during the process that their differences are not as great as they had supposed, so that once the issue is clarified, they can see right away how they can modify their behaviors to benefit their sexual partnership.

This communication procedure involves, for beginners, a fair amount of risk, because they are testing their trust in each other. ("Will he follow the rules and not interrupt?" "Will she shut me down with one of those snide cracks?") But carefully carried out, it shows them that talking about sex need not involve criticisms, blaming, or defensiveness. This discovery in itself often serves to deepen their intimacy, which cannot help but enhance their sexual exchanges.

ASKING FOR WHAT YOU WANT

This really brought some difficulties to the surface.

This activity broke our facade. In fact, it led to our very first fight.

It was a wonderful way to open up some much-needed discussion of our sex life.

After we worked through our initial defensiveness, our discussion led to insights we had never had before.

The activities became an impetus for an evening of sexual experimentation.

A great many sexual dissatisfactions arise from people's not getting what they want. That is, their partners do not behave as they would like, and often it is difficult to ask the partner to try something new or do something different. It may even be difficult to think of what behaviors by your partner may bring about the changes you desire. In this activity, however, that is what you are asked to do.

Part 1: Your Wish List

What are the things you wish your partner would do sexually? Make a list of them. They may be actions that you would like to add to your partnership's repertoire, or to include in it more often than you do now. They may be changes, slight or major, in what your partner is accustomed to doing.

Include in your list anything that you think would give you sexual pleasure, make the occasion more exciting, or leave you feeling attractive and desirable, treasured or at least cared about, and worthwhile as a person. Include tiny little details that would make a difference to you as well as enormous changes that you are unsure would ever come to pass. Word your wishes positively: "I wish you would" rather than, "I wish you wouldn't" or "I wish you'd stop." Concentrate on what you want your partner to *do* rather than *feel* or *think*.

Make your wishes reasonable, things that can be accomplished in your ordinary lives, within your schedules and your budget. Include, within this constraint, whatever you would like to happen; don't leave something off because you doubt that your partner would be willing to do it. If this proves correct, at least you can try to understand your partner better by discussing why he/she feels unwilling; and in any case, you may have underestimated his/her willingness to experiment.

This activity works best if you can come up with a fairly long list, perhaps 25 items. In case you have trouble thinking of that many, here are some examples that may help you add to your list.

- Initiate sexual contact between us more frequently.
- Take more time in foreplay (and/or afterplay).
- Cuddle with me for at least five minutes after a sexual exchange.
- Make a positive comment about my bodily appearance.
- Talk to me more frequently and in greater depth about your sexual needs and interests.
- From time to time, do what you can to create a romantic setting for us, such as dimming the lights, putting on relaxing music, etc.
- Look in my eyes during and after a sexual exchange.
- Share and, perhaps, enact one of your sexual fantasies with me.
- Share an appreciation for a sexual exchange soon after it.
- Ask me what a sexual exchange was like for me.
- From time to time, engage in sensual contact with me without it leading to intercourse.
- Sleep in the nude occasionally and invite me to do the same.
- Watch a sexually stimulating video with me.
- Surprise me with a sexual behavior you do not frequently engage in.
- Talk "dirty" with me during a sexual exchange.
- Arrange, during the day, for a sexual date with me.
- Masturbate to orgasm directly in front of me.
- Concoct a sexual game for us to play.
- Discuss your sexual motivations with me and ask me about mine.
- Ask me about my sexual needs, expectations, and interests.
- Tell me what I might do to enhance the quality of our sexual partnership.
- From time to time, take entire charge of a sexual exchange with me.

- Take a shower, perfume yourself, whatever you think might make you more sexually appealing before initiating sex with me.

Part 2: What Matters Most

When you have made your wish list as complete as you can, number the items on it in order of their importance, with 1 = most important, 2 = next most important, and so forth.

This is apt to be a difficult task when you have a long list. You may have a couple of dozen items and no very clear idea how they rank with you. If so, you can divide this task into steps. First, think of a small group of categories that you can manage, for example Very Important, Sort of Important, Not Really Important (to be abbreviated V, S, and N respectively). Then give one of these ratings to each of the items. When you assign your numerical rankings, start with the items in your most-important category and number them, ignoring the others. After this it may be easiest to look at your least-important items, giving the very least important one your highest number and working backwards. When you have only intermediate items left, you may want to subdivide them further, or perhaps they are few enough that you can now rank-order them without trouble.

Having finished your numbering, by whatever means, you are ready to discuss wish lists with your partner.

Part 3: Comparing Wishes

Start with the wishes you have each chosen as particularly important. As you discuss them, try to touch on these points:

- What do you see by way of advantages occurring from your partner's compliance with your wish?
- How would that enrich your experience of your sexual relationship?
- What might be disadvantageous about the change you wish for?

- If you were to experience your partner differently, how might this affect your feelings and attitudes towards a sexual exchange?
- Is there any way in which you might make your wish even more precise than it appears on your list?
- How does your partner understand your wish? Does he/she know exactly what you want?
- How difficult would it be for your partner to carry out a particular wish?
- What advantages and disadvantages can your partner see in what you would like?
- What might constitute a small but significant step in the direction you would like your sexual partnership to go?
- What promises can your partner make?
- What are you prepared to do that would make it easier for your partner to carry out your wish?

An important part of this process is to make sure that the two of you can agree on whatever changes have already occurred and to express appreciation for wishes your partner comes to fulfill for you. Keep an eye on your progress; you may want to talk together about it regularly, every month for example.

Some couples have used their wish lists as the basis for a contract in which each undertakes to try meeting certain of the other's requests. You may feel too old for gold stars, but when one of the behaviors is undertaken, it should be noted and acknowledged. Whatever the format you choose, make sure that you take special notice of what is happening and share your reactions at regular intervals. In this way, you can be sure that your sexual partnership is no longer on the back burner, that both of you are making continual efforts to improve your sexual circumstances. As needed, you may want to revise your lists.

Even if you do no more than just share your wishes with each other, you are working to promote candor and self-assertiveness between you, which cannot help but improve your sexual fortunes.

FEELINGS

This touched on things we never talked about before, ever!

Try to recall your most recent sexual exchange, from the beginning through to the end. What were your emotions from the moment it appeared likely that you would be having sex? Perhaps certain feelings predominated; or you might have had, instead, a number of different positive or negative feelings, or a mixture of equally strong contradictory feelings. Different feelings, with different degrees of intensity, may have emerged *before* the sexual exchange, *during* it, and *afterward*.

Part 1: Your Own Feelings

Below are listed a wide variety of feelings. In addition, you may be able to think of others that came to you, or that might come to some people but did not happen to you. For this part of the activity, you need to make four columns on a sheet of paper, headed *Feeling*, *Before*, *During*, and *Afterwards*. In the first column, write the numbers 1 through 40 to represent the feelings listed (or copy the list if you like), and underneath write the additional feelings that you thought of.

Next, for each feeling listed, consider whether you experienced it in your most recent sexual exchange. Did it come to you before the activity actually began, during it, afterward, or not at all? How long did it last, and how intensely? For each of the "when" columns, rate the given feeling on a scale of 1 to 10, with 1 meaning a momentary, fleeting, weak, or mild feeling, and 10 meaning a very intense, strong, lasting feeling. Any feeling that you did not experience at all gets a score of 0 for that column. Be sure to give each feeling a number in all three columns.

For example, feeling #10 is Lonely. Suppose that when it became pretty certain you and your partner would be having sex, you were simply pleased and excited about it. You give Lonely a rating of 0 in the Before column. But during your sexual contact, things didn't happen as you hoped, and you began to feel disunited from your partner; and then suppose that afterward you felt deeply, miserably lonely. You give Lonely a high score (say, 8, 9, or 10) under Afterward, and then—to indicate that your feeling had grown—a score somewhere in the middle of the scale under During. Meanwhile, suppose that you weren't aware of any angry feelings at any time: you give Angry (feeling #6) ratings of 0 in all three columns.

1. Aroused/Excited	21. Pleased
2. Tense	22. Appreciative
3. Delighted	23. Happy
4. Uncertain	24. Confused
5. Relaxed	25. Daring
6. Angry	26. Cautious
7. Depressed	27. Frustrated
8. Proud	28. Inadequate
9. Bored	29. Awkward
10. Lonely	30. Disgusted
11. Anxious	31. Warm/Loving
12. Resigned	32. Close
13. Guilty/Ashamed	33. Dutiful
14. Amazed	34. Embarrassed
15. Amused	35. Grateful
16. Upset	36. Stubborn
17. Contented	37. Calm
18. Surprised	38. Satisfied
19. Shy	39. Eager
20. Tender	40. Discouraged

Now looking at your list of feelings, consider these questions:

- Exactly what were you doing that might account for your emotional responses?
- Exactly what was your partner doing?
- Were you surprised to note any particular emotional response, or does it frequently occur?
- What changes, on your partner's part or your own, would help to maximize your positive and minimize your negative feelings?

Part 2: Your Partner's Feelings

Your next task is to imagine what your partner may have felt during your most recent sexual exchange. On a second sheet of paper, use the same list as you did for yourself—adding, again, any other feelings you think of—and assign the items a numerical score for Before, During, and Afterward on the same scale, based on what you could tell about your partner's feelings.

Admittedly, this may be difficult, because many people's feelings are harder to judge during sex than at other times. But it is important to note how your partner *seemed* to you. It will surely be useful to discover instances where you guessed wrong ("I wasn't disgusted! I was worried!").

When you have finished, as well as you can, assessing your partner's feelings, consider these questions:

- What about your partner's behaviors or appearance make you suppose he or she was feeling what you have described?
- How similar were your feelings?
- How do you account for any differences?

Part 3: Sharing Your Feelings

Now, compare lists with your partner and discuss these points:

- How accurate were your perceptions of each other's feelings during that particular sexual exchange?
- How did these perceptions affect what happened?
- If you had one word to express what you usually feel in the sexual arena, what would it be? What one word best describes your impression of your partner's feelings?
- How would you like things to be different?

Part 4: Pay Attention

During the next few weeks, try to notice your emotional reactions during sex as best you can. Make no particular attempt to change what you are feeling. Just pay attention to what is going on inside you and record your impressions soon after your sexual exchanges. This Feelings Log will go far in helping both of you get a clear picture of what is going on inside and between you. To the extent that your Log also contains perceptions of your partner, it can help you each to modify your behaviors during sex so that they convey to each other what you mean to convey. Then you can feel more confident that your partner reads you right.

ACTIONS

This book stresses that it is thoughts and feelings that are crucial to sexual adjustment. But that does not mean that actions are unimportant. What you and your partner *do*—before, during, and after sex—provides the basis for those thoughts and feelings. So it is a good idea to become aware of your behavior patterns and their effects.

Some behaviors are quite obvious: a woman opens her mouth to perform fellatio, a man uses his tongue to perform cunnilingus, partners' hands stimulate and caress each other; lips kiss, deeply or delicately, arms embrace, backs arch, legs brace. But besides what people can do with various parts of their bodies, there are other behaviors, maybe not nearly so obvious, that can account for even more in determining the quality of a sexual exchange.

Part 1: Your Own Actions

Think back over your most recent sexual exchange. Try to recall each thing you did, as minutely as if you had been a camera taping yourself. As you observe each action and the action it leads to, jot down notes according to these questions:

1. **What actions are you engaging in?**
2. **Which of your behaviors are you most aware of?**
3. **What are you trying to convey to your partner? How?**

4. Is there anything different about your behavior that stands out?

5. Are your preliminary behaviors relatively routine?

6. Are you following or are you leading?

7. Are you acting with relative abandon, or do your behaviors seem to be cautious and restrained?

8. How spontaneous do your behaviors seem to be?

9. How inviting, how welcoming are your gestures?

10. How do you see the tempo of your activity?

11. How active are you compared with your partner?

12. How energetic do you appear? How exhausted?

13. Are your motions fluid or are they jerky?

14. Do your behaviors exude confidence or a certain timidity?

15. How mechanical do you appear to be?

16. Are you behaving in accordance with a ritual that has been well rehearsed or are you surprised by what you find yourself doing?

17. Do your behaviors invite closeness or do they appear to create distance?

18. What are you doing with your hands, with your feet?

19. Are you gritting your teeth or is your face relaxed?

20. Are you smiling or are you grim?

21. Do you utter a sound? Do you speak any words at all?

22. Do your bodily gesticulations denote a growing arousal?

23. Do you take charge, call the shots so to speak, careful to allow or disallow certain responses, either your own or your partner's?

24. Where and how do you put on the brakes, determining the tempo and the manner of the exchange?

25. Are you holding or being held? Or is it mutual?

26. Are you gentle or harsh in your behaviors?

27. Did you beckon your partner to the bed, or was it the other way around?

28. Were you the first to undress yourself or your partner?

29. Before this transaction began, did you brush your teeth or take a shower, then down the lights, turn on the stereo?

30. Were there *any* special steps you took by way of preparation?
31. What did you do that conveyed an interest or a resignation over what was to follow?
32. If you said Yes but really meant No, how was that conveyed?
33. Did you initiate the contact or did your partner? How was this done?
34. As you moved on to the next step, how was the transition made? How did you signal your readiness?
35. How did you want to appear to your partner? What behaviors did you choose to create the impression you wanted to make?

Part 2: Your Partner's Actions

Now, focus your mind's eye on your partner. Make another list, this time of what your partner did and in what sequence. Refer again to the questions in Part 1, putting yourself in your partner's place as carefully as you can. In addition, ask yourself:

36. What is my summary of how my partner behaved?
37. Which of his or her actions made the greatest impression on me? What did they convey to me?
38. Which of my partner's actions did I really enjoy? Which turned me off?
39. How different were my partner's actions from my own?

Part 3: Two-Camera Replay

If your partner, working separately from you, has also completed Parts 1 and 2 of this activity, you can now share your awarenesses with each other. Did you list actions of your own that your partner seemed not to notice, or omitted for some other reason? Did you make a shorter list of your partner's behaviors, on the other hand, than he or she recalls doing? What might account for your differing views?

As you discuss your recollections, bear in mind that this is not the time for judgmental commentary, criticisms, or encouragements. Cameras only record; they do not editorialize.

SENSATIONS

> This activity helped us to have the best sex we've had in years. There was no comparison between the impact of what happened and the sex toys, porno films, and fantasy role-playing we've done in the past!

> The barrier of silence was finally lifted!

> It was as though we turned off the autopilot and started actually flying the plane.

> I learned that she likes to hear me make noises during a sexual exchange. I like to hear her heart beating and to feel her perspiration.

> I tend to focus more on touch, and then on sound. She tends to focus more on smell and taste.

> This activity really sparked more meaningful dialogue.

Not only touch but also smell, sight, taste, and sound—messages from all your senses—work together to shape your responses during sex. This activity will help you see which sensory messages register strongest with you, so that you can identify (and possibly work to change) sensations that account for your sexual thoughts and feelings. Another goal might be to expand your capacity to respond to a variety of sensations instead of attending to only one or two of your senses.

Part 1: How Did It Feel?

Divide a sheet of paper into five sections, each one labeled with one of the five senses (touch, smell, sight, taste, sound). Think back over your most recent sexual experience: What images jump out at you? Note down what part each of your senses played, according to these guidelines:

Touch

What can you recall about who was touching whom, and how and when that occurred? Was the touch gentle or harsh? Did it feel good or bad? Was it arousing or was it a turnoff? Where did physical contact take place, on what part of the body? The tongue, lips, the hands, genital parts, ears, hands, feet? Where are you most sensitive? Is that a place you consider to be one of your erogenous zones? Where and how did your bodies meet?

Smell

Were you aware of any particular odors of tobacco, of perfume, of perspiration, of bodily excretions? Were they pleasant or unpleasant? Were you aware at all of how you smelled, or were you attending chiefly to your partner's smell?

Sight

What were you looking at? Your partner? Yourself? The ceiling? How much of what was going on did you take in with your eyes, or were they closed? Were you aware of feasting on each other through your eyes, or did one, or both of you, keep glancing away? Did you see what the two of you were actually doing? Which behaviors could you not get enough of with your eyes? What happened that you chose *not* to observe? Was it the look on your partner's face? Was it your partner's genitals? Was it the red socks your partner was wearing? What visual image was only fleeting or difficult to recall?

Taste

Did the kisses taste like cherries? Were they "sweeter than wine?" What about your partner's genitals? Were they savory, or was their taste repugnant to you? Where did you move your tongue and with what sensory results? How about your mouth, what did it take in? Would you walk a mile for what you tasted during your most recent sexual exchange or would you prefer to sit on the couch watching a rerun? Did you taste anything at all or did you leave this form of sensory input to another day?

Sound

What did you hear during your sexual exchange? The sound of music coming from your stereo? Noise outside on the street? Your partner's breathing, your partner's snore? Sounds of glee? Sounds of sexual excitement? Squeals of ecstasy upon reaching orgasm? Words exchanged between the two of you? Only silence?

Now, try to summarize your notes. Does just one of your senses overshadow the rest? Do you and your partner seem to differ in this regard? Which forms of stimulation elude you or your partner? How might this affect the nature of your sexual exchange, its quality, your interest in it, the degree of excitement that is typically there?

Part 2: A Fuller Picture

If your partner also cares to do Part 1, you can now put together your two sets of notes to see how they combine. The two of you may be surprised to find differences: for example, one of you may relish a sensation that the other dislikes or ignores. A particular sense that is the key to many of your responses may virtually shut down in your partner, or vice versa.

As you compare recollections, you may be able to determine that changing what there is to see or hear or smell would help make a sexual exchange more inviting. You can also identify what actions and what aspects of your surroundings have positive effects and what ones are negative.

In order to build on your self-scrutiny, you may choose to explore why you seem to shy away from certain sensory opportunities and consider what you each might do to make such opportunities positive experiences. If you decide to become masters of sensuality, to tune in to a greater array of sensations, you can congratulate yourselves on coming to your senses in more ways than one!

TIME FOR A CHANGE?

This activity focuses on specifics in your sexual circumstances with the idea that there may be particular improvements that you would like. Before going ahead with it, it is best for you first to have tried some of the others that deal with getting better acquainted with yourself, such as "Thoughts," "Feelings," and "Motivations," because you will be asked to search your mind and heart quite deeply for an understanding of both yourself and your partner, and you will get the most benefit from the activity if you are experienced in self-scrutiny.

Like the other activities in this chapter, this one can be done on your own, with the result that you will know yourself a little better. But you cannot *determine* by yourself what changes, if any, you and your partner should undertake, and particularly not which change should come first. You really need your partner's input for such decisions. Therefore, it is necessary that your partner participate too. And it is also crucial that the two of you fill out Part I entirely separately from each other. This includes being alone in the room, without having each other to glance at, much less consult.

Part 1: Is This O.K.?

Make five columns on a sheet of paper, headed *Item*, *Myself*, *Important*, *My Partner*, and *Difficult*. In the Item column, list the numbers 1 through 14, to represent the elements of your sex life in the list below, with (if you desire) some abbreviation that can remind you what the item is. Below the number 14, list any other elements that you would like to note as important to change or important to keep the way they are.

In each of the other four columns, mark how you feel about possibly changing the particular element. Under Myself, write plus (+) if you would like an increase here, minus (-) if you would like less of it, and O.K. if you don't want a change. Then, under Important, write

V (Very), S (Somewhat), or N (Not Very) for those elements you want changed, according to how important making the change is to you. Next, consider whether your partner seems satisfied or dissatisfied with the given item, and under My Partner write +, -, or O.K. as you did for yourself *and* an importance rating for him/her. Finally, for any item that you think *either* of you wants changed, consider how hard or how easy it would be to change it. Write V, S, or N to show (as for Important) how difficult the change would be.

What to change?

1. How often we have sex
2. How often I make the first move
3. How often my partner makes the first move
4. The different kinds of positions used
5. The amount of time spent in foreplay
6. The amount of time spent in actual intercourse
7. The amount of time spent in afterplay
8. The amount of tenderness displayed
9. The amount of forcefulness involved
10. The amount of talking my partner does during sex
11. The amount of talking I do during sex
12. How often I am interested in having sex
13. How often my partner is interested in having sex
14. How much talking we do about our sexual needs, interests, or concerns

Part 2: Let's Talk It Over

When you and your partner are ready to compare lists, you need to discuss *each* change *either* of you has marked, according to these guidelines:

1. When did you first become aware of wanting this particular change?

2. If you did not express your wish at the time, why?

3. If you made your wish known, what was the outcome?

4. What about you or your partner played a part in what occurred?

5. How similar or different are you and your partner in regard to how you view this particular aspect of your sexual relationship?

6. How similar or different are you and your partner in regard to how *important* it would be to make this particular change?

7. How accurate were you in supposing how important your partner would find a change that you noted?

8. If there are differences between the two of you in regard to how you view this particular matter, how do you account for them? How have you even tried to resolve these differences in the past? How do you account for the outcome?

9. How difficult do you and your partner think it would be for you to make this particular change? What would make it difficult for either of you? What does this say about you, your partner, or your partnership?

10. How hopeful are you that you can make this particular change? Why?

11. If the desired change does not occur, what do you suppose the consequences might be?

12. What benefits would there be if the desired change were made?

Take your time with this. You may want to complete Part 1 one day and begin Part 2 another day. It may take considerable time and effort to address the questions raised in Part 2, so you might decide to limit your discussion to only a few items during any one session. What is important here is discussing each change as something that *might* happen. You are not meant to draw up a rigorous agenda. This activity is only one step towards discovering each other, so that you can more easily talk together about your sexual circumstances.

ACCOUNTING FOR SEXUAL DIFFICULTIES

Very thought-provoking.

We knew more about ourselves than we had given ourselves credit for!

It was scary at first, our first try at any significant communication in many years.

If someone had asked me what turned him on most of all, I wouldn't have had a clue. This activity really helped!

It made him think about our sexual relationship and not just his own arousal.

This started us on the *path* to open communication, not only about sex but about our relationship in general.

He shared with me his huge fear that I might become pregnant. I never knew this was such an issue with him!

All couples, at least now and then, have had difficulties in their sexual lives. They may be temporary, they may be minor, or they may persist and become conscious problems. No matter what your own situation has been, though, it is how you *explain* it that most affects the quality of your relationship with your partner.

In this activity, you are asked to think about your sexual exchanges in general, over the time that has passed. Try to concentrate, not on the specific difficulties you have had, but on what underlying factors might have caused them.

Part 1: Ourselves As Individuals

Below is a list of statements that a person might make to explain why things do not always go smoothly in the sexual domain. You may well be able to think of others that pertain to your own circumstances. On a sheet of paper, make columns labeled *Reason, Myself, My Partner*. In the first column, write the numbers 1 through 27, to stand for the statements listed here, and add any others that occur to you. In the other two columns, you will mark each statement according to how well it applies to you, or to your partner, as follows.

Myself: Consider whether this is true of you—something you might honestly say of yourself—*and also* how much it seems to contribute to any sexual difficulties you have known. Mark V for Very Much a Factor, S for Somewhat— this could mean "quite true, but not often a cause of difficulties" or "sometimes true, and then it's a factor"—or N, Never/Not True/Not a Factor.

My Partner: Now imagine that it is your partner who is making the statements. In this case, "I/me/my" is your partner talking about himself/herself, and "my partner" means you. Write V, S, or N as above. For example, item #5 begins, "I have a negative body image. . . ." If you think that your *partner* feels unattractive *to you*, and that his/her feeling this way accounts for difficulties between you, you would mark #5 with a V in this column.

1. I am highly controlled and inhibited in the sexual domain.
2. I sometimes wish to create distance between me and my partner.
3. I find it difficult to assert myself in the sexual domain.
4. Sometimes I am simply too exhausted.
5. I have a negative body image and find it difficult to believe that I have much appeal to my partner.
6. I often find myself preoccupied with negative thoughts of one kind or another.
7. I do not feel bonded to my partner.
8. Sex is not that important to me any more.
9. I am fearful that a pregnancy might occur as a result of our sexual transactions.
10. I am getting old and not as sexually interested as I used to be.
11. Sex has not been that satisfying to me, so I would just as soon avoid it.
12. My poor health has taken its toll.

13. The various medications I take have adversely affected my sexual functioning.
14. I sometimes wish to withhold sexual satisfaction from my partner.
15. I am sometimes fearful that sex could be physically harmful or painful to me.
16. I am sometimes fearful that sex could be physically harmful or painful to my partner.
17. I would rather be with a different partner.
18. I resent my partner's sexual approaches.
19. I resent my partner's sexual appetite.
20. I have a low sex drive.
21. My emotional state(s) (e.g., depression, anxiety, etc.) make it difficult to enjoy sexual exchanges.
22. Sexual messages from the past make it difficult for me to feel comfortable with my sexuality.
23. During the course of the day I sometimes become upset with my partner and find it difficult to even consider a sexual exchange.
24. I find other aspects of my life more interesting and rewarding than sex.
25. I am not much of a lover.
26. My partner offers me little romance.
27. I find sex with my partner somehow dishonest.

Part 2: Ourselves As Partners

In addition to personal characteristics that you and your partner bring to your relationship, there are factors that pertain to the relationship itself more than to either of you alone. On another sheet of paper, use the same ratings—V, S, or N—as in Part 1 to assess the ten factors listed below. Be sure to add any other descriptions of your life that may interfere with sexual satisfaction. These could have to do with the nature of your partnership, with other stresses within or outside the household, or with conditions over which you have little control.

1. It is very difficult for us to discuss our sexual needs and interests.
2. Our overall relationship is so problematic that sex has become unrewarding as well.
3. We live in too close quarters with very little privacy.
4. My partner and I are mismatched. One of us is raring to go in the morning while the other is raring to go at midnight.
5. We're both so busy that we rarely have time for sexual pleasuring.
6. We're afraid that we'll be overheard by the children or even interrupted by them.
7. Late night shows on television seem to get most of our attention after we retire for the night.
8. It is difficult for us to cast any aspersions on the other's sexual behaviors. We keep our mouths shut to avoid any turmoil or upset.
9. We seem to have put sexual issues on the back burner.
10. We are both pretty naive when it comes to sex.

Part 3: Discussing Our Situation

Now you are in a position to share your responses with each other. Begin by mentioning the factors *in yourself* that might make sexual exchanges not entirely pleasing to you; see "Couple Communication" (p. 297) for how to proceed. Talking over the responses that just one of you made about yourself could well be enough for one session. Some other day you can discuss how you think your *partner* has contributed to the difficulties in your sexual relationship, and later still, give the one who has so far been listening a chance to be speaker. Only the two of you can determine when enough—for today, anyway—is enough.

IDENTIFYING SEXUAL DIFFICULTIES

It helped me take some giant steps toward improving our sex life.

It is very hard—and maybe a waste of time—to imagine any sexual relationship that has no room for improvement, that does not involve difficulties of one kind or another, great or small. There are those whose difficulties amount to technical sexual dysfunctions (for instance anorgasmia vaginismus, erectile failures)—the type of problems typically referred to a sex therapist. But much more frequent are less obvious complaints, frustrations, or regrets.

Part 1: Recent Difficulties

Divide a sheet of paper into four columns headed *Difficulty*, *Myself*, *Effect*, and *My Partner*. In the first column, enter the areas of difficulty from the list that follows—Communication, Interest/ Enthusiasm, and so forth—abbreviating them as convenient. Leave space under each area-label for numbers representing the listed entries and for any other difficulty you think of that falls into that area.

Now consider, for each entry in the list, whether you have experienced it *over the past year*. Under Myself, mark how often this has been a difficulty for you: O for Often, S for Sometimes, R for Rarely, N for Never. Under Effect, mark how badly you think each difficulty has interfered with your sex life: V for Very Much (a severely negative effect), S for Somewhat, N for Not Very Much/Not At All. It is possible to mark N in this column next to an O or S under myself, if you believe the particular item did not count as a problem even though it did happen. On the other hand, it is also possible that a rarely-occurring difficulty (R) can have a strong impact (V). Finally, in the fourth column, write O, S, R, or N to show how you think your partner would mark the frequency of the given difficulty.

Communication

1. **Dissatisfaction with how you and your partner discuss your sexual needs and interests**
2. **A wish that you and your partner would talk about your sexual relationship more frequently**

Interest/Enthusiasm

1. A lack of enthusiasm for sex on the part of your partner
2. A lack of enthusiasm on your part for sex
3. A lack of interest in a sexual exchange with your partner
4. Your partner's lack of interest in a sexual exchange with you
5. A disinterest in improving your sexual circumstances
6. Despair over your sexual circumstances ever improving
7. Wishing sex were more important to you
8. Wishing sex were more important to your partner
9. How levels of arousal rise or fall throughout a sexual exchange
10. Feeling you have to fake sexual excitement, involvement, and pleasure

Initiation

1. Unhappiness over your partner's disinclination to initiate a sexual exchange
2. Unhappiness over your own disinclination to initiate a sexual exchange
3. Your partner's refusal of intercourse when you desire it
4. Your refusal of intercourse when your partner desires it
5. Feeling rejected when your partner does not welcome your sexual advances
6. Your partner's feeling rejected when you do not welcome his/her sexual advances

Birth Control

1. A displeasure with the type of birth control you are using
2. Fears of an unwanted pregnancy

Enjoyment

1. A lack of enjoyment during sexual intercourse with your partner
2. A general unhappiness with your sexual relationship

Fantasies

1. Fantasies of sex with a different partner that are upsetting you in any way
2. Unwanted fantasies that interfere with your sexual enjoyment (involving sadomasochism, group orgies, homosexual ideation, and so on)

Dysfunctions

1. A lack of control over when you reach orgasm (premature ejaculation)
2. A relatively weak and inconsequential orgasm
3. (Males) Relatively weak erections
4. (Males) Difficulties maintaining an erection during intercourse
5. (Males) The loss of an erection prior to engaging in sexual intercourse
6. Finding sexual intercourse physically painful
7. Not reaching orgasm even though you want to
8. Feeling like a spectator during a sexual exchange with your partner
9. Frequent distractions during sex with your partner
10. (Females) Difficulties lubricating prior to sexual intercourse
11. (Females) Not lubricating very much during foreplay
12. (Males) Requiring too long a time to reach orgasm (ejaculatory incompetence)
13. (Females) A vaginal tightness that makes intercourse difficult

Frequency

1. Wishing you had sex more often
2. Wishing you had sex less often
3. Wishing you had a greater say in how often you have sex with your partner

Self Image

1. Feeling like a relatively poor lover
2. Wishing you were more sexually appealing to your partner

Partner Issues

1. Wishing your partner were a better lover
2. Feeling pressured by your partner to reach orgasm
3. Wondering if your partner has been satisfied after a sexual exchange
4. Wishing your partner were more sexually appealing

Feelings

1. Shame/Guilt
2. Fear
3. Inadequacy
4. Disappointment
5. Boredom
6. Disgust

Part 2: Sharing Your Problems

As you and your partner compare responses, consider these questions:

1. How similar or different are the difficulties you see in yourself and in your partner?

2. How might your difficulties contribute to your partner's, and vice versa?

3. How accurate are your impressions of each other? What might account for any of your misimpressions?

4. Do you agree with your partner's estimate of the impact of a given difficulty on the quality of your partnership?

5. Which difficulties do you think might be the easiest to remedy?

6. What changes in the two of you might produce the greatest payoffs?

7. What concrete plans might you make to help alleviate your difficulties?

8. How will you keep track of any the changes you intend to carry out?

Now that you have pinpointed difficulties that you both agree you'd like to get rid of, you may feel discouraged that there seems so much to work on. It will probably be more rewarding in the end, because it will be easier to persist, if you choose to make just one improvement at a time. The activities "Couple Communication" (p. 297) and "Time for a Change?" (p. 315) can help you decide how to start.

SEXUAL PEAKS

I liked the positive focus of this activity.

Even though some of the elements involved were somewhat obvious, the activity helped to bring them out into the open. Our thinking became more focused.

An incredible experience for me.

Think of the times you have felt really good in a sexual exchange, much better than you sometimes feel. These need not be times when the skies fell— simply highlights in your sexual history. They might have occurred with your present partner or with a previous partner.

They might happen to you fairly often, or they might be exceptional moments that you love to remember. This is what is meant by sexual peaks.

Part 1: What Makes It Special

Cast your mind back to one or two of these especially fulfilling sexual experiences. If someone had interrupted you to ask why it was a peak time for you, how might you have answered? Try to write down as many explanations as occur to you. Then number your paper from 1 through 21, to correspond to the statements listed below. For each one, mark how much a factor it was in your delight: V for Very Much, S for Somewhat, N for Not Very Much/Not At All.

1. I am feeling very good emotionally.
2. For some reason I am feeling uninhibited.
3. My partner is doing a good job of stimulating me.
4. I am feeling really close to and appreciative of my partner.
5. I am feeling pleased with my physical appearance.
6. I am feeling a lot of sexual tension and pleased to have an opportunity to gratify myself.
7. I am especially eager to gratify my partner sexually.
8. I am feeling good physically.
9. Things are going well for us outside the home.
10. I am finding my partner very sexually appealing.
11. I am engaging in sex because I really want to.
12. I am not feeling distracted. My head is nowhere else.
13. I am not worried about my performance.
14. I am allowing myself to experience my own pleasure and am not so concerned about how my partner is doing.
15. My sexual fantasies are particularly lively.
16. I feel energetic.
17. We can take our time, not rush.
18. My partner seems to be equally enthusiastic, not unwilling in any way.
19. My partner and I are equally active in the sexual exchange.

20. I am feeling really good about how my partner and I are relating to each other emotionally.
21. I am feeling sexually bold, not so afraid of failure or rejection.

Part 2: Sharing Your Ideals.

When you and your partner have each completed Part 1 and feel that the listed statements plus your own additions pretty well summarize how your sexual peaks feel, you may want to discuss not only your own responses but what you think your partner feels at peak times. Consider these points:

1. What do you think your responses tell you about yourself, about your partner, about your partnership?
2. What clues do they give about what you make of sex and what you need for it to be especially fulfilling?
3. Which factor is the most important of all? How different are you in your priorities?
4. What can the two of you do to make sure that your ideal circumstances get honored in the future? Exactly what steps might you take?

HIDDEN ASSUMPTIONS

This activity prompted us to have one of our most intimate conversations.

We were able to work out an issue I never even knew existed! Some of my hidden assumptions surprised me.

Here is what might prove to be an important activity in which you identify some aspect of your sexual life that is at least moderately upsetting to you. It may be that you notice a lack of sexual interest or responsiveness in your partner; you may wish you had sex more often, or less often out of habit and more often impulsively; perhaps it bothers you that a former lover pops into your mind during sex with your partner; you may feel turned off or emotionally distant because of the way your partner acts. The list could go on and on. You may be able to think of a number of things that you find upsetting to some degree.

Part 1: Tracing Your Thoughts

Now choose one feature of your sex life that upsets you. As the following example indicates, your job will be to discover why you find a particular situation upsetting and to trace the chain of upsetting thoughts as far as you can go, connecting each thought to the next, as the arrows below imply:

- **When we are finished with our lovemaking, I do not feel close to my partner.**

  ↓

  (Ask yourself what this means to you, why this thought is upsetting. Do this with each subsequent thought.)

  ↓

- **We really do not have an honest, authentic connection.**

  ↓

- **If we don't have an authentic connection, maybe we're just biding our time until we end up in divorce court.**

  ↓

- **If we end up in a divorce court, it would mean that I have failed in my marriage.**

  ↓

- **If I fail in my marriage, I am a failure as a human being.**

  ↓

- **This would mean that I am not a really loving or lovable person.**

  ↓

- **If that truly is the case then I'll never find a successful, gratifying relationship with anyone.**

  ↓

- So I'll be lonely and alone for the rest of my life.

↓

- Then people will view me as a sad excuse for a human being.

↓

- I'll lose my friends and I'll forever be an outsider among the people I care about.

↓

- In such circumstances there is no reason to go on living.

This example shows how an initial thought, upsetting in itself, is traceable to a chain of additional thoughts that maintain or even exacerbate our distress. In this chain, we can identify a number of self-defeating suppositions about what constitutes a satisfying life. Among them are the convictions that we can only feel good about ourselves if others think well of us, that we must always live up to others' expectations, and that we must always strive to be perfect *or else*. Having to be perfect or else implies that in order to feel worthwhile, we must never fall short of our standards, that people will never accept us if we are flawed in any way, and that if others reject us, they are always right to do so.

These are beliefs and reactions that we find in our adult selves, but we can be sure that when a given idea or situation really threatens and frightens us, its roots will be found in our childhood. As children, we had no perspective to judge the consequences of our behaviors, our guilt was often quick to overwhelm us, our fears of punishment loomed over us. And somewhere within ourselves we still hold the childish convictions that mistakes and evil doing lead to identically disastrous consequences, that connections with others are all-important no matter what, and that it is only reckless to feel optimistic.

Part 2: Unraveling the Chain

When you have picked out the trail of thoughts that leads from an upsetting sexual event back to its remote and dismal outposts, try to find several points in it where you can halt it by substituting positive statements about yourself or remedies that you could try. In the above example, for instance, the person might well have cut off the destructive monologue by declaring:

> Just because we do not have an authentic connection at the present time, it doesn't mean we're destined for divorce court. Now that I am aware of how important it is for me to feel close during sex, I can share it more fully with my partner. We can talk about it together, maybe with a counselor. As much as it hurts right now, this could be the beginning of an important journey that we have put off for too long. It could breathe new life into our marriage. But even if we do end up getting divorced, that won't mean that I failed, as a spouse or as a person. I'll have tried my best with the relationship we had, and I'll have other opportunities, and I might find a new relationship more congruent with my deepest needs. I'll have learned a lot, anyway. Most people marry again after divorce, so chances are I will too, possibly with better results. I can't help how people want to view me, but most of my friends will probably be supportive or, at worst, indifferent. In any case, I refuse to be controlled by what other people might think. I am ready to deal with whatever happens. I guess I can imagine circumstances where I'd think about suicide, but this isn't one of them!

Upsetting thoughts of one kind or another, especially when we try to sweep them under the rug instead of facing them directly, can play havoc with our sexual lives. When they are not taken on and contended with, we can feel powerless and paralyzed. They can prevent us from taking constructive action and lead but to further estrangement from ourselves and from our loved ones. This activity gives you an opportunity to face down your fears, separate the rational from the irrational, and find the power to take some saving action that will raise your self-esteem, possibly, and provide a remedy.

SEXUAL APPRECIATIONS

> We both came away with more positive feelings about ourselves and each other.

It was like a breath of fresh air. We're looking forward to doing it again.

A wonderful icebreaker for us. We both promised to be more timely about expressing our appreciation of each other. We agreed that waiting ten years was entirely too long!

It's always nice to be stroked!

It warmed us to each other.

After we finished, I wanted to jump all over him. What an aphrodisiac!

Thoroughly enjoyable.

When you think about your sexual relationship with your partner, it is all too easy in the face of besetting difficulties to pass over those features that need no improvement. The difficulties tend to usurp your attention. On the other hand, if your sex life is relatively trouble-free, you may value your good fortune but seldom think to mention it. In either case, telling your partner what it is that you enjoy and appreciate can be important to a fulfilling sexual relationship.

Part 1: What You Like To Remember

Spend a few minutes reconstructing in your mind the story of your sex life with your partner. Try to recall what was memorable about your most recent sexual exchange as well as special ones from the past. Make a list of whatever you have ever appreciated about your partner, whatever has warmed your heart. Ideally, these will be specific recollections of what touched you most about your partner during the sexual moment that took place, but you can also include, more generally, exactly what it is about your partner that has ever been gratifying to you.

Is it something about your partner's physical appearance? Be exact if you can: The texture of your partner's hair? The softness of your partner's skin? The fresh smell of your partner's body? A mouth that felt kissing sweet? The appearance of your partner's genitalia? Perhaps it is a certain look your partner sometimes gives you or a gesture your partner makes, an unusual sound or exclamation, your partner's patience or delight or sexual energy, your partner's appreciation of you, the way your partner initiated a sexual exchange or responded to your invitation, a comment made afterwards, a risk your partner took, a special accommodation that was made, an innovation that surprised and pleased you, a willingness and welcome that was conveyed and the form it took: list just what you liked, without any kinds of wishes or judgments.

To make this list will probably take some time. Allow yourself several days to see if, at a comfortable pace, you can add a few more recollections. Your final list may still be rather short, but this should be no concern: what counts is that you have sincerely gratifying memories to share.

Part 2: What Your Partner Likes To Remember

As you look back over your sexual exchanges, you have probably also recalled a few things that your partner has said or done to indicate appreciation of *you*. If any of these got noted in your list for Part 1, it is time to move them to a separate list. Again, you will probably need quite a bit of time to think of ways in which you have been a source of delight to your partner, but note them down as they occur to you, and search for them carefully.

Part 3: Adding Details

Looking at the two lists you have made, first consider how often it happens that you have experienced the gratifying features of sexual contact that you noted, and mark them O for Often, S for Sometimes, or R for Rarely. Similarly, mark the list of appreciations that you guess your partner has felt. Next, you can further mark both lists according to how deep or strong these feelings are (or seem to be): V for Very, Q for Quite, K for Kind Of. These markings are not really necessary, but they may help you organize what you want to say when you discuss your appreciations with your partner.

Part 4: Appreciations For Each Other

Now you are ready to share your lists with each other. How similar or different are your lists? How accurate are your suppositions of your partner's appreciations? What do your lists tell you about your needs and interests? What do they seem to tell you about your partner's needs and interests? What might they tell you about the nature of your sexual partnership?

During your discussion, be sure to report back to your partner what you hear being said until both of you are satisfied that the message has been accurately received. Tell your partner what a particular appreciation means to you, how it makes you feel, and whether or not it comes as a surprise. It might be helpful for the two of you to agree that each of you will save at least one appreciation of the other to be presented some other day. Meanwhile, you can be on the lookout for more things to appreciate about your partner until you meet for another exchange of appreciations—fairly soon.

ALMOST EVERYTHING YOU'VE ALWAYS WANTED TO ASK

It gave us an opportunity to pose questions we would have felt ridiculous asking otherwise.

It felt very good to get things out into the open.

It helped us conceptualize a problem we had been having in our relationship. The questions brought the problem out about six times.

The questions I found the hardest to answer were the ones that led to the most important discussions.

Chances are you have never felt really free to investigate for yourself or to share with another your sexual values and attitudes, your sexual history, your sexual needs and interests, your sexual concerns and gratifications. The questions that follow give you an opportunity to do just that. When you are in a quiet space by yourself, take out some paper and write out your answers to the questions below. Writing them out is important, because you can produce more thoughtful and careful answers than you could if someone just read you the questions aloud. And some of these questions take a great deal of thought and care. You will probably find it easiest to list your answers over at least half a dozen separate sittings, working on a few of the questions each day.

After you and your partner have finally prepared complete, open, and honest responses to all the questions, discuss with each other what it was like to answer them. Since a chief benefit of this activity is the opportunity it gives you to learn more about each other as sexual beings, start with the first question, tell each other how you answered, and take time to comment on your replies until you both feel you have dealt fully with the question. Then move on to the next. An important word of advice: you and your partner should agree that either of you can postpone any question, either because you are still working on your answer or because you think that it touches on a topic that the two of you cannot comfortably or constructively talk about. Neither of you *must* discuss any particular question before you feel ready to, even if it has to be postponed for months.

1. Given what you know about your partner, what is one thing you might do to make yourself more sexually appealing to her/him?
2. Would you rather be the partner with the greater sexual need and interest who is sometimes frustrated by your partner's seeming *lack* of interest, or vice versa?
3. If your partner does not customarily reach orgasm during a sexual exchange, would you like to be informed of this or do you prefer that it not be talked about?
4. Which would you prefer, a partner who is sexually dysfunctional but emotionally involved with you or a partner who functions very well but remains somewhat detached?
5. What is a chief distraction for you during a sexual exchange with your partner?

6. If you were to give your sexual partnership a title, what would it be?

7. How do you think your bodily appearance affects the quality of your sexual life? What about your partner's appearance?

8. How old were you when you first became aware of your sexual feelings? What was going on at the time?

9. If you are sexually inhibited at all, in what way might that be? How do you account for it?

10. If you have any sexual difficulties at all, do you think they would be there with a different sexual partner? Why? Why not?

11. What might you and/or your partner do that would give your sexual partnership the greatest boost?

12. How hopeful are you that your sexual partnership will change for the better in the not too distant future?

13. Describe a setting in which you would find the prospect of sex most appealing. How does it differ from your customary setting?

14. If your partner had been aware of what your sexual partnership would be like before you ever became involved with each other, do you think he/she would have chosen a different partner?

15. What might your partner do to enhance your sexual arousal?

16. How long should it take for sexual partners to reach orgasm once a sexual exchange has been initiated?

17. In your childhood, prior to going off to school, did anything happen that might have had an impact on your experience of sexuality? What about during your elementary school years?

18. How responsible do you feel for what occurs in your sexual partnership?

19. What sexual behavior(s) have you thought about engaging in but have refrained from doing because of your partner's attitudes or values?

20. How important is sex to the well-being of a partnership?

21. If you have ever thought that your partner would rather be with a different sexual partner, why did you think this might be so?

22. To what do you attribute your partner's sex drive?

23. How much effort have you and your partner made to enhance the quality of your sexual relationship? To what extent have you come to accept the status quo?

24. What about your sexual partnership do you find the most gratifying? The most dissatisfying?

25. How would you rate yourself as a lover or sex partner? How would you rate your partner?

26. Under the most ideal conditions, but not beyond what is truly possible, how frequently would you like to engage in sex with your partner? What keeps that from happening?

27. Since most young people, during childhood and/or adolescence, engage in masturbation, how important would it be for parents to suggest it to their children as a way for them to relieve their sexual tensions?

28. For those involved in an ongoing sexual partnership, how free should they feel to go off by themselves and masturbate? Under what conditions? What proportion of sex with your sexual partner vs. sex on your own would be acceptable to you?

29. Who is more appealing to you, a sexual partner who is exciting and competent but who occasionally fantasizes sex with someone else while having sex with you, or a sexual partner who never fantasizes in this way but who is sometimes inhibited or even dysfunctional during a sexual exchange with you?

30. How predictable are your sexual exchanges with one another? How do you suppose it got that way?

31. What physical position do you prefer the most when having sexual intercourse with your partner? Why is that? What are the advantages and disadvantages of the position you prefer?

32. Which of you is the more active during a sexual exchange

with each other? How does this affect your sexual experience?

33. Which would be worse: to discover that your partner had been sexually unfaithful to you or to be discovered to have been sexually unfaithful yourself?

34. What were the sexual messages your mother gave you? How have they affected you?

35. What sexual messages did your father give to you? How have they affected your sexual partnering?

36. What do you think is your greatest challenge in becoming a fully functioning sexual partner?

37. What are your chief sexual regrets?

38. What sexual situation were you ever in that you resented the most?

39. When were you most afraid in a sexual situation?

40. If you had but one sexual message to give to our nation's youth, what would it be?

41. If you were in search of a partner and advertised yourself in a local newspaper, how would you describe yourself as a sexual human being? How would you describe the kind of partner you were looking for?

42. How much pressure do you feel from your partner to reach orgasm?

43. If you have children, how has their presence affected the quality of your sexual relationship?

44. How do you think your present sexual partnership compares with what you imagine your parents' to have been?

45. How sexually experimental do you consider yourself to be?

46. What sexual experiences during high school had a special impact on you? What about during your college-age years?

47. If you were asked by a good friend to be a sexual surrogate for a member of the opposite sex who was having sexual difficulties, what would be your response? What would be the chief issues for you in considering your friend's request?

48. In what ways and to what extent has your present sexual partnership changed from how it used to be? How do you account for these changes?
49. What was your most enjoyable sexual dream?
50. Have you ever had sexual feelings for a member of the same sex? When? Under what conditions?
51. If it could be guaranteed that three weeks on a tropical island with a sexual surrogate would restore your partner's sexual interest and functioning, would you agree to such a plan?
52. Do you ever wish you'd had more (or fewer) sexual partners prior to meeting your present partner?
53. How hard is it to say "no" to your partner's sexual advances?
54. What is your favorite off-color joke?
55. What advantages do you think might occur from either you or your partner becoming less interested in sex?
56. Think up an appropriate sexual epitaph that might appear on your gravestone.
57. For how much money would you be willing to have sex with a virtual stranger? Consider other conditions under which you would be willing to carry out such an exchange.
58. If you knew for sure that your partner would live ten years longer by having occasional affairs, how do you think this might affect your views of his or her infidelity?

16

Five Stories:
CLINICAL PARADIGMS

Sexual counseling, if it is ever to be successful, requires more than anything else an uncommon honesty on the part of the individuals involved, the therapist as well as the client. Those who are party to this enterprise must get to the point where they can speak their minds and own their most secret agendas, risk shame and embarrassment in a monumental effort to make themselves known to themselves and to the others, and declare their bottom lines.

For the therapist, this might involve insisting that the couple carry out the tasks agreed upon and refusing to meet again until the couple has made good on their promise. At times he may have to call a spade a spade no matter how much this may generate discomfort in the couple: the therapist who is unwilling to risk animus from one or both partners in the effort to redefine the problem or to change the old rules of the partnership will never get the job done. As much as anything else the therapist must model "real talk," be appropriately assertive, and remain confident that no matter what occurs during a clinical exchange, no matter what "mistakes" are made, they can always be rectified if they are ultimately processed and shared.

For the clients, bottom lines will involve taking clear stands with their partners and sometimes with the therapist, declaring what they are willing and not willing to do in behalf of the relationship. Most of all, they must come to see that personal integrity is far more important than interpersonal harmony, that self-respect counts for more than smiles on another's face.

The vignettes that follow offer glimpses into how difficult transparency can be. In fact, it will probably remain the chief challenge of our lives, never entirely accomplished, given our histories of learned evasiveness. We should rejoice in those moments when we, like the couples in these clinical stories, struggle to allow ourselves to be known without apology.

VIGNETTE NO. 1

He, as usual, was sleepy, in what he has called his "therapy coma." It seemed as though he sat there out of a good-natured sense of duty, wishing he could be with us more fully like the "good boy" he always tried to be. Opposite him she, on the other hand, was vigorously alert, her eyes flashing, darting from him to me and back again. I had just reviewed all my clinical notes of our sessions, individual as well as joint, and I knew exactly what I wanted them to address on this particular morning.

Reading over the history of their counseling, I had been struck by how many steps they had taken to remedy their sexual circumstances, not one of which they had maintained. How had all the exercises affected their conscious wishes to draw closer to each other? Had the attendant risks encouraged or discouraged them? It appeared to her that she had to initiate any work they did on their relationship, and this only reinforced her sense that she had been too much like a mother to him, making requests to be either accommodated or resisted, a pattern that had led long ago to her losing respect for him and to his resenting what he had seen as her control.

I knew that for many good reasons their stalemate must require considerable collusion, and because their sexual troubles were by no means of the garden variety sort, I pondered the consequences of a failure to resolve them. The stakes were high, involving not only the quality of their marriage but ultimately his professional success as well.

Given his various predilections for sexual misbehavior, there was trouble in store for the two of them if our efforts could not bear fruit. At this point in our work together I felt I had to alert them, expecting that they would hear my warnings as an expression of a deep caring and respect for each of them.

How could it be, I asked them, that their future life together depended on the success of our efforts, and yet they found it so difficult to set aside time to attend to their relationship? Days would go by without as little as fifteen minutes of "real talk" between them! What were their priorities? How much did any of this matter? What did the risks entail for each of them? I repeated what we had, I thought, discussed so thoroughly before: what would be the payoffs and the costs of full-fledged efforts to turn their relationship around? At first he reacted with his usual nervous laughter, then joked that, given their busy schedules, they might communicate with each other via e-mail. His joking at this point hit her hard: she wanted far more than e-mail from him, and she was tired of taking responsibility for their erratic progress. Her tone of voice made it clear that unless things changed she would be heading for a divorce lawyer.

In the short time we had left, there was not enough time to go over the psychodynamic aspects of their dilemma. Insights of that kind had been gathered and discussed at length in their individual sessions. Would they be willing, I asked, and able to settle upon a time each day for "real talk" between them, for a true engagement of some kind? When, where, how, and for how long could they arrange for such daily meetings? During the evening he would be typically so caught up in his work that scheduling time for such talks would constitute an intrusion. She offered to get up fifteen minutes earlier, but could he get into any meaningful time with her so early in the day? Certainly, he replied, so long as he had downed a cup of coffee before they sat down to talk. Fifteen minutes, I asked, only fifteen minutes to spare for so great a need? Well, she said, there was no way that she could get up even earlier, since it took her forty-five minutes to walk to work and she had to be at her desk eight minutes before eight with the computer booted and ready even though most of her colleagues were nowhere to be seen at that hour. He then offered to feed the cats and clean up from breakfast if that would make for extra time between them. In that case, she responded, she would be willing to leave a little later for work and perhaps jog a little to get there at the mandatory time. I think I'll call them this morning to see how the plan is working out.

Meanwhile I am left with a variety of convictions I constantly need to be reminded of: (a) before involving clients in such enterprises, find out how much time they can (or will) really put in; (b) whenever they put in less time than they have promised, confront, explore, address whatever might be contributing to this resistance until it is fully resolved; (c) warn a couple well ahead of time that the journey they are about to embark on may require more than they are prepared to give, that perhaps their efforts should be postponed or even forgone, that it is always a question of what we are willing to settle for. Clients must be persuaded that an hour spent with me is no cure, and that how they spend their time *between* our visits is what will determine the outcome of our work.

VIGNETTE NO. 2

Sooner or later, I invite everyone working with me on his or her sexual circumstances to tell about his or her most recent sexual exchange, moment by moment, from beginning to end. I accept no euphemisms, no elisions, as we milk those moments for all their possible clues to the client's sexual thoughts and emotions. This is no place for any counselor who worries about being viewed as a nitpicker or voyeur. Any lessons ever learned about modesty, either by the counselor or client, must be parked outside the door. Here and now is where we begin to sift the soil like archaeologists with their sieves, unearthing treasures too easily passed over by a onceover with a garden rake. Usually a client will wince upon discovering that I insist on details he or she can hardly bear to recall, much less share with a virtual stranger.

He reports: "Typically we make plans to take showers and then go lie down together. We'll use a crystal pumpkin or a pillow to indicate our interest in having sex. I guess that seems crass and unromantic. It makes sex feel perfunctory, not something that happens out of the moment. [I ask him to imagine and describe the scene in the present tense.] I'm feeling nervous. Will I fantasy or not? She would hate it if I did. In fact she made me promise to tell her if that happened, but I usually keep it to myself and end up feeling guilty. I'm wondering how well I'll perform and whether or not she'll reach orgasm. All the while I'm thinking she's only doing this for me. More than that, she's afraid that if she doesn't I might act out again. [He'd been arrested more than once for exhibiting himself in public.] I rub her shoulders and actually want to suck on her entire body, but she complains that this feels so slimy and wet. I'm wondering if she's getting aroused and if this will require cunnilingus. The prospect of performing oral sex is nerve-wracking. Will she enjoy it? Will we even get to the passionate stage where both of us are really into it? I keep feeling that it's all a farce. Since I think she's not really enjoying oral contact that much, I can't lose myself in what's going on between us. Am I taking too long? Will it not be long enough? She's tense, probably because she's feeling pressure from me to reach orgasm. That's when I stop and decide to have intercourse. When I mount her, she appears neutral. I want to kiss her, but she would be grossed out by that since my mouth is full of her vaginal juices. So I kiss her, but not deeply. As I prop myself up on my elbows, I'm thinking she's thinking this had better end. If I go more slowly she might finally come. Maybe it would be better if I chose a faster pace and stuck with it. If there's no positive sign from her I'll just focus on me and reach orgasm. On the other hand if things are looking positive from her end, I'll go for *her* orgasm. Above all, I don't want to fantasize. Will I or won't I? How extensive will the fantasies be? I just know I'm going to fantasize [being teased and humiliated by a female stranger]. So already it's a downer for me. Since I won't report it to her, I'm being dishonest. These negative feelings continue after I ejaculate. I feel bad about wanting to stop. She's not reached orgasm, and I should really keep going. I feel selfish. I should be more attentive to her. I've been gratified, and she hasn't been. Even though I feel physically relaxed and enjoy holding her, I feel selfish too. How long should I lie there? How soon can I get up without hurting her feelings? I think she wants me to stay close to her, but I want to watch TV. So I stay with her five to ten minutes. But she knows I want to get up and go."

There is so much here, so much that needs attention, so many avenues to explore, a host of thoughts and feelings that tell so much about these people and their partnership! Not bad for a beginning. We are beginning to filet the fish. Here and there, a few parts of the skeleton are exposed. But what to focus on first with him? That he is squeamish about being frankly sexual? That he fears and dreads having fantasies? That with all his preoccupations, he can't be spontaneous? That he feels guilty and ashamed to be who he is? That his detente with his wife contributes to the very circumstances he tries so hard to avoid? That he must try to assure his wife that he is normal while resenting her desire to control his thoughts, his feelings, his behaviors? That he seems to balance his pleasure and gratification against hers, instead of seeing them as complementary? I see that there must be many more directions of inquiry than these, but even so, every one of them begs further explanation, suggests endless trails of thoughts and feelings waiting to be discovered and then discussed more fully. His descriptions of future sexual episodes will provide more information to take into account. Eventually some saving insights will appear. Important risks will be identified, though perhaps none greater than the one already begun: exposing all the secrets of one's mind and heart to another human being.

VIGNETTE NO. 3

I am astonished! The two of them can hardly wait to begin our session. I haven't seen them in almost a month, and when I greeted them in the waiting room I am taken with her looks: she is actually glowing. Both of them are euphoric, full of an energy I have never seen before. They sit down together in a way that betokens an uncommon welcome from each to each, and I am not about to suggest that he sit opposite or on another couch, my usual recommendation for couples who usually avoid each other's eyes. Something significant has happened in them or between them since our last meeting, and I am all ears.

Hardly able to contain herself, she begins to report so many changes that it is all I can do to keep track of them. First she exults in a sexual resurrection that has taken place in her, a surge of sexual feelings that she'd been sure would never be recovered in this lifetime. Although she was afraid that he would reject her out of hand if she told him of her transformation, she has already shared the news with him, of how tired she has been of being a sexual neuter, of hiding herself from him. She has begun "body work"—deep massage—with a local specialist in that realm, and for the first time *ever* has begun to connect with herself, to find pleasure in her body without shame or guilt. In going to the masseur, she challenged parental taboos about owning her body; now masturbation, which she previously begrudged her "unruly" body, has become a veritable physical and emotional "meltdown." In addition to this major change, she has lost another eight pounds, and is now two dress sizes smaller than when we began; further, she has declared a "divorce" from her young son, who has been her primary emotional focus, much to the boy's (and her husband's) discomfort. It's a new dawn for all three of them!

His comments are just as enthusiastic. His wife has not only returned to the marriage bed, she has leapt joyfully into it. Now that he can see how she is revived, he can get over his guilt about playing into her cadaver-like state. Not only that, but he can now talk freely about what it was like to peep in windows and seek out impersonal sex in men's rooms. He has already begun to let her into this hidden part of himself, testing his old convictions that if she really learned who he was she would recoil in horror. Today he speaks of his mother's life-long assaults on his personal integrity, of how their relationship amounted mostly to her screaming demand that he meet her needs and ignore his own. The only way he was able to force any autonomy at all was to go underground, to engage in thoughts and wishes and behaviors that he was sure were not on his mother's agenda for him. He has treated his wife the same, he says: superficially accommodating her while the hideous stranger inside would not let her in on what he was up to. For him the question has always been, what can I reveal about myself safely and still be joined? And further, if I find it so hard to look at myself, how can I ever really look at you?

What a delight to hear all of this coming from the two of them! My delight, however, is tempered somewhat by the fact that her breakthrough has occurred at the hands of a "body work" practitioner

I hardly know and in the space of only two sessions! I had not really considered the potential benefits of such an intervention. I had not even recommended him to her! But hard on the heels of this thought comes my realization, that the progress they are so excited about did not really happen all at once. It never happens that way, as much as the counselor and client(s) may wish for such a possibility. We have had fully sixty-nine sessions, individual and conjoint, and over the course of them much spadework has been done, other secrets have been revealed, other personal truths discussed, various remedies attempted, risks taken, a step forward sometimes followed by a step or more backwards. That is the way this works when more than sexual issues get addressed.

She had been to ten therapists before me, had gained sixty pounds in the process, and had stayed angry at him from the time they had tried to have sex without the fog induced by drugs or alcohol. Although she blamed him for not being aggressive enough, she was not at all sure that she could handle much more than a sexless marriage. She had no bottom line to declare. Having been a therapist herself, she was quick to identify and analyze his psychosexual circumstances with hardly a glance at herself, her pockets of shame, her dependency on him, or her use of anger to hide her pain. It was not until three months into our journey that he finally shared with her and me the fact that he had had many anonymous sexual contacts with other men throughout their marriage. This news only strengthened her conviction that *his* issues were the problem and that this was where the focus should be.

After exclaiming, "I want to be a woman before I die!", she did not return for a month and was then still confused about how she might pursue such a goal. I did not see her again until two more months had passed, when she reported using trance tapes to control her eating and finding it all but impossible to exercise; yet a month after that she was ready for a divorce, having lost hope that he would ever become her lover. Next over a series of weekly sessions, among other things she recalled that in her first love relationship she had felt like a woman but was ultimately rejected. In an effort to avoid such painful consequences in her future, she started armoring herself, as she had done before against her father's verbal assaults. When I urged her to focus more on herself than on her husband, she recalled that when she was twelve, an older boy visiting the family had done all but rape her. This trauma she shared with the Virgin Mary alone, saying daily Ave Marias for a year. From it had come her fears of any male's being even remotely seductive toward her and her apprehension over ever being seen as a seductive female. Out of that life-defining moment had come her resolve to always be in charge. Was it any wonder that twice she had chosen to marry males who were singularly unaggressive sexually?

Subsequent sessions involved deep scrutiny of all the ways she covered up a host of insecurities, her fears of being hurt masked by her anger toward him for his failure to initiate intimate contact, her fear of becoming too dependent on him, her embarrassment over not being gainfully employed, and her constant complaints over *his* unwillingness to move off dead center when, in fact, she was rebelling at her obvious need to exercise and control her eating.

Finally changes began taking place. She started exercising, joined Overeaters Anonymous, and looked terrific. Her anger and depression began to abate. She was, as she put it, "ready to fly," eager to process opportunities for closeness which had run aground. She was ready to eroticize their relationship and to push for greater intimacy.

One "experiment" involved their masturbating in separate rooms, focusing on photos of each other, and reuniting in their bedroom after their orgasms. Another was to engage in fantasies of being together, looking into each other's eyes, trying to communicate their love. An elaboration of this involved an experiment in which they spent a minute looking into the other's eyes, remaining silent but making a non-verbal sexual request.

After these "experiments" they agreed to share their answers to the questions found throughout the book, carefully writing them out ahead of time. This endeavor showed them that they shared several problems. Each was afraid the other would recoil from their personal truths, each felt sexually deficient, each longed for the other's compassionate understanding.

Well before consulting the "body work" specialist, she had come to acknowledge, even to expect, that she helped maintain their painful sexual circumstances. By owning these truths, she had prepared the ground for cultivating.

None of this could have happened, of course, without the vital contribution of his efforts. First and foremost and throughout his meetings with me had been the risks involved in discovering who and where he was coming from, his daring to be more than a "marketable self," to use Fromm's term, to declare himself despite his childhood terror of being abandoned by those he depended upon. It was hard for me to even imagine what it must have been like for him to inform her of his bisexuality. When I learned about all his revelations to her, he became a hero to me. Could I have done what he did?

As we explored together the formation of his sexual conflicts, aims, and purposes, when he brought in to me the nude pictures of males he had assembled from the Internet, discussed his long-abiding shyness with girls, the emasculation he had endured during high school, the deep fears he still had of merger with his mother and abandonment by her, considered the differences he experienced between sexual episodes with men versus women, he was able to pour out his guilt and shame, to mention with feeling all the unmentionables of his life. Our discussion shifted from his attempt to understand his sexual orientation to his terror of intimacy and his uncertain identity. Out of this emerged highly tentative and unreliable experiences of adulthood, of declaring himself, of taking charge.

As he waxed, she had seemed to wane, and he was not sure what to make of her pain, confusion, and dependency on him. This was not the woman he married and thought he needed. He could no longer define himself as the sole problem in their marriage. No longer could he look for validation by "scrambling to be as she wanted me to be." He refused her demands that he move out of their house. At work he wrote with a newfound authority and became less careful about what he did or said.

Joining Sexual Addicts Anonymous, he was overwhelmed by others' honesty and began seeking male friends. He was growing tired of his sexual fantasies and of what he found on the Internet. Finding out that perhaps he was a bona fide male, after all, he now wanted to see if he could function sexually outside a men's room stall. His first baby steps involved telling her of his morning erections, approaching her with his erect penis, suggesting they engage in sensual massage.

He went to work on declaring himself to others in no uncertain terms. There were excessive drafts of letters he planned to send to his mother, written in his own "voice" and not in response to *her* needs. He needed to speak to his siblings as well in a no-nonsense tone. Operation Forthright, as we called it, was also directed at his colleagues in SAA to whom he would bare his shame. There were "leveling" statements he came up with every day over the course of two weeks that he shared with me. In a daily journal he logged the occasions when he could have shared more of himself with others and held back instead. A giant step was made when he put his foot down regarding his wife's exchanges with their son. No more would he allow the kind of emotional incest his own mother had inflicted on him. Unquestionably, he was ready to challenge some core rules in the marital relationship. He called her on her self-evasiveness and took the lead in writing up their question-answering exercise. He told her how afraid he was to be so self-revealing and invited her to be just as plain-spoken.

Clearly, no one who has been party to today's momentous change can claim exclusive credit for it. In fact, it has not been sudden at all. Perhaps the logjam has been broken; only time will tell, and if it has it is surely because of two people's daring resolve that there was so much at stake, they could not do otherwise.

VIGNETTE NO. 4

The handsome 60-year-old sat and spoke as if he had been given a death sentence in the first of a dozen sessions we had together. He began every utterance with a sigh. The lines on his face told of longstanding burdens that were now about to finally overwhelm whatever spirit he had once had. His first wife—"my buddy, my best friend"—had died three years before of ovarian cancer: "I lost 74 pounds during the time she was in the hospital, and when the end came I just crawled into a hole. I tried painting and drawing, tried returning to the woodworking I'd enjoyed, but soon I just gave up."

This is what he shared with me that day, from the Intake form I always use with my clients.

1. At the present time, generally how *depressed* would you say you were? (He rated himself a 10 on the ten-point scale.)

2. What symptoms might indicate the extent of your depression? His answer: No desire to live, no apparent future, feel antisocial, spend a lot of time in the dark.

3. At the present time, generally how *anxious* would you say you were? (Again, a rating of 10.)

4. What symptoms might indicate the extent of your anxiety? His answer: Not knowing where I'm headed, not knowing if I will recover from the depression, not knowing if I can maintain my new marriage, not knowing if I will remain alive, not knowing if I will recover any sexuality.

5. Can you identify any events in your life which may have precipitated your present emotional circumstances? When did they occur, and what were the circumstances? Answer: My wife died in 1993 after an eight-month fight with ovarian cancer. I sat in her hospital room for three months watching her die, feeling really helpless. I felt guilty for being alive after she died. I've had great difficulty dealing with her death and the events afterwards. I've been extremely depressed ever since.

6. What medical conditions are you dealing with at the present time? What medications are you taking for them? Answer: Tests and biopsies are being performed on me to determine if I have prostate cancer.

7. Are you presently taking any psychopharmacological medications for your mood state? What are they, what is the dosage? By whom were they prescribed? How long have you been taking them? Answer: Not currently. I took Paxil for about three months in 1996, but this was discontinued due to side effects.

8. What particular psychosocial stressors are you currently dealing with, e.g., marital difficulties, separation/divorce, living alone, economic problems, etc.? Answer: I lived alone for four

years. As of three months ago I have been in a new marriage, living in a new location, and we may be relocating out of state. There have been some sexual difficulties together with health problems and worries.

9. On a scale of 1 (in danger of hurting yourself or others) to 100 (superior functioning), how would you rate yourself at the present time? (He rated himself a 50 on the scale, indicating serious symptoms—suicidal ideation, etc.—and serious impairment in social functioning).

10. How would things have to be different for you to be satisfied with your emotional/social adjustment? Answer: Elimination of the depression. Elimination of the sexual difficulties due to the depression. Must feel I have a reason to exist, something to live for. I want to be out of the black hole I've been in for the last four years. I need to be able to be productive and creative. I must be in control of my life, emotions, and thoughts. I have a wonderful new wife and want to have a good happy marriage.

11. How many sessions do you think will be required for your full recovery? Answer: I have no idea. I just want to be back to normal.

12. Please list some of the subgoals that might be established for you over the course of treatment/counseling. What would these require of you? of me? Answer: I need to *completely* recover from the death of my wife and eliminate the guilt I feel about remarrying. This should result in improving my marriage and sexual difficulties. I have to overcome the depression. You must help me make the above happen.

Exactly what was his first wife like? I asked him to fill out questionnaires as though he were presently married to her, one for himself, the other as he supposed she would have answered. These responses indicated that at least in the beginning his first wife had been far more certain about marrying him than he was about marrying her. For her, unlike him, it had been very much a matter of love at first sight. Although he sometimes wondered if she was the right person for him, she never had such doubts. And she maintained that confidence to the end. Throughout the marriage that had contented her so, he experienced her as nurturant and protective toward him. Her delight in him extended to her sexual domain as well, where, according to him, both were ideal lovers, extremely satisfied, and there was simply no room for improvement. They had sex at least once a day, and she would have liked it even more often. Their sexual repertoire included every form of sexual delight. She was easily aroused and had multiple orgasms through coitus alone or, if this was their pleasure, through delectable oral-genital contact. She found him extremely sexually appealing, as he did her, and there was no question but that her best sexual experience had been with him.

It was not until our fourth session that he revealed the extent of her claim on him. Sometimes she was extremely jealous of any attention he might give to other women, and on her death bed she asked him to promise that he would never remarry; but if he did, he must at least make sure that his new partner would never experience the sexual joy she had known with him! He had done his best to keep that promise until now. During the three years since his wife's death, he had experimented sexually with an old girlfriend over the course of four months, but that had come to naught, and there was comfort in that.

It was not until he met his new wife-to-be that his former loyalty was truly tested: "We really clicked!" She'd been married before, unhappily, in a relationship that fell far short of what he had known in his, especially in regard to sex. Even now, in her new marriage, she sometimes found it difficult to become highly aroused, attributing this to her need to be in control, to certain sexual inhibitions, and to blood-pressure medication she was taking. In addition, she reported in her questionnaire, she was not always comfortable about declaring her sexual needs to her new husband. He, in turn, could not help but notice her sexual reticence, and commented that not only did he always have to initiate sexual contact but he had to put forth most of the sexual effort as well. There were times when he experienced the most intense orgasms of his life — "we don't have sex, we make *love!* — but all too often this was not the case. Instead, her sexual passivity had led him to question, for the first time in his life, his sexual competence and attractiveness. Since he had told her about the sexual feats and gratifications he enjoyed in his first marriage, his mounting failures in relation to her had become a principal source of embarrassment and humiliation.

Never before had he been sexually unconfident. Not once had he experienced an erectile failure. Never had he doubted his wife's sexual pleasure and gratification and gratitude to him. Unlike his mother, who "made me the lowest form of life", who never told him she loved him and never gave him a hug, his first wife had showered him with assurances that he was worthwhile to a female; but now in his sexual nightmare he had begun to question that. There were a few times that he avoided sex entirely. Usually, however, he would make a point of approaching his second wife at least daily, desperate in his attempt to restore his sexual dignity, terrified by the prospect of failure, and regardless of his momentary sexual appetite.

His first wife was not, however, the only intruder. During our first conversation he had alluded to a former lover of his second wife's, who lived nearby. It seems that on the very first night he attempted sexual contact with his wife-to-be, the telephone rang. It was "him", and with "him" emerged an ongoing agony of doubt over his new partner's fidelity. She had maintained contact with "him" during the first five months of her relationship with her husband-to-be who sat fuming over all the evidence of her former one: a gift here, a magazine there, old love letters, a coffee-table book. When he began to take umbrage over the ex-suitor's telephone intrusions, she "laughed in my face," assuring him that "he" meant nothing at all to her and not to worry. Even after the marriage the calls continued, and too often the image of her old "friend" would crowd his mind as he attempted sexual congress. It was only when the two of them could get away from her turf, as they did for two weeks on a trip to Texas, that his symptoms vanished: "Sex was excellent. We had intercourse every day! There were no problems with erections. I could be spontaneous, I didn't even need her to stimulate me!" Upon their return, however, the symptoms reappeared. As he reported in his log:

12/22: She wasn't into it, and I lost my erection.
12/23: Half-assed.
12/24: We showered together; she masturbated me.

12/26: All right.

12/27, 28, 29: Failures.

12/30: Oral sex again, three hours, erectile problems.

12/31: Attempted intercourse but lost erection.

1/1: Nothing worked.

1/2: Played around, lost my erection, cunnilingus.

1/5: My erection was fine at first, then lost it!

The log ended, "Why go on? Is there any reason to hope that things will be different? Should I just abstain?"

Not until he prevailed upon her to return her ex-lover's books did my client's mind began to ease. There were still times when, upon entering her, he'd imagined it was the other man's penis and not his own. Talk about spectatoring! Three weeks later, he absolutely insisted that her ex-lover not hang around the premises in any form, and the two of them removed all the mementos from the past, fancy presents and all, and hurled them into the trash barrel. Some he took into an empty field and blew up to smithereens (a far better end than one I had envisioned only a few weeks before, when he had sat outside the ex-lover's house in his truck, the same gun cocked, and wrestled with the impulse to do his rival in).

This is not to say that my client's torment was entirely gone. There were more reports of sexual failures. He still used firm versus weak erections as the criterion of his masculine worth. Pleasing his wife and reassuring himself that he could still perform sexual magic remained the point of much of his sexual contact. He continued to devour the literature for ways to "keep it up." He begged to be hypnotized. Meanwhile, he drew his new wife into his frenzy, confronting her about her sexual inhibitions, chiding her for not initiating sexual contact, entreating her to perform fellatio. The pressure was about as much as she could bear: "He's so insecure! He reads all kinds of things into what I do or don't do. He doesn't have a life of his own. He never wants me out of his sight. I really think that if something happened to our relationship, he'd commit suicide!" Her impressions agreed with mine.

From the beginning it was clear that if this unhappy man did not begin to define his problems in terms that went far beyond his failure to perform whenever and however he liked, we would be in for a long spell of unremitting agony. That became the challenge. Would it require the professional services of one more expert than I and perhaps more patient with his stubborn hold on self-destructive beliefs? I unloaded on him while he listened dutifully, recording every word on the tape machine he had been bringing with him to our sessions:

- You must examine whatever you are doing or saying to yourself that maintains your long history of low self-esteem.
- You are far too dependent on your wife. You must do all you can to enlarge your circle of friends who care.
- Your self-preoccupations and concerns about being a perfect lover have made your sexual life a travesty. Whatever love you may feel for your wife cannot possibly be communicated to her by this modus operandi.
- Stop your mind-reading. Much of what you suppose your wife is thinking and feeling is no more than your own projections.
- You need medication for your depression and an exercise program as well.
- You must get yourself a life. This will probably entail your moving to a new environment, back to your own turf if that's what it takes, where you can invest yourself in some rewarding activities.

Along with these admonitions come the recommendation that they process their sexual exchanges—share what they think and feel and want during sexual contact, read over the manuscript of this book and discuss the questions it raises, and try being physically close after agreeing ahead of time that coitus would not take place.

Who is to say what comment or direction hit the target? Counseling in this and other areas of people's lives will probably forever remain more an art than a science. Whatever the reasons, by the time we got to our last three sessions, my client could report "tremendous changes." There had been gut-wrenching talks between the two of them. Her lover had been exorcised from his mind, and he was focusing on her instead. He was feeling less depressed, due perhaps to the Welbutrin that had been prescribed. They were making plans to move back to his old house in a different town, and he had already started getting the property back into shape.

Unfortunately, in the sexual arena, the results were more mixed. Back to his old tricks, my client was now on cloud nine, reporting strong erections and counting an array of sexual "successes." To be sure, his wife could report during our last conjoint session that there had been much more communication between the two of them and that sexual exchanges were not nearly so frantic. She was especially pleased that he had become less preoccupied with her reaching orgasm. What he had *not* done, however, was to enjoy sensual contact with his wife without proceeding to intercourse when his erections allowed it. (*"I've always taken advantage of my erections."*) Out of fear that his current erection might be his last he "never passed up an opportunity." He had yet to draw close without engaging in coitus if there was an opportunity to do so; he had yet to engage in coitus and, deliberately forgoing orgasm, let his erection subside. We had no further meetings. As far as he was concerned, they were no longer needed. Perhaps he was right. The chances are, he was wrong.

VIGNETTE NO. 5

Things were going from bad to worse to absolutely awful, for both of them. He had gone to one counselor after another, only to quit in rage at being misunderstood. His wife of twenty-six years had made life unbearable: she'd threaten to leave, he'd beg her not to; the stress made him suicidal, and when it led to a heart attack, he finally agreed to divorce. Now his second marriage, two years along, was in trouble. He had consulted a psychiatrist, who supplied medication and referred him to me for intensive counseling.

That was a need of long standing indeed. It might have helped in his first marriage; or earlier, perhaps when his beloved son, only ten years old, had "accidentally" strangled himself, leaving a distraught father with grief and guilt unassuaged by annual cemetery visits complete with Christmas tree; or earlier yet, when he was three and his sister was born, leaving him feeling displaced and unwanted, the more so as successive babies came. It seems that his siblings were hurt by whatever was unfortunate in the family, just as he was himself. A brother, incurably despondent, committed suicide in young middle age. His sisters apparently cannot shake the self-loathing that over time had become his own daily portion.

Other boys did not choose him for their team or call him to play after school. In adolescence he never dated anyone enough for her to count as a girlfriend, and most weekends he was alone. Later on, his three most significant relationships with women would be character- ized chiefly by their feeling smothered by him and withdrawing from his desperate attempts to hang on to them. On one occasion he drove all day and night non-stop across country, to find and plead with a woman who had gone into hiding. Nor could he please other people in his life. At work he had repeated difficulties with superiors and colleagues. None of these clashes was serious enough to force his departure, but he had been transferred out of one post after another, feeling unwanted and embittered. Even as we met for the first time, he was facing the prospect of another unwanted move and of having to make it alone if his marriage did not improve. His entire life seemed to be hanging in the balance. All would be lost if our venture should fail.

His view was that everything important to him depended on his ability to get his wife sexually interested. The trouble, as he saw it, was that she came from a sex-phobic environment. Sex had been taboo for her not only in girlhood but beyond. Catholic schools, followed by eight years in a convent, had reinforced all the taboos she had ever learned at home. She had never even gone out with a man until she was twenty-nine, and had masturbated for the first time much later than that. During one relationship, to which she had felt more committed than her partner was, she became pregnant, had an abortion, and vowed never again to get into those circumstances. He had known all this about her before their marriage; but, because at first she did have sexual interest in him, he had had reason to believe that she would realize he was different from the other men she had known and would allow him to lead her to a more promising land. He would make up for all the sexual deprivation she had endured. She, of course, would be forever grateful for his sexual wizardry and his undying love and, thus, she would never leave him. He would be able to relax in this all-encompassing success. Alas for dreams! Before their second anniversary she had become stone cold. He had tried to "fix" her to no avail. Now it would be up to me, as far as he was concerned, to convince her that she had no reason to be so sexually fearful, and that her inhibited, unwelcoming response to him was wrong for both their sakes. He added, unnecessarily, that if I could not bring all this about, he still had his old option of killing himself.

Because he had brought up so much during our first session, I asked him to fill out a form I use at various junctures during therapy. It reads: "Describe what was addressed during our last meeting: problems/issues, their sources, their possible remedies, steps you need to take, risks you are willing to take and their potential benefits, assignments (if any) given and agreed to, etc." His description of what took place during our first two meetings tells it like it was for him, almost to the last detail:

> You said that I was angry about what was going on between me and my wife. What was that based on? I am *not* angry all the time. We really need to discuss this more. Whenever I feel I'm under attack or rejected, I get angry. It's because it makes me feel so anxious. Most of the anger is toward myself. I feel guilty, ashamed, embarrassed, and foolish. The fear of rejection is probably the bottom line. I get so frightened that I can't think clearly, and I end up not being able to communicate effectively.
>
> The fear of her leaving me is like the fear of death. There's a paralyzing cold fear in the pit of my gut. I feel nauseated, like I'm going to throw up. It's like the feeling I'd have if I were standing blindfolded in front of a firing squad waiting to be executed. The adrenalin starts pumping. I try desperately to find a way to reduce my fear. I'll talk to her, try to analyze what's going on between us for hours at a time. This makes her even more angry, so again I try to get her to understand and this makes her even more upset. I become beside myself. We both want desperately to find harmony between us, but we don't know what to do. It's at that point that I start feeling guilty. I'll apologize, beg to be forgiven, take all the blame and promise to do better in the future. I'm also feeling humiliated and totally

without value. This goes on until I finally crash in despair and exhaustion.

I think I've done pretty good in controlling my anger over the last few years. I tell myself I'm not going to spend anymore of the time I have left on this earth in anger. It just isn't worth it. So I try to keep active. I try to shift my focus to love. I'll listen to meditation tapes, I'll try not to care. As far as I'm concerned, my wife is the most wonderful person I have ever known in my life. She is so kind and nurturant and generous. I really *love her*!

He went on:

We discussed the ways I believe she shuts down sexually. In other words, the problem as I see it:

> She won't let me touch her nipples.
> She won't let me touch her pubic area.
> She won't let me touch her anal area.
> She won't let me make any sexual advances when we're in the car or when I'm on the phone.
> She doesn't want to watch X-rated movies with me.
> She is reluctant to get into a sauna or hot tub with me and my friends.
> She doesn't like to go nude, even in the house.
> She doesn't like to discuss sexual fantasies.
> She doesn't like to wear clothing that reveals her shape.
> She doesn't like spontaneous sex, never more than once a week, and nowhere but in bed.
> She almost always turns me down when I ask for sex other than Saturdays at 9:00 A.M.
> She doesn't like to not wear a bra or panties.
> She likes her frumpy housecoat which hides everything.
> I have brought home innumerable sexual self-help books; but she refuses to look at them with me, especially if they have pictures.
> She won't watch movies that have sex scenes in them.
> She thinks I'm perverse because I like sex.
> She only likes sex in the missionary position.
> She doesn't like to take too long with sex. She says it feels too much like work!

She doesn't like me to go down on her because it takes too long.

She only enjoys climaxing with her vibrator. I have only been able to get her to climax three times by going down on her.

She says she is not interested in sex any more and wishes I'd drop the subject. She says that all I think about is sex and that she's sick of hearing about it.

The idea of a sexual threesome disgusts her!

I don't feel free to do anything sexually with her unless I ask for permission. I don't ask any more. It's humiliating to be turned down.

She says I don't turn her on any more.

He wound up with:

You said I was coercing her into sex by my anger and hurt and insisting on discussing our sexual problems with her and asking her to do things she doesn't want to do, etc. I can't remember the whole list!

This bothers me. I don't feel I've tried to *force* her to have sex with me. That makes me sound like a perverted creep. Sure I've been very frustrated and angry, but that's because she's not interested in having sex with me. She has *no trouble* saying No. She does it all the time. I've tried to find ways to interest her in sex, but nothing seems to work.

I *do* accept your basic premise, however. What I have done has only made the situation worse. I don't want to control, manipulate, or coerce her in any way. What am I to do? I don't want to spend the rest of my married life in this unnatural sexless situation we have now. I'm desperate! I want to respect her right to say No, but don't I have a right to my feelings and needs?

We don't see sex the same way. She sees it as a reward or gift for good behavior. If I have crossed her in any way, she withholds sex, and I have to serve out my sentence. To me, that is very controlling and manipulative. It is very important for you to know that I do not think she is intentionally vindictive or manipulative. I don't think she's even aware she's doing it.

You said she's not obligated to have sex out of duty,

commitment, or anything other than her own desire. You said anything else is a form of rape. You said that if I want sex and she doesn't, I should masturbate.

You said I am not to discuss sex with her, ask for sex, or make any sexual advances. The only way I am to have sex is when she decides on her own she wants it. I agreed to your proposal. However, it seems to me I might as well forget having sex in my marriage. At least before we had it occasionally. I thought she wanted it too, but I guess I was wrong. I'm concerned we'll never have sex again. She sees no reason for it. With these new rules, there will not even be a *pretense* at sex, there will be nothing. You said that many of my beliefs about her are invalid. I hope so. If I'm in error I want to get it correct.

When I told you about the candles and the music I arranged for us so that we would have a romantic atmosphere, you suggested I was trying to manipulate her. Nothing could be further from the truth. I just *like* these things. I enjoy it. I don't think *she* feels I'm manipulating her with those things either.

I have the feeling you see me as a manipulative bad person and her as a victim. I'm very sorry about that. I'm *not* trying to control her. I think it's important that she be happy and have her needs met. I also want my needs met. I want our relationship to work. I know it's easy to see me as a bad guy and her as O.K. In some ways I see it that way also. I think both of us have a lot of changes to make.

Good for him! It took a lot of courage to report his thoughts and feelings as he did. Not only had he been courageous, he had been plain and candid, whether it looked pretty or not. While he protested my suggestion that perhaps he was a little bit more than angry at a predicament he believed had been foisted upon him by a wife who refused to cooperate with his plans for her, his later description of his circumstances confirmed my original impressions. Underneath his anger, of course, lay his fears and his sense of impotence. He had become boxed in by his definition of the problem—it was her lack of sexual interest much less enthusiasm—and could not see past his explanation for it, which was that she had been crippled by her upbringing and also needed to exercise power and control over him. Meanwhile, *his* behaviors were innocent of complicity, indeed were the "normal" expressions of a caring, loving husband. He refused to admit any self-interest in his strivings and stuck to his conviction that the remedy for their ills lay in a sexual "cure" for her. When I asked him to list the things she could do that would demonstrate her caring for him, his answers remained entirely consistent with that view: "allow me to touch, caress, and massage her; kiss me first; let me go down on her; be spontaneous with sex and affection; touch me even if it leads to sex; place her hand on me and leave it there . . . anywhere!; join me in the hot tub and sauna; be sensual and erotic for my benefit; free herself up to experiment sexually." Talk about a one-track mind! It would take several months before I could persuade him that I was on his "side" as much as hers; only then did he come to broaden his view.

At the same time that I was meeting with him for individual sessions, I was meeting with her as well. Her first session with me came the day after his, and I had developed more than a mild curiosity about her. Her first assertion was not surprising: "I can't be myself!" There was his undisguised wish that she convert to his religion so that they could be together in "The Kingdom." There was his pleading that she go caving with him, go canoeing with him, go wilderness camping with him, share hot tubs with him, and, of course, be sexual with him. "I have no freedom. He wants me to do everything with him!"

As if this were not bad enough, whenever she did not go along with his requests she would end up feeling not only estranged from him but from herself as well: "What I've become in this marriage is not me!" she exclaimed. She had always viewed herself as generous and kind, a stranger to anger and resentment. She had always taken pride in being more concerned about others' needs than her own: "He's so unhappy with me. He feels I don't pay enough attention to him and that I don't want to spend time with him. When he gets upset over this, I try to patch things up, try to reassure him, but it never works. These long discussions are exhausting me!" Clearly, she needs time and space for herself, but she is not ready to actually demand it of him.

Meanwhile I suggest that she respond to his requests with, "Let me think about it," no more of the reflexive accommodations in which she has wasted herself as a human being. And, since he has already begun to ask her what goes on in her sessions with me, I make another suggestion: tell him that she will share such information only when she chooses to and if she thinks it might be helpful. These will not be easy tasks for her. Having her way feels too "unloving and selfish." Asking for what she wants seems brutal in the face of another's need for reassurance from her that she cares.

For her, the cardinal sin is to fail another who needs her. Thus, she continues intermittent contact with the few men she was involved with prior to her marriage, through notes, telephone calls, sometimes even meetings, in which she assures her ex-lovers that they are still her friends. Looking back on the time she first met her husband, she will recall how she ignored all the warning flags because she was more concerned that she not disappoint him. He had experienced so much of that with other women, she was not about to join their company. She could not live with herself if she added anything more to his sense of rejection. If that meant marrying him, so be it!

Clearly, this dear woman was at her wits' end! Having run through her usual repertoire of coping with others who are upset with her, she simply did not know what to do! She had begged and pleaded in the face of her husband's relentless intrusiveness. Whenever he expressed his exasperation with her, whenever he kept asking her if she really loved him, whenever he tried to paw her in bed no matter where (on her body) or when (during the night), however he launched his erotic program for her, she would try her best to be patient with him, would try to answer his fears with reassuring responses, and would sometimes grit her teeth and cooperate, "give in just this once" just to calm him down. It never worked, of course, and, in fact, her occasional acquiescence served as intermittent reinforcement of his behavior, making the pressure he put on her even *more* likely to recur. He could not help but sense her unwillingness to engage, and the more impatient she appeared, the more insecure he became and, predictably, the more insistent as well.

It would become my job to convince both of them that the use of coercion is numbered among the chief interpersonal errors we make in our dealings with others. There may be Pyrrhic victories from time to time, but the battle is lost, by the coercer who will never be convinced that the partner's response comes from the heart and is not due chiefly to wanting to escape the pummelling, and by the coerced who will never learn his or her true responses except for a mounting anger, resentment, and feeling of alienation. Self-forfeiture in the interests of keeping the peace does no good for anyone. In the case of this anguished couple, each had to learn the truth of this contention and actually experience the payoffs from the changes that had to be made. And it should be pointed out, the challenge would be not greater for him than for her. Progress could only be made hand in hand.

My suggestion to her—that she not automatically respond to his requests and that she share with him what went on in our sessions only if she wanted to—were only the beginning of an effort to identify and declare her bottom lines with him: What do I want? What can I not tolerate? What behaviors on his part do I insist on? What changes do I think would begin to improve my feelings about the partnership? What temporary remedies might help? What must I make loud and clear to him about where I'm coming from? Individuals without such bottom lines are badly off in any context but perhaps especially so in the sexual domain. Without bottom lines, self-esteem leaks away. Without the willingness to give up a relationship once it has become totally unendurable, the relationship will inevitably become moribund. In this relationship, either she grudgingly permitted his unwanted intrusions or else she would express her annoyance, or even anger, but then back down and apologize for being so testy. And he knew full well she would! Thus, one of my first homework assignments for her was to begin jotting down her bottom lines. What about his constant interrogations? How intolerable had they become? What had to be changed? How about his constant requests for sensual and sexual contact? What brakes was she ready to apply, what requests was *she* prepared to make of *him*?

Slowly but surely some bottom lines appeared. Concrete requests began to emerge. First, she was able to report how intolerable his interrogations of her and his attempts to convert her sexually had become. He was to limit these to fifteen minutes once a day, at an acceptable time and place. She promised to listen to him, ask him questions, but say nothing by way of reassurance. There would be no effort to calm him down. Next, she would be willing to be engaged sexually, but only two times a week (Tuesdays and Saturdays), in a romantic setting: they would begin by her massaging him after they showered together, proceed to oral-genital contact (her initiating first), and include the use of a vibrator, with him taking an active role in that regard. These sessions were to take place at a reasonable hour, while she was best prepared for them, and would last no more than a half-hour to an hour. There would be no more videos for her to share with him, no more porno left around for her to look at. All these new rules she was setting down were to be regarded as an experiment and to be reassessed after a month. I asked her also to look for opportunities to disappoint him just a little during the course of a week, to start a frontal assault on the guilt and fear she experienced when she did not meet others' requests of her.

You can be sure that her husband was not entirely pleased with her newly minted declarations! From the beginning he had felt that sooner or later I would ally myself with her against him, that I too would view him as a sexual predator and "creep". He had already indicated this suspicion in his write-up of our first individual session. At least he had not bolted, as he had other counseling situations. Over time he allowed us to move beyond his sexual preoccupations and frustrations and into his lifelong fears of abandonment by those he'd grown (too) dependent on, into considerations of how other women, his first wife and a previous lover, had had similar complaints, had both felt smothered by his attentions, had both been put off by his desperation.

He listened attentively as I suggested the need for him to be in better shape, emotionally and physically, to deal with what lay in store for him: my partial remedies for the terrible stress he was under included taking regular exercise, getting enough sleep, using the relaxation tape I'd made for him, spending time each day in meditation, and meeting with a psychiatrist for consultation and possible prescription. From time to time I joined with her in her assignment to share her appreciations of him. These included how he was holding up under pressures that would sink many a less courageous man, the times he helped with dinner, the work he was doing in the house to prepare for their move, and especially, how he was honoring her bottom lines and had backed off sexually. I reiterated her commitment to him, no matter what, her report that her best sexual experience had occurred with him, and I shared her ideal sexual scenario with him, making it clear that under certain conditions she could muster up some sexual enthusiasm.

Perhaps my most powerful intervention was made when I shared my identification with him, when I made it clear that I knew what it was like to be terrified when another seemed displeased with me or would erect walls between us. I told him all about how I had had issues of my own like this, how I had gone into therapy to deal with them. By some miracle he took heart in this comparison: now he could believe that I did respect him. It became easier for him to talk about his depression, his humiliation over not providing his wife with what she needed, his feeling beaten and overwhelmed. His sense of himself as a social invalid came through loud and clear. He no longer regarded me as the enemy, chiefly responsible for the changes he was seeing in his wife, and eventually was even able to express appreciation for the sexual contract they devised. True, sex was now limited; but at the same time, it was scheduled, and knowing this, he no longer badgered her. She had set limits and he was actually relieved. His obsession had eased up considerably. There were, as there must be, payoffs along the way: "The other day she put her arms around me and kissed me! I almost cried." There was the growing realization that he and she, given their histories and temperaments and needs, were simply different. Period! No reason to take these differences personally and no sense in trying to change her all around—a lost cause, in any case.

It was then, and at his urging, that we decided to all three meet together for the remainder of the time they had left in town. The four months we had spent in our individual sessions had been well worth it. She had been able to hold pretty well to her bottom lines without too much guilt and, therefore, without animus. She knew she had a right to herself and found this so reassuring that her old resentments had begun to melt away, replaced by some appreciations for him and even budding sexual interest. She had reviewed her sexual history and could see it was typical for her that initial sexual interest in him had waned after a few months, never to return. There was a hint of homosexual interest, but this was by no means a chief impediment to her sexual difficulties with males, including her husband, whom she was now beginning to view as handsome, if overweight. He, meanwhile, would own the panic he felt whenever he felt she was rejecting him and was able to trace his feelings of low self-worth to their origins in a variety of contexts. He was able now to share his fears with her and get beyond his anger and accusations. They had begun to work on communication with the exercises in this book. They decided they needed to do all they could to promote friendship between them, to focus on the positive and give each other strokes, and that she was to take the lead in activities that heightened their togetherness.

Their progress became readily apparent as they sat together for the first time (except for our initial visit) with me. This would be our last month together before they moved south, but they said they would like to come back and meet with me from time to time after that. They seemed to be much more relaxed and spontaneous. There was obvious humor and good will. Out of all the pressures they were experiencing over the move—exactly where they would live? when should she end her job? would they go off together or would he go first while she concluded details here?—they began to hone their negotiation skills. They brainstormed and returned to structured communication exercises. Never too far was the issue that had brought them in to me, but now they spoke in quite different terms: she spoke of her guilt and shame over the anger she'd often felt toward him, and he readily acknowledged his crippling fears of abandonment.

During our last session I asked each of them to report whatever progress they thought they had made:

> **He: There has been a lot of progress. I don't let everything get to me, only occasional blow-ups. Although our sexual situation has a way to go—it's not perfect by any means—there has been a tremendous improvement. She seems to be more willing to have sex. Things are not so stressful between us. My anxiety has been reduced by eighty percent! I think that scheduling times for sex has really helped. I'm pressing her less, not trying to persuade her to have sex all the time. I find myself wanting to reward her by being more considerate of her wishes. Sometimes she even lets me touch her breasts. Last night, when I asked her if we'd have sex, she said No. I said, O.K., even though it was Saturday. I'm not sure she'll ever want sex.**

She: Last week I did. In fact, I really got into it. I enjoyed arousing him. He went down on me, and that felt good. I can even orgasm now even though it takes a lot of fantasies and concentration. There's a lot less pressure coming from him. I just feel more comfortable. When he touches me, I know it doesn't mean we'll have sex.

He: She seems to be getting close to real sexual enjoyment.

She: Sometimes I'm really receptive.

He: There seems to be a real shift going on. I see her as far less punitive.

She: I've *never* felt punitive. It's just that I have other priorities.

He: Last week I *almost* got a freebie! Sometimes it seems she really wants to do it, in fact even looks forward to it. She's more imaginative. She asks for things. She takes the initiative!

She: The biggest thing is how I experience him. I can't want sex if I'm pissed off at him! Right now I'm feeling a lot of respect for him for how he's handled all the stress we've been under. He really perseveres. I don't know how he does it. He's got more stamina than I have!

When I asked him what it was like to hear her talk like this about him, he replied:

It's hard for me to take her compliments. If I believe her, I may end up feeling duped or I'll be afraid it won't last since I'll goof up sometime, and then the loss of her respect will be even more painful. I'm so familiar with the dark side of me, I guess I sometimes think she loves and respects me only because she doesn't really know me, and that she'll lose respect for me when she does.

Honest declarations on both their parts. Peering beneath the outsides of themselves and each other, they discovered a compassion and respect that had not been there before. Transparency with oneself and with another has a way of doing this.

Annotated Bibliography

GENERAL

Beck, A. T. (1988). *Love is Never Enough*. New York: Harper & Row.
A leader in the field of cognitive psychology, the author does a masterful job of applying its principles to a deeper understanding of couples' circumstances and to the alleviation of their difficulties.

Blumstein, P. and Schwartz, P. (1983). *American Couples*. New York: Morrow.
A must for any clinician working with couples, this book reports findings from the authors' survey of a very large number of couples. In addition to discussing how these couples managed money and work, it focuses on respondents' reports on their sexual lives.

Burns, D. D. (1989). *The Feeling Good Handbook*. New York: Penguin.
Although the author does not deal directly with sexual matters per se, he provides extremely useful information about negative feeling states, how to measure them and how to alleviate them by means of cognitive restructuring. His discussion of communication is especially relevant for those who would be more transparent with their partner.

Comfort, A. (1972). *The New Joy of Sex*. New York: Pocket.

A classic in the field of human sexuality, this book, filled with beautiful illustrations of various sexual postures and scenarios, stresses the importance of sensuality and of the role of play in sexual exchanges.

Hartman, W. and Fithian, M. (1972). *Treatment of Sexual Dysfunction*. Long Beach Center for Marital and Sexual Studies.

A further elaboration of the Masters and Johnson approaches to the treatment of sexual disorders, this book contains useful information for any clinician interested in a broader view of clients' difficulties and in a wider range of interventions.

Kaplan, H. S. (1974). *The New Sex Therapy*. New York: Brunner/ Mazel.

This and the author's other books should be required reading for any clinician who would enlarge his/her perspective on sexual functioning. Unconscious as well as conscious thinking is considered here in some detail, and the importance of effective communication is stressed.

Masters, W. H., Johnson, V. E., and Kolodny, R. C. (1982). *Human Sexuality*. Boston: Little Brown.

This carefully crafted textbook on the length and breadth of human sexual experience explores the biological, psychosocial, behavioral, clinical, and cultural perspectives of what it means to be sexual. Much-needed attention has been given to such matters as gender roles, loving relationships, and sexual fantasy. Research findings and suggested additional readings round out the smorgasbord of useful information.

Offit, A. K. (1977). *The Sexual Self*. New York: Lippincott.

The author does an excellent job of pointing out the complexities of human sexual experience and the extent to which our sexual lives reflect who we are to the core.

Walker, R. (1996). *The Family Guide to Sex and Relationships*. New York: Macmillan.

This is a useful and informative book that covers the waterfront when it comes to sexual matters. The author discusses everything from sexual communications to sexual problems and does not withhold helpful advice in regard to the many different features of sexual experience.

INTIMACY

Barbach, L. (1984). *For Each Other: Sharing Sexual Intimacy.* New York: Signet.
Taking up from where she left off in *For Yourself,* the author considers ways in which men, and especially women, can make their sexual needs and interests better known to their partner with the goal of enhancing their sexual partnership.

Etkes, D. (1995). *Loving with Passion: Your Guide to the Joy of Sexual Intimacy.* Claremont, CA: Claremont Publishing.
Sex is described as a wondrous gift for loving partners but also a fragile one that can only be preserved through mutual respect and open communication.

Goldhor-Lerner, H. (1989). *The Dance of Intimacy: A Woman's Guide to Courageous Acts of Change in Key Relationships.* New York: Harper & Row.
The author, who also wrote *The Dance of Anger,* rightly bemoans the fact that far too many women sacrifice their truest selves in so-called service to a relationship. She defines intimacy as a relationship "in which neither party silences, sacrifices, or betrays the self and each party expresses strength and vulnerability, weakness and confidence in a balanced way." A very important book for women.

Hendrix, H. (1988). *Getting the Love You Want: A Guide for Couples.* New York: Harper & Row.
An enormously interesting and insightful book on the conscious and unconscious elements involved in our search for a mutually satisfying partnership. That search is thought to involve the attempt to resolve unfinished issues of past relationships with our original caretakers. Communication exercises, designed to help the reader obtain a more accurate image of their partner, are an outstanding feature of the book.

Hooper, A. *Anne Hooper's Sexual Intimacy.* (1996). New York: Dorling Kindersley.

Maintaining that intimacy is as much about emotional exchanges as it is about sex and that the two are by no means synonymous, the author stresses the importance of early childhood experiences in forming adults' capacities for bonding with others.

Pearsall, P. (1987). *Super Marital Sex: Loving for Life.* New York: Ballantine.

Filled with self-tests, marriage tests, and questionnaires, this book is designed to deepen a couples' level of intimacy in their sexual exchanges. Describing super marital sex as "the most erotic, intense, fulfilling experience any human being can have," the author makes it clear that sex includes far more than genital performance and engagements. In his later book, *Sexual Healing*, the author sustains his assertion that sexuality "includes how we think, feel, behave, and believe on the most personal level."

Rubin, L. B. (1983). *Intimate Strangers: Men and Women Together.* New York: Harper & Row.

In this book, highly regarded by marital therapists over the years, the author examines the differences between men and women as they affect their capacities for genuine intimacy and sexual fulfillment. Found in the roots of childhood, differential patterns mean that, "for men, the erotic aspect of any relationship remains forever the most compelling, while, for women, the emotional component will always be the more salient."

Sager, C. and Hunt, B. (1979). *Intimate Partners: Hidden Patterns in Love Relationships.* New York: McGraw Hill.

Although now out of print, this book remains one of my favorites in its exploration of our hidden emotional and sexual expectations of our partners. A special feature involves advice as to how couples can create more conscious sexual covenants in order to find a more intimate and satisfying partnership. Track this book down by any means at your disposal!

Schnarch, D. M. (1991). *Constructing the Sexual Crucible: An Integration of Sexual and Marital Therapy.* New York: Norton.

A must read for any self-respecting clinician, although probably not so easily accessible to the average client, this book provides many fresh looks at many different aspects of human sexuality and questions a number of long-held assumptions and perspectives. The author leaves few stones unturned in his considerations of intimacy including more than casual reference to the spiritual dimension of sexual experience.

———— (1997). *Passionate Marriage*. New York: Norton.

The author, borrowing from the object-relations perspective on human relationships, stresses the need for self-differentiation and differentiation from one's partner. According to him, intimacy develops only through conflict, self-validation and unilateral disclosure. While there are no exercises, the book's interesting case material and the author's highly personal sharing of his own circumstances make the reading a treat, even inspirational!

MALES/FEMALES

Bader, E. and Pearson, P. (1988). *In Quest of the Mythical Mate*. New York: Brunner/Mazel.

In discussing couples' relationships from an object-relations point of view, the authors stress the importance of self-differentiation and of differentiation from one's partner for establishing a truly adult partnership.

Castleman, M. (1983). *Sexual Solutions: A Guide for Men and the Women Who Love Them*. New York: Simon & Schuster.

This is a plea to couples (especially to men) that they not be so genitally focused. Entire bodies are given ample attention and sex is not begun so abruptly.

Chichester, B. and Robinson, K. (1996). *Men's Health Life Improvement Guides: Sex Secrets, Ways to Satisfy Your Partner Every Time*. Emmaus, PA: Rodale.

According to the authors, sexual disinterest on the part of the female partner is the result of the male's failure to do what he can to promote truer levels of intimacy. While sexual technique may be important, far more important is the male's ability to share a sense of mystery and wonder when he engages a woman sexually.

Danoff, D. (1993). *Super Potency: How To Get It, Use It, and Maintain It for a Lifetime*. New York: Time Warner.
Challenging the male reader to "reclaim the power that belongs to every man", the author asserts that super potency, a mark of a male's self-confidence, happens first in the mind and not the bed, and that penis power is much more a matter of what occurs "between the ears" than between the legs.

Farrell, W. (1986). *Why Men Are the Way They Are*. New York: McGraw Hill.
Focusing on the dynamic between men and women, this author maintains that the symbiotic nature of sex roles will not be changed until men own their feelings of powerlessness and vulnerability and are able to share their true circumstances with women.

Goldberg, H. (1987). *The Inner Male: Overcoming Roadblocks to Intimacy*. New York: New American Library.
In three previous books the author explored the dangers of traditional masculinity, described the relationship between men's and women's expanding gender identities and social roles, and examined the cost of traditional relationships for men and women alike. This one attempts to explore and recognize the manifestations of what he terms the "gender unconscious," defined as the enormous power of our psyches and based upon the gender conditioning that determines how we see ourselves as men and women.

Gray, J. (1995). *Mars and Venus in the Bedroom: A Guide to Lasting Romance and Passion*. New York: HarperCollins.
Following his other popular books on the differences between males and females, the author now writes about sexual relationships in a book which will purposely "launch your love life into orbit." Its optimistic outlook is conveyed in chapters devoted to the rekindling of passion in long-term monogamous relationships and advice as to how to keep the music of romance alive. The special plea is to appreciate how different are the needs of men and women in bed.

McCarthy, B. (1988). *Male Sexual Awareness*. New York: Carroll & Graf.

Confronting the myths of what many believe is required of the male for successful sexual congress, the author stresses the need for flexibility and pleasure-oriented approaches to intimacy. He reiterates this theme in *Couple's Sexual Awareness: Building Sexual Happiness*, written with Emily McCarthy (1990) and published by Carroll & Graf.

Zilbergeld, B. (1992). *The New Male Sexuality*. New York: Bantam.
In a follow-up to his previous work in this realm, the author stresses the importance of a male's ability to be appropriately self-assertive, to be a better listener, to initiate sexual contact in ways that honor his partner, and to resolve problems which inevitably arise in the sexual domain. A lot of useful advice and information here.

WOMEN

Barbach, L. (1976). *For Yourself: The Fulfillment of Female Sexuality*. New York: Signet.
A classic in the field of female sexuality, this book invites the reader to become well aware of her body and offers a step-by-step program by which to enhance her pleasure and satisfaction without requiring the ministrations of a male partner.

Boston Women's Health Collective. (1992). *The New Our Bodies, Ourselves*. New York: Touchstone.
Almost half of the book's 750 pages are devoted to female sexuality and reproduction. Blending factual information with personal experiences, it makes an effort to include as many women's experiences as possible. For example, in addition to diversity in age, ethnic, and socioeconomic backgrounds, there is an excellent section on the sexuality of women with disabilities. An excellent reference for all women.

Heiman, J. R. and LoPiccolo, J. (1976). *Becoming Orgasmic: A Sexual and Personal Growth Program for Women*. New York: Simon & Schuster.
An extremely useful book for women who would own their own sexuality. It invites the reader to consider her sexual history, to

explore, discover, and become more comfortable with her body, and to share her discoveries with her partner. Well-designed exercises enhance self-pleasuring as well as sexual contact with another.

MASTURBATION

Dodson, B. (1987). *Sex for One*. New York: Harmony.
Taking the shame out of masturbation, the author argues convincingly that the cultural denial of masturbation sustains sexual repression and makes for hardships across the board for those who would be more fully sexual. Emphasis is given to loving oneself and getting more in touch with what is physically and emotionally arousing through masturbation. An excellent source of information about female perspectives on sexuality.

FANTASIES

Friday, N. (1992). *Women on Top*. New York: Pocket.
This is an update of the author's previous exploration of women's sexual fantasies which were described in *My Secret Garden*. The numerous actual fantasies of women which comprise the book are divided into three sections: seductive, sometimes sadistic, sexually controlling women; women with women; and insatiable women who cry for more!
Kronhausen, P. and Kronhausen, E. (1969). *Erotic Fantasies: A Study of the Sexual Imagination*. New York: Grove.
The authors have compiled a survey of sexual fantasies through the ages. These mental aphrodisiacs are mined for what they tell us about their psychological and cultural origins. A classic in the field.

SENSUALITY

Anand, M. (1989). *The Art of Sexual Ecstasy*. New York: Putnam.
When the author terms the "ecstatic response" is based upon our

ability to bring ourselves fully into the sexual movement as the "most honored guest in your own heart, a guest worthy of respect, a lovable companion." A special plea is made that we move beyond conformity to the one-dimensional attitudes and behaviors of conventional masculinity and femininity in the ways we go about making love.

Lacroix, N. (1989). *Sensual Massage*. New York: Henry Holt.
This is a good resource for anyone wishing to give or receive a sensual massage. It explores all the basics in that regard with helpful directions and illustrations of the mechanics involved. The aim is to help a couple feel more present and comfortable in their bodies.

Steinburg, D., ed. (1992). *The Erotic Impulse: Honoring the Sensual Self*. New York: Jeremy P. Tarcher.
This interesting collecting of essays by such authors as Nancy Friday, Betty Dodson, Allen Ginsberg, and Rollo May explores society's distrust of erotic impulse. The social suppression of every form of erotic interest and behavior by religious, political, and economic forces is made plain. Its remedy is less certain.

BODY IMAGE

Engel, B. (1995). *Raising Your Self-Esteem: How to Feel Better About Your Sexuality and Yourself*. New York: Ballantine.
The author points out the ways in which shame in the sexual arena affects a person's self-confidence, body image, sexual desire, sexual functioning, and the ability to form intimate relationships. She believes that sexual fulfillment comes from learning that physical intimacy is no shortcut to emotional intimacy, from focusing on one's own physical pleasure, and from learning the importance of touch and learning how to communicate one's sexual needs. The book addresses both men's and women's issues.

Rodin, J. (1992). *Body Traps: Breaking the Binds That Keep You From Feeling Good About Your Body*. New York: Morrow.
This book would rid us of preoccupations with our own and

others' physical appearances and challenge us to give up the self-defeating quest for physical perfection.

MYSTICISM

Meldman, L. W. (1997). *Mystical Sex: Love, Ecstasy, and the Mystical Experience.* Rockport, MA: Element.

This book grasps very well the importance of being in the present moment, of total absorption in the here and now, and of sexual experience as an opportunity to experience the oneness described by mystics of every religious persuasion.

COMMUNICATION

Gottman, J. A. *A Couple's Guide to Communication.* Champaign, IL: Research Press.

The author reports on research pertaining to communication, including the nature and importance of feedback, how leveling can be conducted, and the content and feeling components of the messages we give and receive. More than passing reference is made to the importance of communication in the sexual sphere. A classic in the field.

Klein, M. (1990). *Your Sexual Secrets.* New York: Berkley.

Addressing the issue of whether or not to share sexual secrets with our partner, the author focuses on the various motivations for self-disclosure. Inappropriate and unhealthy reasons including taking revenge, relieving guilt, and testing the relationship. Much better reasons would include the desire to draw closer, improving sexual compatibility, expressing a need, and the wish to initiate a change in the sexual arena.

McKay, M., Davis, M., and Fanning, P. (1983). *Messages: The Communication Book.* Oakland, CA: New Harbinger.

A complete discussion of the skills required to become an effective communicator. The reader is left with no doubts about the monumental importance of communication in everyday life, regardless of the context. How to listen, how to assert ourselves, and how to disclose ourselves are among the skills spelled out.

Miller, S., Miller, P., Nunnally, E. W., and Wackman, D. B. (1991). *Talking and Listening Together*. Littleton, CO: Interpersonal Communication Programs.

If there were only one book that I would recommend to clients in need of improving their communication patterns, this would be it. Using questionnaires, exercises, and worksheets to help the reader develop self-awareness, listening skills, and ways of resolving conflicts, this book really cuts to the chase, and its treasures are easily accessible to all of us desperately in need of them.

Tannen, D. (1990). *You Just Don't Understand: Women and Men in Conversation*. New York: Ballantine.

The basic premise of this book is that men and women are so profoundly different that when they speak to each other it is like "trying to communicate across two different cultures." The author's insights into this phenomenon can go far in removing the animus that so often characterizes male–female contact.

EXERCISES

Hooper, A. (1992). *The Ultimate Sex Book*. New York: D. K. Publishing.

You may find the numerous detailed, illustrated exercises and techniques designed to enhance sexual performance quite beneficial. Topics include fantasies, masturbation, orgasms, and intimacy; all are illustrated by individual case histories.

Keesling, B. (1993). *Sexual Pleasure*. Alameda, CA: Hunter House.

Stressing the importance of playfulness and sensual enjoyment on the part of lovers, this book offers numerous exercises designed to enhance these features of sexual exchange. It is supposed that sexual fulfillment requires chiefly the enjoyment of touching (one's self or partner) and of being touched, as well as making love without anxiety or guilt. Dozens of bonding exercises and explorations are provided.

McCarthy, B., Ryan, M., and Johnson, F. (1975). *Sexual Awareness: A Practical Approach.* San Francisco, CA: Boyd & Fraser.

There are many useful exercises here, chiefly involving physical touch and pleasuring. These basics, as the authors point out, will not be enough for couples in too much conflict, whose communication has become highly destructive and who are experiencing major sexual or psychological difficulties. The authors make good use of case studies in their consideration of sexual communication, feelings, and functioning.

Renshaw, D. (1995). *Seven Weeks to Better Sex.* New York: Dell.

This seven-week program contains a host of questionnaires and exercises designed to promote sexual confidence and pleasure and to reach a better understanding of how our attitudes influence our behaviors. The general goal is to help couples draw closer to each other, enhance their communication, and gain greater sexual satisfaction.

Rey, C., ed. (1997). *Love and Sexuality.* New York: Carroll & Graf.

This mammoth book on how people connect sexually is especially useful to anyone interested in enlivening his/her sexual partnership. There are love-play suggestions galore, which you may or may not find far-fetched.

Stock, G. (1989). *The Book of Questions: Love and Sex.* New York: Workman.

This small book, crammed with thought-provoking questions about relationships and sexuality, provides the kind of structure often needed by couples who want to get a conversation going about sexual expectations, values, and experiences.

Index